Internet teaching is very bored teachers.

*Page 6
*Page 13

P 21 Risky

D. LaMont Johnson
Cleborne D. Maddux
Editors

Technology in Education: A Twenty-Year Retrospective

Technology in Education: A Twenty-Year Retrospective has been co-published simultaneously as *Computers in the Schools*, Volume 20, Numbers 1/2 2003.

Pre-publication REVIEWS, COMMENTARIES, EVALUATIONS . . .

"Wow! What a pleasure! I could not put it down. There are chapters in this book that should be required reading for every teacher, administrator, and school board member that seeks technology solutions for learning. For once we have an immensely readable, enjoyable, and well-documented recount of the technology events that have shaped American education. The book reveals what has worked, what has not worked–and most importantly, why."

Jay Blanchard, PhD
Professor, Psychology in Education
Arizona State University

The Haworth Press, Inc.

Technology in Education:
A Twenty-Year Retrospective

Technology in Education: A Twenty-Year Retrospective has been co-published simultaneously as *Computers in the Schools*, Volume 20, Numbers 1/2 2003.

The *Computers in the Schools* Monographic "Separates"

Below is a list of "separates," which in serials librarianship means a special issue simultaneously published as a special journal issue or double-issue *and* as a "separate" hardbound monograph. (This is a format which we also call a "DocuSerial.")

"Separates" are published because specialized libraries or professionals may wish to purchase a specific thematic issue by itself in a format which can be separately cataloged and shelved, as opposed to purchasing the journal on an on-going basis. Faculty members may also more easily consider a "separate" for classroom adoption.

"Separates" are carefully classified separately with the major book jobbers so that the journal tie-in can be noted on new book order slips to avoid duplicate purchasing.

You may wish to visit Haworth's website at . . .

http://www.HaworthPress.com

. . . to search our online catalog for complete tables of contents of these separates and related publications.

You may also call 1-800-HAWORTH (outside US/Canada: 607-722-5857), or Fax 1-800-895-0582 (outside US/Canada: 607-771-0012), or e-mail at:

docdelivery@haworthpress.com

---

such as the Internet, the World Wide Web and various software packages to further research and statistics. You will explore on-going debates relating to the theory of research, research methodology, and successful practices. Information Technology in Educational Research and Statistics *also covers the debate on what statistical procedures are appropriate for what kinds of research designs.*

Educational Computing in the Schools: Technology, Communication, and Literacy, edited by Jay Blanchard, PhD (Vol. 15, No. 1, 1999). *Examines critical issues of technology, teaching, and learning in three areas: access, communication, and literacy. You will discover new ideas and practices for gaining access to and using technology in education from preschool through higher education.*

Logo: A Retrospective, edited by Cleborne D. Maddux, PhD, and D. LaMont Johnson, PhD (Vol. 14, No. 1/2, 1997). *"This book–honest and optimistic–is a must for those interested in any aspect of Logo: its history, the effects of its use, or its general role in education." (Dorothy M. Fitch, Logo consultant, writer, and editor, Derry, New Hampshire)*

Using Technology in the Classroom, edited by D. LaMont Johnson, PhD, Cleborne D. Maddux, PhD, and Leping Liu, MS (Vol. 13, No. 1/2, 1997). *"A guide to teaching with technology that emphasizes the advantages of transiting from teacher-directed learning to learner-centered learning–a shift that can draw in even 'at-risk' kids." (Book News, Inc.)*

Multimedia and Megachange: New Roles for Educational Computing, edited by W. Michael Reed, PhD, John K. Burton, PhD, and Min Liu, EdD (Vol. 10, No. 1/2/3/4, 1995). *"Describes and analyzes issues and trends that might set research and development agenda for educators in the near future." (Sci Tech Book News)*

Language Minority Students and Computers, edited by Christian J. Faltis, PhD, and Robert A. DeVillar, PhD (Vol. 7, No. 1/2, 1990). *"Professionals in the field of language minority education, including ESL and bilingual education, will cheer this collection of articles written by highly respected, research-writers, along with computer technologists, and classroom practitioners." (Journal of Computing in Teacher Education)*

Logo: Methods and Curriculum for Teachers, by Cleborne D. Maddux, PhD, and D. LaMont Johnson, PhD (Supp #3, 1989). *"An excellent introduction to this programming language for children." (Rena B. Lewis, Professor, College of Education, San Diego State University)*

Assessing the Impact of Computer-Based Instruction: A Review of Recent Research, by M. D. Roblyer, PhD, W. H. Castine, PhD, and F. J. King, PhD (Vol. 5, No. 3/4, 1988). *"A comprehensive and up-to-date review of the effects of computer applications on student achievement and attitudes." (Measurements & Control)*

Educational Computing and Problem Solving, edited by W. Michael Reed, PhD, and John K. Burton, PhD (Vol. 4, No. 3/4, 1988). *Here is everything that educators will need to know to use computers to improve higher level skills such as problem solving and critical thinking.*

The Computer in Reading and Language Arts, edited by Jay S. Blanchard, PhD, and George E. Mason, PhD (Vol. 4, No. 1, 1987). *"All of the [chapters] in this collection are useful, guiding the teacher unfamiliar with classroom computer use through a large number of available software options and classroom strategies." (Educational Technology)*

Computers in the Special Education Classroom, edited by D. LaMont Johnson, PhD, Cleborne D. Maddux, PhD, and Ann Candler, PhD (Vol. 3, No. 3/4, 1987). *"A good introduction to the use of computers in special education. . . . Excellent for those who need to become familiar with computer usage with special population students because they are contemplating it or because they have actually just begun to do it." (Science Books and Films)*

You Can Do It/Together, by Kathleen A. Smith, PhD, Cleborne D. Maddux, PhD, and D. LaMont Johnson, PhD (Supp #2, 1986). *A self-instructional textbook with an emphasis on the partnership system of learning that introduces the reader to four critical areas of computer technology.*

Computers and Teacher Training: A Practical Guide, by Dennis M. Adams, PhD (Supp #1, 1986). *"A very fine . . . introduction to computer applications in education." (International Reading Association)*

The Computer as an Educational Tool, edited by Henry F. Olds, Jr. (Vol. 3, No. 1, 1986). *"The category of tool uses for computers holds the greatest promise for learning, and this . . . book, compiled from the experiences of a good mix of practitioners and theorists, explains how and why." (Jack Turner, Technology Coordinator, Eugene School District 4-J, Oregon)*

Logo in the Schools, edited by Cleborne D. Maddux, PhD (Vol. 2, No. 2/3, 1985). *"An excellent blend of enthusiasm for the language of Logo mixed with empirical analysis of the language's effectiveness as a means of promoting educational goals. A much-needed book!" (Rena Lewis, PhD, Professor, College of Education, San Diego State University)*

Humanistic Perspectives on Computers in the Schools, edited by Steven Harlow, PhD (Vol. 1, No. 4, 1985). *"A wide spectrum of information." (Infochange)*

Technology in Education:
A Twenty-Year Retrospective

D. LaMont Johnson, PhD
Cleborne D. Maddux, PhD
Editors

Technology in Education: A Twenty-Year Retrospective has been co-published simultaneously as *Computers in the Schools*, Volume 20, Numbers 1/2 2003.

The Haworth Press, Inc.

New York • London • Victoria (AU)
www.HaworthPress.com

Technology in Education: A Twenty-Year Retrospective has been co-published simultaneously as *Computers in the Schools,* Volume 20, Numbers 1/2 2003.

The development, preparation, and publication of this work has been undertaken with great care. However, the publisher, employees, editors, and agents of The Haworth Press and all imprints of The Haworth Press, Inc., including The Haworth Medical Press® and Pharmaceutical Products Press®, are not responsible for any errors contained herein or for consequences that may ensue from use of materials or information contained in this work. Opinions expressed by the author(s) are not necessarily those of The Haworth Press, Inc. With regard to case studies, identities and circumstances of individuals discussed herein have been changed to protect confidentiality. Any resemblance to actual persons, living or dead, is entirely coincidental.

Cover design by Jennifer M. Gaska

Library of Congress Cataloging-in-Publication Data

Technology in education : a twenty-year retrospective / D. LaMont Johnson, Cleborne D. Maddux, editors.
    p. cm.
    "Technology in Education: A Twenty-Year Retrospective has been co-published simultaneously as Computers in the Schools, volume 20, numbers 1/2 2003."
    ISBN 0-7890-2199-4 (hard cover : alk. paper) –ISBN 0-7890-2200-1(soft cover : alk. paper)
    1. Educational technology–History. 2. Computer-assisted instruction–History. I. Johnson, D. LaMont (Dee LaMont), 1939- II. Maddux, Cleborne D., 1942- III. Computers in the schools.
LB1028.3.T39693 2003
371.33–dc21   2003010480

Indexing, Abstracting & Website/Internet Coverage

This section provides you with a list of major indexing & abstracting services. That is to say, each service began covering this periodical during the year noted in the right column. Most Websites which are listed below have indicated that they will either post, disseminate, compile, archive, cite or alert their own Website users with research-based content from this work. (This list is as current as the copyright date of this publication.)

Abstracting, Website/Indexing Coverage . . . . Year When Coverage Began

- *Academic Abstracts/CD-ROM* **1994**
- *Australian Education Index <www.acer.edu.au>* **2000**
- *Child Development Abstracts & Bibliography <www.ukans.edu>* . . . **2000**
- *CNPIEC Reference Guide: Chinese National Directory of Foreign Periodicals* **1995**
- *Computer Literature Index* **1993**
- *Computing Reviews* **1992**
- *Contents of this publication are indexed and abstracted in the ProQuest Education Complete database, available on ProQuest Information & Learning <www.proquest.com>* **1994**
- *Current Index to Journals in Education* **1991**
- *Education Abstracts. Published by The HW Wilson Company <www.hwwilson.com>* **1992**
- *Education Digest* **1991**
- *Education Index <www.hwwilson.com>* **1999**
- *Education Process Improvement Ctr, Inc. (EPICENTER) <www.epicent.com>* **2000**

(continued)

(continued)

* **Exact start date to come**

Special Bibliographic Notes related to special journal issues (separates) and indexing/abstracting:

- indexing/abstracting services in this list will also cover material in any "separate" that is co-published simultaneously with Haworth's special thematic journal issue or DocuSerial. Indexing/abstracting usually covers material at the article/chapter level.
- monographic co-editions are intended for either non-subscribers or libraries which intend to purchase a second copy for their circulating collections.
- monographic co-editions are reported to all jobbers/wholesalers/approval plans. The source journal is listed as the "series" to assist the prevention of duplicate purchasing in the same manner utilized for books-in-series.
- to facilitate user/access services all indexing/abstracting services are encouraged to utilize the co-indexing entry note indicated at the bottom of the first page of each article/chapter/contribution.
- this is intended to assist a library user of any reference tool (whether print, electronic, online, or CD-ROM) to locate the monographic version if the library has purchased this version but not a subscription to the source journal.
- individual articles/chapters in any Haworth publication are also available through the Haworth Document Delivery Service (HDDS).

Technology in Education: A Twenty-Year Retrospective

Contents

ABOUT THE EDITORS

D. LaMont Johnson, PhD, Professor of Educational Technology in the College of Education at the University of Nevada, Reno, is a leading specialist in the area of educational computing and related technologies. He is the founding editor of *Computers in the Schools* and is Program Coordinator of the Information Technology in Education program at UNR. He has co-authored 10 books with Cleborne D. Maddux, including *Distance Education: Issues and Concerns* and the textbook *Educational Computing: Learning with Tomorrow's Technologies,* now in its third edition. A popular speaker and conference presenter, Dr. Johnson is active in several professional organizations concerned with advancing the use and understanding of educational technology.

Cleborne D. Maddux, PhD, is Professor of Education in the Department of Counseling and Educational Psychology at the University of Nevada, Reno, where he teaches courses on statistics and on integrating technology into education. He has co-authored 10 books with D. LaMont Johnson, including *Distance Education: Issues and Concerns* and the textbook *Educational Computing: Learning with Tomorrow's Technologies,* now in its third edition.

INTRODUCTION

D. LaMont Johnson

The Dream Machine

SUMMARY. This article presents a brief retrospective from the editor's point of view covering 25 years of *Computers in the Schools*. The author then presents some of the ideas relating to obstacles that have prevented a more thorough immersion of information technology in education. Finally, the article introduces the authors and articles that comprise the remainder of this anniversary volume. *[Article copies available for a fee from The Haworth Document Delivery Service: 1-800-HAWORTH. E-mail address: <docdelivery@haworthpress.com> Website: <http://www.HaworthPress.com> © 2003 by The Haworth Press, Inc. All rights reserved.]*

KEYWORDS. Microcomputer, creativity, technology, WebQuests, assessment, evaluation, research

A little over twenty years ago, I was a young professor, eager to make my way in academia by establishing a specialized interest that would allow me to

D. LAMONT JOHNSON is Editor, *Computers in the Schools*, and Professor, University of Nevada, Reno, Department of Counseling and Educational Psychology, Reno, NV 89557 (E-mail: ljohnson@unr.edu).

[Haworth co-indexing entry note]: "The Dream Machine." Johnson, D. LaMont. Co-published simultaneously in *Computers in the Schools* (The Haworth Press, Inc.) Vol. 20, No. 1/2, 2003, pp. 1-10; and: *Technology in Education: A Twenty-Year Retrospective* (ed: D. LaMont Johnson, and Cleborne D. Maddux) The Haworth Press, Inc., 2003, pp. 1-10. Single or multiple copies of this article are available for a fee from The Haworth Document Delivery Service [1-800-HAWORTH, 9:00 a.m. - 5:00 p.m. (EST). E-mail address: docdelivery@haworthpress.com].

publish, which I understood to be the coin of the realm. It came to my attention that a colleague, also a new professor at my university, had a computer in his office. Having established a love affair with mainframe computers in my graduate student days, I was naturally eager to see this "computer-on-a-desk." And so it was that I came to visit Jerry Willis, who had an office on the next floor up from mine. My initial impression of Jerry's SOL, a very early microcomputer sold by *Processor Technology*, which he had built himself from a kit, did not exactly leave me spellbound. What Jerry patiently tried to explain to me was that the computer had a powerful central processing unit (CPU) that could manipulate data in all sorts of interesting ways, but in its present stage lacked a means for getting data in and results out. Jerry's enthusiasm for his machine, however, made a lasting impression on me. I didn't realize it at the time, but what I was looking at on Jerry Willis's desk was a "dream machine." I didn't think of it as a dream machine in the sense of the beauty and power I might associate with an automotive dream machine. I saw it as a dream machine because of its ability to invoke dreams in the minds of visionary educators who saw endless potential for altering traditional notions of teaching and learning. I was one of those who instantly became a disciple of harnessing the power of the computer to improve education.

After I had worked with Jerry for a couple of years in convincing our department chairman to let us offer some course work relating to the use of what we then called microcomputers in education, the Haworth Press called and asked if we would be interested in starting an academic journal dealing with this new phenomenon. The proposed title of this new journal was *Computers in the Schools*. Jerry, at the time, was under contract with another publishing company and so the opportunity fell to me to become the founding editor of this publication, which is now celebrating its 20th year. At the time, Cleb Maddux was also a new faculty member at our university, and he immediately became and has remained a valued and trusted associate of this new journal.

As I look back over the past 20 years of *Computers in the Schools*, I realize just how fitting my use of the term "dream machine" really is. From the very beginning of this movement to make technology a partner in education, we have been dreaming of what could happen. In other words, it seems to me that we are constantly looking ahead. It reminds me of when I was in my growing up years, the big important things were always just on the next horizon or around the next bend. Interest in harnessing the power of a machine to improve technology, of course, did not begin with the invention of the microprocessor or the launching of *Computers in the Schools*. The dream machine, as I am using the term here, goes back about as far as you want to look. In fact, there were many dream machines before the microprocessor came along, but the microprocessor stands as a singular landmark in the history of technology in education because it took the computer out from behind the glass-walled, air-conditioned fortress and placed it on the teacher's desk. Innovations over that past 20 years have not only placed computers on teachers' desks, but also on students' desks, and even in their backpacks. The advent of the microcomputer was seen by many educators as the breakthrough that would finally make it possible to realize some long-held dreams that had previously been shackled by technological restraints.

Now after 20 years, not much has changed in terms of our dreaming—we are still dreaming! The technology we have to work with today is vastly superior to Jerry's SOL computer, and many teachers across the country are working magical tricks with technology in their classrooms, but we definitely aren't there yet. The vast majority of students still spend less than one hour per week on a computer in their school. Interestingly enough, many of these students have personal computers, which they use several hours per day in learning activities. In a recent meeting I attended, a technology specialist for a K-12 school district complained that most of the computers that had been placed in classrooms were not even being turned on. The overarching dream invoked by the dream machine was what we now refer to as "integrating technology into the classroom." Our vision was that we would one day be able to peer into any classroom and see teachers and students making creative and efficient use of these wonderful teaching and learning tools. This 20th anniversary publication of *Computers in the Schools* will provide a retrospective of where we are, where we have come from, and where we are going with regard to this dream.

In this introduction, I want to do two things. First, I want to present a potpourri of thoughts and ideas I have gained over the past 20 years that relate to our achieving the dream of integrating technology into the classroom. Second, I want to introduce the 11 articles that constitute the remainder of this issue in order to provide a perspective for the reader.

My interest in using technology in education began before I ever saw a microcomputer. Having come from a school psychology background, I not only understood intellectually, but felt emotionally, through face-to-face contact with many children who were experiencing school-related problems, that people learn in different ways and at different rates. I became convinced through my work as a school psychologist that we could improve on the way we organized teaching and learning to meet more diversified learning styles. Shortly after I saw my first microcomputer, I began to think that this machine, the dream machine, might just be the tool that could revolutionize traditional classroom instruction. My interest in seeing classroom instruction change soon became embodied in the phrase "technology integration." Progress in technology integration has been slow, but in the past few years, I have been in classrooms where wonderfully exciting and effective teaching and learning was taking place and these experiences have heightened my optimism that the revolution I, along with many others, began dreaming about over 20 years ago will eventually come to pass.

During a recent summer institute designed to present ideas about how to use technology to meet state standards, I witnessed a remarkable presentation by a third-grade teacher. This young teacher had thoroughly integrated technology into his classroom and he had done it using just technology tools, PowerPoint and the Web. Within minutes after he began his presentation, the audience forgot what tools he was using and became mesmerized by the creativity and inventiveness he had brought to his classroom. He demonstrated bells and whistles, but showed how they related to and enhanced his ability to provide his students with deep understanding of concepts and mastery of skills. At the end of the presentation, this young teacher informed his audience that, at the end of the school year, his and a fellow technology-using colleague's classes scored highest on the statewide standardized achievement test in their very large elementary school.

We now have much of the technology we need to bring about significant changes in America's classrooms. We have and are developing technology integration models that illustrate how to enhance classroom learning with technology. We are beginning to see some evaluation results demonstrating that thorough emersion of technology brings about improved learning and in some cases, we have been able to show this with standardized test scores. Why then are computers and related technology equipment gathering dust in so many classrooms? Let me offer a few thoughts on this question.

STARTING FROM THE WRONG PLACE

I was recently involved as an outside evaluator for a PT3 grant at a major university. While visiting the project, I had the opportunity to spend some time with the dean of the college of education at that university. This dean was a seasoned veteran in the business of education and was in his final year before retirement. During the time I was there, the PT3 project was conducting a summer institute where the theme centered around using WebQuests in the classroom. The dean took me aside one day and asked me if I would be interested in seeing some of the work he had done over his career. After viewing some very interesting projects, he brought out a box filled with large, portfolio-size envelopes and asked me to look inside one of them. Inside I found a document describing a small group exercise with a social studies problem to be solved. Also in the portfolio were copies of numerous documents that, when studied carefully, would yield insights and clues for solving the problem. The way the problem was structured made it obvious that there was no one correct solution, but rather the solution depended on certain directions the group decided to take based on their study of the related documents. The dean then explained that he had developed these teaching materials for a pre-service methods course he used to teach.

After surveying the materials for a time, I enthusiastically informed the dean that what he had here was a WebQuest before the invention of the Web. He then gave me a "wise old owl" look as if to say, "Yes, now you are catching on." He then continued to teach me by telling me that he thought we technology enthusiasts–which he, himself, admitted to being–were starting from the wrong place. His point was that by using the materials contained in his portfolio envelopes, he was able to get his pre-service teachers to think about a different way to approach the teaching of social studies. He asserted that, once he got future teachers to think in this new model, getting them to use technology would require only showing them the World Wide Web. He believed that, once they saw the Web, they would automatically see that it provided a more powerful and efficient portfolio of resources for a problem-solving learning experience. Finally, the dean summarized my lesson by musing that maybe we would have better success if we started with the teachers who were ready to use technology, meaning they were already practicing teaching methods that naturally lent themselves to adopting technology. He contrasted this approach to trying to convince all teachers to change their teaching methods so they could begin using technology.

THINKING WITH THE TOOL

Probably the most common excuse I hear from teachers for not using the technology available to them is lack of time. "I just don't have time to fit it in," they often say. I realized one day that there was a missing element in our approach to making converts for classroom technology use. I believe that, when we use the appropriate technology efficiently and well, we save time–we save time in the sense that we can do more with less time. I realize that much has been said about people actually working longer hours with technology than they did previously, but I think it can be shown that this is a result of wanting to do more because more can be done. In trying to illustrate my point, I use one of my first experiences with a microcomputer. The first time I saw a word-processing program in action, I was convinced that it was a tool that would work for me. I was, as a young professor, in a business where I had to publish to survive and progress. I liked writing, but it was a laborious task. I did not type well enough to be very efficient, so my writing tools were a pencil and a yellow legal pad. I would write out my document then give it to a secretary to type. I would then edit it and ask the secretary to type it again. This sequence would continue until I was too embarrassed to ask for one more revision. I quickly saw that, despite my poor typing skills, a word-processor would give me control over my own writing destiny. So I began. It was slow at first. I would still start with pencil and yellow pad, then I would enter my text via the keyboard. After my first few tries, my wife informed me that I was wasting time. She maintained that it was actually taking me more time to get a refined document than it did using the old method. She was probably right, but I was stubborn. My typing skills soon improved, and I made the transition from composing on paper to composing on screen. Once I got to this point, I had control. By then, I had improved my efficiency as a writer a hundredfold and the old method seemed like an arcane relic. What I realize now is that I gradually conditioned myself to think with a keyboard and screen–they provide the atmosphere for my writing creativity. Now whenever I have writing to do, I need my writing tools: keyboard and screen.

I can trace numerous similar experiences with various computer skills. PowerPoint, for example, seemed awkward and time consuming the first time I used it. I used to enhance my teaching by writing and drawing on the chalk-board as I talked or by preparing crude overlays to be used on an overhead pro-jector. In those days, preparing a professional quality overlay (i.e., slides) was difficult and very time consuming. I immediately saw the value of PowerPoint, which would allow me to use color, graphics, animation, sound, and video to create highly professional slides at my keyboard and screen. Getting started, however, wasn't easy. After working with the software for a while, I gained proficiency. Then, over time, it became my presentation tool. I began to think with the tool–when I needed to develop a presentation, I automatically went to my presentation tool and, in that environment, my presentation creativity would come alive. Let me refer back to my third-grade teacher friend whose primary technology tool is PowerPoint. PowerPoint has become such a com-fortable tool for him that he can do almost anything with it, and it is as much a part of his teaching style as a chalkboard is to many other teachers.

I believe that too often we are exposing teachers to new tools and new ideas without providing an atmosphere where those tools and ideas can be mastered. Sometimes it is like attending a concert and then being expected to play a vio-lin solo, having never played the violin before. I think many teachers fail to see the benefit of using new technology tools because they never make the tools their own–they never get to a point where they think with the tool.

STARTING WITH THE RIGHT TOOL

A few years ago I talked to a teacher who had taken one of my courses where we emphasized authoring systems as valuable teaching tools. I asked this student if she found much application for such software in her classroom. Her frank reply was "none at all." I remembered how difficult it was during that course to try to convince the students that the time and energy they were putting into mastering the software would pay off when they got into their classrooms. Later, I developed a course where we investigated ways to use the Internet and the World Wide Web to integrate technology into the curriculum. In this course, I found that no convincing was necessary. Both prospective and practicing teachers immediately saw the potential of these tools to enhance and enrich teaching and learning experiences. All of this started me thinking about a relationship between the amount of personal investment required by a teacher to begin integrating technology using a given application and the de-gree to which that application was functional in terms of integration. I concluded that there is an interesting relationship between the personal investment of time and energy by the teacher and the degree to which the application can be used in a breadth of situations. Applications that require little time to master and are readily available to be used in a variety of lessons seem to have the most power to bring about changes in the degree to which teachers will integrate technology into their classrooms. On the other hand, applications that require a great deal of time and effort to master and are only relevant in a small segment of the curriculum do not seem to have much power in terms of convincing teachers to use them.

I am now convinced that, if we want to turn teachers on to using technology, we should start with the applications that have the lowest personal investment and the highest degree of functionality. I think the application that best meets that description is the Web. Show sincere and dedicated teachers the Web and you have caught their interest.

THE NEXT BIG CHALLENGE

One thing we can be confident of is that an emphasis on using technology in education is here to stay. I say this primarily because of the tremendous push from federal and state governments in the past few years. The PT3 grant initiative from the federal government probably gave the strongest signal of all that the educational technology movement is being taken seriously. With educational technology with us in such a forceful way, our next great challenge will be to demonstrate that all of the promises, all of the hopes, and all of the dreams are real–we can really improve teaching and learning with technology. The No Child Left Behind Act of 2001 clearly mandates that innovative practices by state and local education agencies must build in assessment strategies to demonstrate effects on student achievement. We have known this was coming for a long time. Politicians and the general public want to know if the tax dollars being spent on technology for schools is yielding a fair return. In this, we face a dilemma. It is almost certain that results based on standardized tests alone will not show that technology improves learning. Yet, the No Child Left Behind Act pushes schools more and more toward evaluating teachers and students on standardized test scores. I think our next great challenge, in order to continue the momentum we started with the dream machine, will be to prove that we are affecting student achievement with legitimate and acceptable measuring systems that go beyond standardized tests. Unless the educational technology advocates develop these methods, they will not be developed and we will never have a chance to prove our dream. I am not sure how we will do this or what these new measuring systems will look like. I strongly suggest, however, that we look to technology itself to help find the answer. If technology can help us teach and learn, it should also be able to help us demonstrate our effectiveness.

The electronic portfolio assessment technique gets us going down the right path, but we must expand on this and find additional methods also.

THIS VOLUME

In this, the 20-year anniversary publication of *Computers in the Schools*, we are taking a retrospective look at the dream machine. Which dreams came true, which are in the process of coming true, and which were ill conceived from the start? I will introduce each of the remaining 11 articles that make up this collection in order to provide the reader with an overall perspective of its contents.

Twenty years ago, in the first issue of *Computers in the Schools*, Jerry Willis wrote the feature article. The title of that article was "Educational Computing: Current Status and Future Directions." Now, in this 20-year anniversary collection, we are pleased to publish a retrospective view by Jerry entitled "Instructional Technologies in Schools: Are We There Yet?" In this article, Jerry explains how he missed some important trends in educational technology and how he predicted some things that didn't come to pass. He then draws a distinction between empirical and ideological arguments for using technology in the schools and develops an argument that it is really ideology, not empirical evidence, that has driven most of the debate on whether technology can improve teaching and learning and discusses various educational ideologies and the positions they take on using technologies in the schools.

The next article in this collection is written by a long-time friend and colleague who has offered significant contributions to *Computers in the Schools* since the very first issue. Cleborne Maddux, who is co-editor of this volume, has served as Research Editor for *Computers in the Schools*, and has personally reviewed every research-based submission to the journal. In the article he wrote for the first issue of *Computers in the Schools*, Cleb expressed his concern that educators not just run out and purchase computers because they were there, but rather that a solid research tradition be started so that arguments for and against using technology in education might be based on research evidence. In this volume, Cleb explains that he believes technology has had little impact on education in general and describes some of the stages of research he thinks the field of educational technology has experienced. He further explains that having been sidetracked by many events and attitudes, we have never really reached a point where we can answer the important questions in the field of educational computing with research.

I am pleased to include in this anniversary volume an article by a distinguished educator, Dwight Allen. In his article, Dwight takes the position that technology really has changed education and society in some dramatic ways. He celebrates some of the advances in education brought about by the advent of the World Wide Web, but also expresses regret for the fact that the potential of present-day technology has not been fully taken advantage of, and that its power is not universally available.

Glen Bull, another early dreamer about the potential of technology in education, along with two of his colleagues, Randy Bell and Sara Kajder, also addresses the hits and misses relating to predictions made 20 years ago. These authors, however, clearly demonstrate that they have not grown tired of dreaming. They speak of the day when every student will carry a personal computer and the reality of total technology immersion in classrooms will finally occur. They speak also of trends that they think must occur in educational software and explain the benefits of a new trend, open source software, which they think will have a major impact on how we use technology in education.

As we planned the content for this anniversary collection, we wanted at least one article that reviewed the contents of the previous 19 volumes of *Computers in the Schools* and summarized some of the trends and issues that have been debated and discussed since 1984 when the first issue was published. I asked another long-time friend and colleague, Nancy Wentworth, to do this and she enlisted Rodney Earle, a colleague of hers, in this endeavor. Nancy and Rodney have done a masterful job of helping us look at some of the trends in what we have been reading and writing about for 20 years with regard to our dream of improving education with technology.

No scholarly effort by an old-time professor would be complete without at least one contribution by a former graduate student. I am fortunate to have a close working relationship with two of my former graduate students, Leping Liu and Norma Velasquez-Bryant. Together they have also looked at some of the trends and issues from the contents of 20 years of *Computers in the Schools* and have developed a model that explains a great deal about our slow progress in reaching that state of total integration of technology we have anticipated.

When I think of the predictions we made 20 years ago that missed the mark completely, the technology skills of entering college freshmen is one of the first to come to mind. I remember many conversations with my colleagues centered around the idea that college of education courses designed to make future teachers technologically literate (i.e., teaching basic skills) would have a very short life because soon, very soon, all students entering the university would already be technologically literate. Amazingly, this has not happened even after 20 years. Paul Merrill, also an early contributor to *Computers in the Schools*, has gathered data on the students entering the computer literacy class at his university and has summarized this data to illustrate what has happened with regard to this one early prediction.

During the very early stages of planning for this publication, I ran into another long-time friend and early advocate of educational technology at a national meeting. Karin Wiburg, who has published widely in the field and who has made several significant contributions to *Computers in the Schools* over the years, suggested that we should include at least one article addressing the equity issues relating to technology and education. I asked Karin to provide us with an overview and update on this important issue.

At the 2002 SITE conference in Nashville, I made a brief presentation where I talked about this anniversary volume and invited some young professors to contribute work. Part of my motivation was to counterbalance the content of the publication, because I anticipated that much of the collection would be filled by the work of old timers. In response to this request, Tara Jeffs and four of her colleagues, William Morrison, Trinka Messenheimer, Mary Rizza, and Savilla Banister, compiled a very fine retrospective analysis of trends and issues relevant to the use of technology in special education.

While the majority of pages in this collection are filled with retrospective analyses, the final two articles focus on very current trends that, when considered with a retrospective eye, illustrate just how much progress we have made in 20 years. The first of these two articles by Ward Mitchell Cates, Betsy Price, and Alec Bodzin illustrates some of the effects technology can have when immersed appropriately into science teaching. The second article by Lee Montgomery illustrates one way we are truly using information technology to do new things in new ways by exploring effective ways to use digital portfolios for student assessment.

GENERAL ARTICLES

Jerry Willis

Instructional Technologies in Schools: Are We There Yet?

SUMMARY. Some predictions made by the author 20 years ago, in the first issue of *Computers in the Schools*, are revisited. The author explains how he didn't see some trends that developed and how he predicted things that never came to pass. A distinction is made between empirical and ideological arguments for using technology in the schools. Numerous problems associated with relying on empirical evidence to make the case for educational technology are iterated. Ideology, not empirical evidence, drives most of the debate on whether technology can improve teaching and learning, and various ideologies are discussed. *[Article copies available for a fee from The Haworth Document Delivery Service: 1-800-HAWORTH. E-mail address: <docdelivery@haworthpress.com> Website: <http://www.HaworthPress.com> © 2003 by The Haworth Press, Inc. All rights reserved.]*

JERRY WILLIS is Professor of Curriculum and Instructional Technology, Iowa State University, College of Education, Center for Technology in Learning and Teaching, Ames, IA 50011 (E-mail: jwillis@jerrywillis.net).

[Haworth co-indexing entry note]: "Instructional Technologies in Schools: Are We There Yet?" Willis, Jerry. Co-published simultaneously in *Computers in the Schools* (The Haworth Press, Inc.) Vol. 20, No. 1/2, 2003, pp. 11-33; and: *Technology in Education: A Twenty-Year Retrospective* (ed: D. LaMont Johnson, and Cleborne D. Maddux) The Haworth Press, Inc., 2003, pp. 11-33. Single or multiple copies of this article are available for a fee from The Haworth Document Delivery Service [1-800-HAWORTH, 9:00 a.m. - 5:00 p.m. (EST). E-mail address: docdelivery@haworthpress.com].

10.1300/J025v20n01_02

11

KEYWORDS. Instructional technology, empirical, conservative, progressive, critical theory, ideological, critical theory of technology

In 1984 I was a confident young professor who had just made the transition from educational psychologist to educational computing specialist. The field was new and I was novice enough to agree to write a paper for the new journal, *Computers in the Schools.* My paper was titled "Educational Computing: Current Status and Future Directions" (Willis, 1984). In it, I talked about the status of computing in general and said we were in the middle of a transition from a *high priest* model of computing dominated by computer scientists to what I called the *citizen participant model.* By 2000 that transition was so complete that even talking about the high priest model of computing seems a little archaic.

I also talked about the revolution in microcomputer technology, particularly LSI, or large-scale integration, that makes personal computers possible. Today we take for granted advances in integration that allow a few million more transistors to be placed in an integrated circuit. I also talked about the revolution in software that would make computers *user friendly.* I was not accurate about that. I did not anticipate how far the possibilities of computing would take us in the 20 years since I wrote that paper. We have traded user friendliness for sophistication. If we want the power of a program like PhotoShop or Adobe Premier, we must pay for it by giving up some ease of use. Even the most popular program, Microsoft Word, is not really easy to learn and use, in part because it has grown fat and heavy with features that were not even dreamed about in 1984.

In that 1984 paper I also talked about the three main thrusts of computers in schools: computer literacy, drills, and use of computers to teach strategies (e.g., the Logo movement). I also tried to tell the future and predicted that computer literacy would be a standard expectation for high school graduates and that the emphasis would be on "learning to use applications programs rather than programming" (p. 11). That comes close to being true. Most students do graduate from high school today computer literate, and only a small percentage today take programming classes.

I also predicted that computers would be much more widely used "throughout the school curriculum" (p. 10). That is also true, but computers have not become ubiquitous in American schools. It is still unusual for a teacher to regularly integrate technology into the learning experience. I was wrong when I predicted that "the computer will play a central role in the curriculum." Information technology is important, but it is still not "central" in most schools today.

Another prediction I made was that "by the turn of the century the American school system will play a smaller role in society than it does today. Education will be a lifelong task for most citizens; and learning will increasingly become a regular part of life in the home, the office, and the factory" (p. 11). That prediction seems to have been fulfilled (Hiemstra, 2002). Most of us are involved in many types of informal and formal learning long after we leave school and university classes. Many workers, including auto mechanics and brain surgeons, must regularly update their skills through formal professional development training. This trend also means there are many types of jobs available today for specialists in teaching, learning, and computers. They work in schools, in higher education, in industry, in government, and in a diverse range of organizations from museums to military combat groups.

I am fairly satisfied with the predictions I made 20 years ago, but I am disappointed in what I did not see or did not understand. I missed completely at least three major uses of computers in education today. For example, I did not foresee the use of computers and information technologies to provide information. To cite just one personal example, about 40% of the citations in this paper refer to papers and books that are online. None of the papers in the first issue of *Computers in the Schools* in 1984 cited a single online paper.

A second trend I missed was use of information technology for communication. The idea of the World Wide Web and the creation of a language for formatting documents, hypertext markup language (HTML), began with the work of Tim Berners-Lee in 1989 while he was working at CERN, the European Center for Particle Physics. By 1991 Berners-Lee had all the rudimentary components of his electronic system of document sharing, and the World Wide Web was born. He created it for his colleagues around the world, but it has become the foundation for a revolution that may be more influential than the original invention of the personal computer. Today the Web is not only a source of information, it is a major means of personal and professional communication. The World Wide Web is also the foundation for the rise of another movement–distance education. Today thousands of colleges and universities offer everything from individual courses to complete undergraduate and graduate degree programs "over the Web." Virtual schools and virtual universities are discussed widely today and are also becoming a reality.

There are other trends and issues I missed in that 1984 article, but I want to focus on one of them in this paper. In the original paper I pointed out that there were already theoretical debates about the proper role of computers in education. As I saw it then, "The debate pits the behaviorally oriented learning theory group against the Piagetian cognitive developmentalists. Behaviorists view drill and practice programs and tutorial software as desirable and beneficial" (p. 7). I then discussed the work of Papert and the Logo movement. Today the Piagetian group would be called constructivists and the behaviorists would be called "direct-instruction" advocates, or in the words of one advocate, Diane Ravitch, "instructionalists." In 1984 I argued that we should not let theory get in the way of creative development. "Theories, by their very nature, are unproved, usually unprovable, and thus are often more troublesome than helpful in the birth of a new field. Now is the time for experimentation, for creative efforts to expand the range and type of applications for computers in schools. It is not a time for bickering over how well a project or program meets the requirements of a particular theory" (p. 8). I still believe that, but I also think such a statement is incredibly naive. The debates between constructivists and behaviorists are examples of a much broader and more fundamental debate about the nature of learning, even about the nature of knowledge and knowing. Then, as now, the approaches and perspectives we take on the role of computers in education derive from ideology much more than from research. It is that point I want to discuss in this paper. In the following section I will contrast two opposing views of computers in education. The optimistic perspective is based on modernism. As Hlynka and Yeaman (1992) put it, "The defining characteristics of modernity seem to be a faith in science, in the positive benefits of technology, and in the belief that progress is inevitable and good." Confidence in the usefulness of computers in schools is, to a great extent, an expression of a modernist perspective or ideology. On the other hand, skepticism about the roles and relevance of computers in schools is often an expression of a "postmodern" ideology. Hlynka and Yeaman describe a postmodern perspective on educational technology this way: "Educational technology can no longer be perceived as neutral or as leading inevitably to progress" (p. 8). In this paper I want to make two major points–that there is no possibility that we will make decisions about the proper role of computers in schools by relying on "objective research" for answers, and, conversely, we cannot avoid bringing ideology into the discussion. I will end the paper with a discussion of what we, as consumers of ideas about computers in schools and as creators and advocates of those ideas, can do.

SOME BACKGROUND

In 1984, when the first issue of *Computers in the Schools* was published, the landscape of computing in America was quite different. Four of the most popular computers of the day were the VIC-20, the Commodore 64, the Apple II, and the Atari. Compared to today's models these machines were pitifully weak. They were slow and had very little memory. The VIC-20 had only 5K of RAM, but even the 65,536 bytes of RAM in the Commodore 64 was only 1/4000th of the RAM in a typical middle-range computer today. Other components including the disk drive, the video display, and the sound system are all far superior in today's models.

In spite of the limitations of computers being sold the first year *Computers in the Schools* was published, they were very popular. Twenty-two million Commodore 64s were sold in 1983. Computers were such a phenomenon that instead of naming a man of the year for 1982, *Time* magazine named a "machine of the year"–the personal computer. The magazine (Friedrich, 1983) began their tribute to the computer with the comment, "By the millions, it is beeping its way into offices, schools and homes" (p. 6). *Time* magazine waxed eloquent about the potential of computers, but even their predictions about computers fell far short of what really happened over the past 20 years. In 1982 there were approximately 5.5 million computers in use, and *Time* estimated that 80 million would be in use "by the end of the century." Actually, the figure was 600 million, more than seven times the optimistic estimate of *Time*. Of those 5.5 million computers in 1982, only about 100,000 were in schools, one for every 400 students. By contrast, in 1998 there are almost nine million computers in schools (The Future of Children, 2001).

WE'VE COME SO FAR: ARE WE THERE YET?

In the 20 years since *Computers in the Schools* began publication, the equipment has become amazingly more sophisticated, cheaper, and easier to use. And, there are more than 90 times the number of computers in schools! Add to those facts the Internet revolution and the growing number of multimedia resources for education, and we should be fulfilling Seymour Papert's 1984 prediction that

> There won't be schools in the future . . . I think the computer will blow up the school. That is, the school defined as something where there are classes, teachers running exams, people structured in groups by age, following a curriculum–all of that. The whole system is based on a set of structural concepts that are incompatible with the presence of the computer. . . . (Papert, quoted in Clark and Wentworth [1997, p. 9])

Papert's prediction, which was probably more of a wish than a prediction, has not come to pass in the 18 years since he made it, and there are few indications that it will be fulfilled anytime in the near future. Papert's prediction is not the first one to be "off the mark" when it comes to the impact of technology on education. Jost Lowyck and Jan Elen (1998) collected a number of quotes about technology over the past 80 years. They all reflect the optimism of the believer, and, from the vantage point of hindsight, also tell us how often we miss the mark when predicting the future. For example, in one now-famous quote in 1922, Thomas Edison predicted that in a few years virtually all education could be done with his new invention, film:

> I believe that the motion picture is destined to revolutionize our educational system and that in a few years it will supplant largely, if not entirely, the use of textbooks. (Oppenheimer, 1997)

Virtually every communication technology that has become popular over the past 100 years has been touted as the technology that will revolutionize education: film, radio, television, computers. The famous Harvard psychologist, B. F. Skinner, even predicted that mechanical devices would drastically change education:

> I believe that teaching machines are destined to revolutionize our educational system and that in a few years they will supplant largely, if not entirely, the use of teachers. (Skinner, 1968, p. 1)

There have always been advocates for technology in education. I remember wandering through the musty shelves of the East Carolina University library a few years ago and finding dusty volumes of the papers delivered at the National Education Association annual meetings in the mid-1800s. There, in one paper, the author spoke enthusiastically about the impact information technology would have on education. He was talking about steam-powered printing presses.

At the same time there have been advocates, even evangelists, of technology in education there have also been critics who doubted either the effect or the purpose of technologies in education. Larry Cuban and Michael Apple are two contemporary critics, but there are many. Cuban's two books, *Teachers and Machines: The Classroom Use of Technology Since 1920* (1986) and *Oversold and Underused: Computers in the Classroom* (2001), are strong critiques of the roles computers play in education. The view of many critics is aptly summed up in a quote from Todd Oppenheimer's (1997) paper, "The Computer Delusion":

> There is no good evidence that most uses of computers significantly improve teaching and learning, yet school districts are cutting programs–music, art, physical education–that enrich children's lives to make room for this dubious nostrum, and the Clinton Administration has embraced the goal of "computers in every classroom" with credulous and costly enthusiasm.

Oppenheimer's paper, published in *The Atlantic Monthly*, remains one of the sharpest, most concise, and clearest criticisms of the rush to "computerize" American education. He, and other critics like Cuban and Apple, generated considerable smoke as well as fire in the debate over whether computers are actually a benefit or an expensive distraction that pulls money away from legitimate school needs. The critics, especially Cuban, often use predictions from supporters of technology that were made years ago and were, in hindsight, clearly wrong. And, of course, proponents of technology often write replies to the critics. For example, Bonnie Bracey, a respected leader in the field of educational technology, had this to say:

> As Todd Oppenheimer was researching material for his article, "The Computer Delusion" in the July 1997 issue of *Atlantic Monthly*, he took

time to interview me. I shared my experiences as a member of the National Information Infrastructure Advisory Council with him. After years of fighting to get even the most rudimentary technology for teachers, I was so very hopeful that this article would pave the way for more technology adaptation in the classroom. Needless to say, I was quite shocked when I finally read Oppenheimer's words.

What I didn't understand of what I read is Oppenheimer's contention that teachers, administrators, and school children see technology as just a glamorous tool, a toy. Where did Oppenheimer get this idea? It certainly wasn't from a recognized educational authority or a facilitator of educational technology, such as, say, a Chris Dede, a David Thornburg, a Sally Ann Law, a Jenny Grogg, a Marilyn Schlief, a Robert Pondiscio, a Mark Leon, a Larry Anderson–people in the world of education–people who understand the classroom and technology's place in it or who facilitate, observe, the transfer of technology to education from telephones to the many kinds of technology that are component parts of the information highway. (Bracey & Galus, 1998)

Say It Ain't So, Joe!

The heading above has entered the American English lexicon via the infamous "Black Sox" baseball scandal in 1919. Shoeless Joe Jackson was the charismatic but illiterate left fielder of the Chicago White Sox, a member of a team that seemed destined for baseball greatness. However, against Cincinnati in the baseball World Series, they played so poorly that rumors began that some members of the team were being paid to lose. An investigation turned up proof that the Series had been fixed. One of the young boys in the courtroom to hear the testimony of their hero, Shoeless Joe Jackson, supposedly asked him to "Say it ain't so, Joe." Today we use that term when cherished beliefs about anything are challenged.

Both sides in the discussion of whether information technology, especially computers, is a worthwhile addition to the classroom might ask that question when presented with arguments to the contrary. Both sides believe strongly in their views and find it hard to even consider the possibility that they are wrong.

Actually, the arguments on both sides have come in two forms: empirical and ideological. It is important to distinguish between the two.

Empirical Arguments

American psychology, and American education, has tended to try to answer questions about whether something works or not by deferring to research. This is certainly true when it comes to questions about computers in schools. Thousands of individual studies have been published on the question of whether computers in schools are beneficial or detrimental.

While there are many studies, scholars generally acknowledge that no single piece of research will ever "prove" anything. However, there is a procedure called *meta-analysis* that attempts to get at the truth of a question by systematically aggregating the results of many different studies to arrive at a conclusion. For example, Bayraktar (2002) conducted a meta-analysis of the "effectiveness of computer-assisted instruction in science education." This study, which looked at research about high school science instruction, used data from 42 studies. Bayraktar concluded that computer-assisted instruction was effective in science education. Another recent study by Soe, Koki, and Chang (2000) looked at the effect of CAI on reading achievement. This meta-analysis found 17 research studies that met the criteria for inclusion in the analysis. The authors concluded, "CAI does have a positive effect on reading achievement (p. i). These two studies are some of the more specialized meta-analyses. Most of the best known and most often-cited analyses cast an even broader net. Almost all of the more general meta-analyses used similar procedures to Soe, Koki, and Chang (Bangert-Drowns, Kulik, & Kulik, 1985; Kulik, Bangert-Downs, & Williams, 1983; Kulik, Kulik, & Bangert-Drowns, 1985; Kulik & Kulik, 1991; Ryan, 1991) and also reported the general conclusion that computers are "good" in schools. The 15 or so meta-analyses of computers in schools are cited over and over in the literature to support increased use of technology in education. For example, the widely cited Milliken report (Schacter, 1999) begins its discussion of the data with a meta-analysis by James Kulik (1994). The report also reviews a large number of the strongest research studies on "computers as learning tools."

The Problem with Empirical Evidence

The idea of answering a question such as "What is the impact of computers in American schools?" by systematically analyzing all the relevant research seems, on the surface, to be very appealing. What could be better? Why shouldn't you use an objective, scientific method to arrive at the answer to an important question? Isn't that better than relying on the subjective opinions of teachers and either advocates or critics? Actually, the answer may be no, it isn't. That is because of a serious flaw in meta-analytic techniques that is, to a great extent, shared by the individual studies they are based on. In a nutshell, the problem is this: Meta-analytic studies draw conclusions by combining the results of many different studies. If the studies do not research the "same thing" then the meta-analysis is invalid. If some studies were about apples and others about oranges, there is no basis for aggregating the results from the studies. This problem was pointed out in a discussion of meta-analyses of the impact of different forms of psychotherapy.

> In our review of psychodynamic psychotherapy . . . , we acknowledged 2 meta-analyses of brief dynamic psychotherapy and STDP [short-term

dynamic therapies] . . . , but we indicated our concern that in both instances, interpersonal psychotherapy (IPT) was included within the broader term, brief dynamic psychotherapy (p. 193).

Unfortunately, this practice is repeated in Leichsenring's review. Statistical approaches like meta-analysis use the principle of aggregation to their advantage to pool findings from a range of research settings. However, unless there is consistency within the category across which information is being pooled, this singular advantage can become a liability. (Kennedy, Segal, Lam, & Whitney, 2002, p. 193)

The crux of the problem, as noted in the quote, is that the researchers who conducted the meta-analyses included studies about two different kinds of psychotherapy and thus invalidated the analysis. The same is true of meta-analyses about computers in schools. When you combine studies about the impact of simulations with studies that looked at the impact of drill-and-practice programs, the conclusions are simply not valid. We would laugh at a meta-analysis that tries to answer the question, "Does medicine help sick people?" Why? Because there are many types of illnesses and many types of medicine. The same is true with regard to computers in education. There are many types of "education" and many ways computers can be used in education. We will never be able to answer the general question: "Is the impact of computers in education positive?" because there is no single entity called computers in education. There are many forms of "computers in education" just as there are many forms of medicine. In the case of computers in education and "medicine," it does not make sense even to try to answer a general question about effectiveness.

For example, in their analysis of research on computers and reading, Soe, Koki, and Chang (2000) comment that the ways computers can be used in reading instruction are diverse, and they mention several uses, including drill and practice, tutorials, and "dialogue." However, when they conducted their meta-analysis, they combined the results of all the studies and drew one general conclusion–that computers are good to teach reading. They made that general conclusion in spite of the following differences across the studies:

1. Age and grade of students: from first grade to eleventh grade
2. Type of tests used to determine success
3. Type of students studied: minority, disadvantaged, rural, urban, etc.
4. Duration of treatment: from one month to more than one school year
5. Type of hardware and software used
6. Type of instructional strategies and procedures used

I have not singled this study out because it is unusual. It is, in fact, typical in the way it combines studies of many different ways to use computers in schools and then comes up with a general conclusion about computers and education.

Common practice, in this case, is unfortunately not good practice. It simply does not make sense to treat a drill-and-practice study of teaching vocabulary words or the use of commas as if it were the same as a study of the impact of electronic books or collaborative writing software.

Similar problems plague many, if not all, the individual empirical studies that are used in meta-analytic research. Mandinach and Cline (1997) looked at the research on the impact of technology in education and concluded that most of the studies to date are very weak. They often ask simplistic questions–"Does it work?"–and often use research designs that are inappropriate. Mandinach and Cline argue that the impact of technology on education is a complex and multifaceted question. They are hopeful that in the future longitudinal studies using complex designs will help answer questions about the impact of computers on education. I am not so confident. The traditional "scientific method," when applied to educational computing, is an attempt to "prove" the effect, or lack thereof, of a particular type of instructional technology: drill and practice, tutorials, simulations, distance education, WebQuests, information resources, Web sites, e-books, video cases, problems, collaborative learning support, PowerPoint lectures, and so on.

The empiricist's solution to the problems with current research on computers in schools is to do better studies. If you can't find the truth about "computers in schools," then do good studies that ask questions like "Are WebQuests effective ways to use computers in schools?" Wouldn't well-designed studies about specific ways to use computers give us the truth about that particular application? Unfortunately, they won't. In her 1993 autobiography Gertrude Stein talked about going back to Oakland, California, to see her childhood home. However, when she looked for the house she lived in, she could not find it. Her comment was "There is no there there" (Tenderbuttons, 2003). The same is true of empirical studies of WebQuests, simulations, distance education, e-books, and any other form of computers in schools. There is no *there* there. By that I mean the terms are all very elastic. If you do a search of the Internet for any of those terms I mentioned and then read the specifics of what each author means by them, you will discover that they all cover such a wide and diverse range of educational strategies that no single instance of say, WebQuests, can represent the entire category. No single example is sufficiently typical enough to allow us to generalize from the research study to other examples of that type. Empirical research thus cannot prove anything; it is only one source of information among many. A thoughtful teacher's story about how he or she used a particular form of WebQuest may be as useful, if not more useful, than a research study that attempts to prove that WebQuests are effective. There are too many variations, too many contextual variables, too many forms of WebQuests, to allow us the luxury of proving anything about them.

Now, if empirical research will not answer the question, what will? For better or worse, the way most of us answer the question is ideological.

It Is Ideology, Not Research, that Drives Most Positive *and* Negative Critiques

The title of Armstrong and Casement's (2000) book is *The Child and the Machine: How Computers Put Our Children's Education at Risk.* In it they marshal their argument that computers are detrimental to education.

Armstrong and Casement's well-written book begins with a comment about the importance of research in the debate about computers:

> As I began research for this book, I discovered that what had been excluded from the debate was scientific evidence. Proponents often claimed this research bolstered the argument for computer-based education, but in reality it struck a far more cautious, if not critical note. . . . One question was foremost in our minds: do computers improve the quality of instruction in schools? This question needs a clear answer, supported by real evidence. . . . So far the most that can be said about computer-based instruction is that vast sums have been lavished on a technology whose educational potential has yet to be proven. We can only guess the long-term effects of computers on young children's development. (p. xii)

In spite of saying that we don't have the research to answer the question, the authors spend another 200 pages doing just that. Though the book purports to be based on a review of the research, it is really an ideological critique of computers in education. The tone, language, interpretations, and slant of the book are all designed to reinforce the subtitle, *How Computers Put Our Children's Education at Risk.* There is really no effort to provide a balanced view of computers in education–the goal is to convince the reader that computers are ineffective, risky, and "counterproductive" in schools.

Critics of computers in schools are not the only ones who approach the topic from an ideological basis. Consider Apple Computer's "K-12 Effectiveness Report" Web site (*http://www.apple.com/education/k12/leadership/effect.html*). According to Apple, "Effectiveness Reports provide easy access to important research findings about the effectiveness of technology in education. Each summary consists of a description of the role that technology plays in addressing a particular grade level and subject area, a list of the major research findings, full citation for the findings, additional useful readings, and places for educators to call or visit." That is true. The site does have summaries and conclusions from research studies of computers in schools, but all of them are positive. Apple's site is just as selective as Armstrong and Casement's review of the research in their book!

This is not an isolated phenomenon. We all approach research with our own biases and preconceptions. We have no God's Eye View, as the philosophers call it, that allows us to step outside our own biases and experiences and look at the world objectively. Even "objective" research is subjective! Does that mean we should stop doing or reading empirical research? No, it does not. It simply means that we need to be aware of possible biases and preconceptions when reading research. One of the more enthusiastic summaries of the available research is a study by Sivin-Kachala and Bialo (1994) entitled *Report on the Effectiveness of Technology in Schools 1990-1994*. The authors concluded, "Recent research consistently demonstrates the value of technology in enhancing student achievement." This study has been widely cited by proponents of computers in schools. However, it is always good to keep in mind that the study was funded by the Software Publishers Association. It is not likely the SPA would have accepted a report that said computers did not have a positive impact on education. Research about computing, *any* research, must not be considered an objective source of truth on a topic. It is simply one source of information, and it is best thought of as an effort to convince others that the conclusions of the authors, and possibly the sponsors, are believable.

Ideology and Testing: Another Example

Ideological critiques are not something new. They are, in fact, common in education. On a recent, extended trip to Turkey to work with some universities there, I took two books on testing in American schools. The two books could not have been more different in their answer to the "problems" of American education. One book was written by a Republican business leader and former Xerox CEO, David Kearns, and James Harvey (2000). It was a doctrinaire critique of American education in the tradition of conservative critics. With a forward by President George Bush, the book purports to provide a review of the research on schooling to show how bad schools in America are and how additional testing (referred to as *accountability* and *standards*) will solve the problem.

There is no doubt that the Kearns and Harvey book is ideologically based. They consistently criticize Deweyian progressive and constructivist approaches to education, and find methods advocated by them unacceptable or problematic. In one of the final chapters, Kearns and Harvey conclude that, if American education is going to prosper, "much greater accountability is needed in American public education" (p. 180). And they conclude that "the best way to hold schools accountable for their performance is to institute a statewide testing program, with the results for individual schools and districts made public" (p. 180). Further, they believe that "It is time to stop letting educators pull the wool over their own eyes. A little sunshine on how well our students are performing will work wonders to raise achievement" (p. 180). I do not have space to deal with all the errors in this concept of testing as the salvation of education. It is a logical extension of the "factory model" of education that emerged from Frederick Taylor's time and motion studies in the 1920s. My point is that this book is not based on research; the foundation is ideological.

The same is true of another book I took on my trip to Turkey. The title, *Standardized Minds: The Higher Price of America's Testing Culture and What We Can Do to Change It* (Sacks, 1999), is written by a liberal. While both books are about testing in American schools and both claim to support their positions with research, their conclusions about testing and schooling could hardly be farther apart. Instead of deciding that the research supports more testing, Sacks found that

> the evidence revealed the very troubling and costly effects of our growing dependence on large-scale mental testing to assess the quality of schools, one's merit for college, and a person's aptitude for many different jobs. In light of the evidence, I was dumbfounded that mental testing was continuing to carve out an increasingly entrenched and unquestioned position in our schools, colleges, and workplaces. (p. xi)

These two books, each thoughtfully written and supposedly based on the available research, reach opposite conclusions about testing in America. Sometimes they even cite the same examples to make their opposing points! If you still have doubts about whether ideology or research guides educational policy, reading these two books should convince you of the critically central role of ideology in policymaking and educational practice. (And, if you would like to read another book about the impact of implementing statewide accountability testing, I recommend Dale and Bonnie Johnson's book, *High Stakes: Children, Testing, and Failure in American Schools,* 2002.) One reader, in a review published by the online bookseller, Amazon (http://www.amazon.com), described the book as

> a critical, passionate, firsthand account of the 2000-01 school year in a Redbud, LA, elementary school, where teachers are among the lowest paid in the nation and 98 percent of the students qualify for free or reduced-price breakfast and lunch. Under Louisiana's accountability bureaucracy, the school is regulated, monitored, assessed, and labeled. The authors challenge the effectiveness of using standardized tests to make decisions in a school that lacks basic amenities and suffers from excessive student and teacher stress. They provide numerous examples, clear descriptions, and a deep appreciation for the role of teachers to illustrate the dire consequences of this emphasis on testing.

Competing Ideologies: Progressive and Conservative

There is nothing new in saying that there are two competing ideologies that vie for control of the policies and practices of American education. In a report of progress toward reforming American education, the Hudson Institute pointed its finger at one likely culprit:

When it comes to instructional philosophy, however, all the dominant approaches can be traced to a common ancestor: the progressive-education movement that arose in the early part of this century.

Strategies that heed this orthodoxy are described with such phrases as "student-centered," "child-centered," "learner-centered," "developmentally appropriate," "discovery-based," "self-directed," "constructivist," and the like. Their names, details, and emphases vary. These features, however, are less important than what their common dogma *excludes*. Practices that are deemed "teacher-directed" or "knowledge-based" or that involves "direct instruction" are most certainly *not* welcomed by contemporary instructional theorists. The pedagogic tent, it turns out, is not very big at all. (Finn & Ravitch, 1996)

I will quote the Hudson Institute report extensively because it illustrates how deeply ideology is entrenched in our views of education. The report on education reform is written from a conservative ideological perspective and is a cogent, confident expression of that viewpoint:

The reigning orthodoxy demands not only obeisance, but also the exclusion of dissenters. The results of rigorous studies and pilot projects that don't conform to progressive ideology are dismissed, while airy speculation, vacuous theories, and sloppy evaluations that buttress the prevailing wisdom are published in Ivy League education journals. Unproven methods are thus imposed on thousands of America schools. The failures that often follow are predictably attributed to lack of funding or time (no matter how much of either was available). Other excuses include lack of faith, inadequate staff development, ignorant parents, or a malevolent society. Never is it admitted that the concept itself may be flawed and the method ineffective, much less that different methods were ruled out and never tried.

The "child-centered" version of progressivism from which so much of today's constructivism flows is hostile to standards, assessments, and accountability. In the child-centered classroom, teachers are supposed to "facilitate," not teach. Teaching is scorned as didactic, almost authoritarian. Objective knowledge is replaced by learner-constructed knowledge, as though each child is ideally situated to reinvent what has been painfully learned by humankind over the centuries.

Because of the overwhelming preference for progressivism among education-school faculty, few researchers evince interest in what we now term "instructivist" programs, no matter how successful they appear to be, even with disadvantaged and low-achieving students.

Variously called "direct instruction," "mastery learning," "explicit teaching," or "precision teaching," these classroom strategies have key points in common. Teachers who use them are specific about what students are expected to learn, and they communicate these expectations clearly to their pupils; virtually all school time and energy are focused on the desired learning; testing provides frequent feedback on progress; success is rewarded; failure is not accepted; and effort continues until the goals are attained.

Despite their unpopularity among education-school faculty, instructivist methods seem to produce solid results, especially for children who need help in learning to read, write, and cipher. They start by assuming that the teacher knows something that children need to learn. They rely on carefully planned and purposeful teaching. They hinge, above all, on high-quality instruction by knowledgeable instructors. That's why we call this philosophy instructivism.

The Hudson Institute report was written by two very well known conservative critics of education, Chester Finn and Diane Ravitch. Their ideas are not random positions about specific issues in education. Their ideas "hang together"; they are a family of ideas that devolve naturally from the conservative ideology they hold true. I could select another report or paper that represents the ideas of a progressive educator and point out the same thing about his or her ideas. Progressives have a different set of foundational beliefs, and their educational policies and practices devolve naturally from them. Again, ideology is at the heart of important educational issues today.

Today conservative and progressive ideologies are associated with movements like those indicated in Table 1. Table 1 is admittedly overly simplistic and the two columns lump together many different movements that share many beliefs but differ on important issues as well. However, the list does illustrate the point that ideology is at the core of educational policy and practice today. It is also at the heart of educational computing. Ironically, the lists for conservative and progressive ideologies both include important roles for computers. Neither side sees computers as detrimental to education, but the role computers will play is radically different. I was once asked to participate in a project to develop an "ideal" high school that would be based on new models of teaching and learning, and infused with technology. The project was funded by one of the computer manufacturers and it was organized by a foundation. I was horrified to hear the plans for computers outlined by one of the foundation officers after a few days of meetings. His vision involved creating a standardized curriculum that would be taught by all teachers of a particular subject. Then the curriculum would be broken down into weekly and daily units. Once a week, on Friday, the students would go to the computer lab and take objective tests over the content of their courses. The computer system would then

TABLE 1. Conservative and Progressive Ideologies

Conservative		Progressive	
Content Issues			
1.	Back to basics	1.	Flexible learning
2.	State standards	2.	Teacher/student control
3.	Objective knowledge	3.	Constructed knowledge
4.	Reverence for the past	4.	Irreverence
5.	Teacher/society-determined goals	5.	Student/group-determined goals
6.	Phonics-based reading	6.	Whole language
7.	English immersion	7.	Bilingual education
8.	Content-centered education	8.	Constructed knowledge
9.	Correct answers	9.	Multiple perspectives
10.	Focus on mainstream America	10.	Multiculturalism
11.	Teach facts, truths	11.	Teach ideas, alternatives
Evaluation Issues			
12.	Standardized testing	12.	Portfolio assessment
13.	Computers for testing, tutoring, and training	13.	Computers for self-directed learning
14.	Accountability	14.	Excellence
Pedagogy Issues			
15.	Traditional, teacher-centered teaching	15.	Student-centered teaching
16.	An established canon of content	16.	An open, evolving canon
17.	Competition	17.	Collaboration
18.	Rugged individualism	18.	Group processes
19.	Drills, tutorials, etc.	19.	Simulations, problems, Internet
20.	Teaching as a technical skill	20.	Teaching as an art
21.	Teach	21.	Facilitate
Policy Issues			
22.	School choice, charter schools	22.	Support for public schools
23.	Melting pot mentality	23.	Diversity
24.	No "special" treatment	24.	Gender, ethnic equity

analyze the data and provide printouts to the assistant principal on Monday morning that showed him/her which teachers were meeting the goals for the courses and which were not. A teacher who regularly failed to meet objectives would be provided with remedial professional help; and, if that failed to bring up the test scores, he or she would be fired. While this proposal was drastic, it is in line with conservative ideology. I, as a progressive, found it abhorrent.

Take a look at the two lists in Table 1. Then consider the implications of each ideology for how computers are used in education. Take one example: competition versus collaboration. It would not be difficult to use computers to support competitive educational activities. And, it would not be difficult to create computer resources that support collaborative learning environments. The question is, Which effort will be funded, encouraged, supported, and nurtured by teachers, schools, school systems, and state and national governments? Take another difference: teach facts, truths versus teach ideas, alternatives. Integrated Learning Systems are a natural way of teaching simple facts and skills in an effective, automated way. They are not so good, however, at helping students understand ideas and alternatives.

Each of the differences between conservative and progressive approaches to education has implications for educational computing. And, when choices are made between these alternatives, the choice will not be made on the basis of objective research; it will be a battle of ideologies.

The Case of Critical Theory

Thus far, I have presented a simplistic picture of the debates over computers in schools. In my discussion, they have involved two broad groups–conservatives and progressives. The situation is actually much more complex than that. For example, some conservatives see computers as a problem; others see them as benefits if they are used "correctly." This emphasis on "correct" use is at the heart of another ideology, critical theory. Critical theorists take a neo-Marxist view of technology use and argue that it is being used today in American schools to support methods of teaching and learning that are detrimental to both students and teachers.

David Blacker (1995), using the term *instrumentalism,* described critical theory this way:

> Instrumentalism is anti-technology insofar as it considers present usage to be overwhelmingly driven by morally suspect motives; technology is problematic, but *only as it is currently employed.* Technology's liberatory potential awaits societal change, usually of fairly major proportions. Most anti-technology instrumentalism in education is Marxist in provenance and takes the form of socio-political critique. Following Andrew Feenberg's philosophical statement of this general position, it might be called a "critical theory of technology" (CTT).
>
> CTT typically regards all other views of technology as so many smokescreens behind which certain social groups, usually identified as the patriarchy, the capitalists, or some other cultural elite, advance their agendas of domination. A focus on the tools themselves aids in maintaining privilege by deflecting critical scrutiny away from the real motive forces of society, the economy and those who control it.

Blacker further divides critical theory into two types:

> In educational theory, two more or less distinct levels of CTT may be identified. First-level CTT corresponds to a straightforwardly unrecon- structed, Marxist analysis. Although I know of no comprehensive state- ment of first-level CTT in education, Bowles's and Gintis's *Schooling in Capitalist America* suggests that technology, like schooling, essentially functions as a superstructural variable dependent upon the economic base of society and those who control it. And while these authors claim to allow for a certain amount of dialectical interplay between base and superstructure (as any but the most vulgar Marxist should), they never- theless counsel unequivocally that technology itself is mostly beside the point: "If meaningful educational reform requires a transformation of production relations, as we believe, we must begin by creating a new so- cial structure, not a new technology" (p. 69). One does not liberate to- day's oppressive classroom by altering its physical structure, but rather by teaching liberating things for tomorrow's liberated society. Sec- ond-level CTT shares with the Marxist view the contention that at pres- ent technology serves elite groups and that the task of a radical pedagogy is to uncover how and why this happens. But it differs markedly by not regarding technology as a *neutral* tool in the service of hegemonic power; technology is non-neutral in the sense that, as it is currently con- stituted, it has demonstrably prejudicial *effects* and, therefore, works to privilege some groups at the expense of others. . . . Elites not only use technology as a club, but use it also to conceal that there is any clubbing going on at all. It provides a perfect weapon–effective yet invisible. And the more value-neutral we regard it, the more invisible it becomes. (Blacker, 1995)

Leading critical theorists who emphasize the role of technology in educa- tion and society include Michael Apple (1992) and Andrew Feenberg (2001), but there are many others. Another critical theorist (Streibel, 1991) described the way computers influence education this way:

> Computers tend to legitimize those types of knowledge that fit into their framework and delegitimize other types of knowledge. . . . Hence, com- puters tend to legitimize the following characteristics of knowledge . . . : rule-governed order, objective systematicity, explicit clarity, non-ambi- guity, non-redundancy, internal consistency, non-contradiction (i.e., logic of the excluded middle), and quantitative aspects. They also tend to legiti- mize deduction and induction as the only acceptable epistemological methods.
>   By way of contrast, computers tend to delegitimize the follow- ing characteristics of knowledge . . . : emergent goals, self-constructed

order, organic systematicity, connotation and tacitness, ambiguity, re-
dundancy, dialectical rationality, simultaneity of multiple logics, and
qualitative aspects. And finally, they tend to delegitimize the following
epistemological methods: abduction, interpretation, intuition, introspection, and dialectical synthesis of multiple and contradictory realities.
(p. 317)

Because space is limited I will not attempt to provide a well-rounded and
exhaustive view of this ideology and the way critical theorists look at computers in education. However, for those who wish to read more about educational
technology from the critical theory perspective, I recommend the books and
papers of authors like Ann De Vaney, Robert Muffoletto, Neil Postman, and
Michael Streibel.

What Do You Do as a Consumer of Ideas?

I would like now to expand on the idea that ideology is at the center of debates about computers in schools. Ideology is often associated with politics.
However, I do not mean that everything can be explained on the basis of
whether you are a Republican or a Democrat (or Conservative, Liberal, or La-
bor if you are in the UK). Political philosophies are expressions of broader,
more fundamental belief systems. So are psychological and educational theories. There are, in fact, ideological families that have specific applications at
different levels of thought and practice. For example, in Table 2, the three columns represent three ideological families: conservative, progressive, and critical. However, those names apply only at the level of educational ideology. At
other levels, such as philosophy of science, different terms are used. Each column is thus a "family" of beliefs, and at each level in this table the beliefs and
values are expressed in ways that are meaningful at that level. I have also included in this list a leading proponent or two of each ideology at each level.

These are, of course, not the only ideological families, but they are the most
active and influential in American education, and in the field of educational
computing. Although I am a strong believer in the middle, progressive, ideological family, I am not suggesting that you adopt that ideology. What I am
suggesting is that you always ask yourself, what is the ideological position of
the author of this book, paper, or presentation? If, as I believe, there is no such
thing as objective research that will definitively answer basic questions about
computers in schools, then all of our research, our arguments, and our pontifi-
cating about computers is tinged with and influenced by our ideology. And, if
you are to be a good consumer of all the sound and fury about computers in
schools, you must be able to see both what the author means and the context,
the background, the framework in which the author worked out his or her conclusions. It is only with this dual understanding–of meaning and context–that

TABLE 2. The Three Ideological Families

Educational Ideology		
Conservative	Progressive	Critical
Diane Ravitch	John Dewey	Michael Apple
Educational Pedagogy		
Instructivism/ Direct Instruction	Situated Cognition	Emancipatory/Liberation
Siegfried Engellman	John Seeley Brown, Paul Duguid, Allan Collins	Paulo Freire/Michael Apple
Psychological Theory		
Behaviorism	Constructivism	Postmodern/ Critical Psychology
B. F. Skinner	John Bransford	Rom Harre
Research Methodology		
Quantitative/Empirical	Qualitative/Interpretive	Critical Research Methods
Donald Campbell	Yvonna Lincoln/Egon Guba Norman Denzin	Phillip Carspecken Peter McLaren
Philosophy of Science		
Empiricism/Positivism/ Realism Post-Empiricism/ Post-Positivism	Interpretivism/ Cultural Relativism Sociological Philosophy of Science	Critical Realism
Sir Karl Popper/D. C. Phillips	Thomas Kuhn	Christopher Norris
Philosophy		
Realism/Empiricism	Democratic Pragmatism	Neo-Marxism
Positivism	Constructivism	Critical Theory
D. C. Phillips	Richard Rorty, Ludwig Wittgensetin	

you will be able to learn the most from the vast and growing literature in our field.

What Do You Do as a Person of Influence?

A second issue is, What do you do when you want to influence others? There are really two answers to that question. If you wish to influence those within your own ideological family, then you use the forms, language, and procedures that your group values. For empiricists, it will often be hard-nosed research done carefully on topics the group considers important. However, for interpretivists, it may be detailed case studies, interviews, or observations, and your method of communication may be stories told richly and with feeling.

If you wish to have a wider impact, to influence people who may not share your ideological beliefs, the process is much more complex. There are the unethical approaches, which many, if not most, politicians take. Use the language and terminology of opponents but attach your own meaning. Focus on the fears and concerns of your audience and present your view as a solution, even if that is not true. Enhance your position by tearing down the opponent or the opponent's position with spurious accusations or claims.

But what if you want to honestly influence others? In my view you must consider what the target group considers worth listening to. Is it research? Then do the research or find research that is relevant to the question? Is it bold narrative? Case studies? Reflective statements? Political statements? Petitions? Voter opinion? Pressure from interest groups? Public hearings? Special events? Lobbying? Dialog? Debates? Center reports? Policy statements? Organizational position papers? Invited conferences? Press releases? Something else? Empirical research is one of many ways to influence others, and it is, in most cases, one of the least effective. Other forms of influence are likely to be more powerful and more effective. The trick is to match your methods with your purpose and the audience you wish to influence.

IN CONCLUSION

In the 20 years since *Computers in the Schools* began publication, the field has expanded, become more sophisticated, and more integrated into the fabric of education. For much of that time most of us have assumed that empirical research is an important, even critical, aspect of advancement and influence. A careful study of these past 20 years, however, suggests that ideology, not research, is the most powerful influence on both whether and how computers are used in education. If that is true, we must be continually aware of the role ideology plays in efforts to influence us, and also take it into consideration when trying to influence others.

REFERENCES

Apple, M. W. (1992). Computers in schools: Salvation or social disaster? *Education Digest, 57*(6), 47-52.

Armstrong, A. & Casement, C. (2000). *The child and the machine: How computers put our children at risk.* New York: Robin Lane Press.

Bangert-Drowns, R., Kulik, J., & Kulik, C. (1985). Effectiveness of computer-based education in secondary schools. *Computers in Human Behavior, 12*(3), 59-68.

Bayraktar, S. (2002). A meta-analysis of the effectiveness of computer-assisted instruction in science education. *Journal of Research on Technology in Education, 34*(2), 18-32.

Blacker, D. (1995). *Philosophy of technology and education: An invitation to inquiry.* Retrieved October 25, 2002, from http://www.ed.uiuc.edu/EPS/PES-yearbook/94_docs/BLACKER.HTM

Bowles, S., & Gintis, H. (1976). *Schooling in capitalist America.* New York: Basic Books.

Bracey, B., & Galus, A. (1998). *Bonnie responds.* Retrieved October 25, 2002, from http://www.tnellen.com/ted/tc/bonnie.html

Clark, M., & Wentworth, C. (1997, April 17-19). Constructivism and the development of multimedia applications. *Proceedings of the 30th Annual Small College Computing Symposium* (pp. 8-33). University of Wisconsin-Parkside. Retrieved October 25, 2002, from http://www.doane.edu/crete/academic/science/phy/SCCPAP.htm

Cuban, L. (2001). *Oversold and underused: Computers in the classroom.* Cambridge, MA: Harvard University Press. Available from http://www.hup.harvard.edu/catalog/CUBOVE.html

Cuban, L. (1986). *Teachers and machines: The classroom use of technology since 1920.* New York: Teachers College Press.

Feenberg, A. (2001). *Critical theory of technology* (2nd ed.). Oxford, UK: Oxford University Press.

Finn, C., & Ravitch, D. (1996). Education Reform 1995-1996: Part IV. Instruction: The Tyranny of Dogma. Indianapolis: Hudson Institute. Retrieved October 25, 2002, from http://www.edexcellence.net/library/epciv.html

Friedrich, O. (January 3, 1983). Time Man of the Year: 1982–The Computer. *Time Magazine,* p. 6.

Hiemstra, R. (2002). *Lifelong learning: An exploration of adult and continuing education within a setting of lifelong learning needs.* Fayetteville, NY: HiTree Press.

Hlynka, D., & Yeaman, A. (1992). *Postmodern educational technology.* ERIC Digest, EDO-IR-Syracuse, NY: ERIC Clearinghouse on Information Resources. Retrieved October 25, 2002, from http://www.csu.edu.au/research/sda/Reports/pmarticle.html

Johnson, D., & Johnson, B. (2002). *High stakes: Children, testing, and failure in American schools.* Lanham, MD: Rowan & Littlefield.

Kearns, D., & Harvey, J. (2000). *A legacy of learning: Your stake in standards and new kinds of public schools.* Washington, DC: Brookings Institution Press.

Kennedy, S., Segal, Z., Lam, R., & Whitney, D. (2002, March). Re: Short term dynamic therapies in the treatment of major depression. *The Canadian Journal of Psychiatry, 47*(2), 193-194. Retrieved October 25, 2002, from http://www.cpa-apc.org/Publications/Archives/CJP/2002/march/letters2.asp.

Kulik, J. (1994). Meta-analytic studies of findings on computer-based instruction. In E. L. Baker & H. F. O'Neil, Jr. (Eds.), *Technology assessment in education and training* (pp. 7-33). Hillsdale, NJ: Erlbaum.

Kulik, J., Bangert-Drowns, R., & Williams, G. (1983). Effects of computer-based teaching on secondary school students. *Journal of Educational Psychology, 75,* 19-26.

Kulik, J., & Kulik, C. (1991). *Effectiveness of computer-based instruction: An updated analysis.* Ann Arbor: University of Michigan, Center for Research on Learning and Teaching.

Kulik, J., Kulik, C., & Bangert-Drowns, R. (1985). Effectiveness of computer-based education in elementary schools. *Computers in Human Behavior, 1,* 59-74.

Lowyck, J., & Elen, J. (1998). *The learner in the centre of world-wide learning: The promised Land of ICT.* Paper presented at the European Conference on Computer Assisted Language Learning, Leuven, Belgium. Available from e-learnit.fi/nettped/NettpedagogikkTS2.pdf

Mandinach, E.B., & Cline, H.F. (1997). *Methodological implications for examining the impact of technology-based innovations: The corruption of a research design.* Paper presented at the annual meeting of the American Educational Research Association, Chicago.

Oppenheimer, T. (1997, July). The computer delusion. *The Atlantic Monthly Online Edition.* Retrieved October 25, 2002, from http://www.theatlantic.com/issues/97jul/computer.htm

Ryan, A. (1991). Meta-analysis of achievement effects of microcomputer application in elementary schools. *Educational Administration Quarterly, 27*(2), 161-184.

Sacks, P. (1999). *Standardized minds: The high price of America's testing culture and what we can do to change it.* Cambridge, MA: Perseus Publishing.

Schacter, J. (1999). *The impact of educational technology on student achievement: What the most current research has to say.* Santa Monica, CA: Miliken Family Foundation. Available from http://www.mff.org/publications/publications.taf?page=161

Sivin-Kachala, J., & Bialo, E. (1994). *Report on the effectiveness of technology in schools 1990-1994.* Conducted by Interactive Educational Systems Design, New York, NY. Commissioned by Software Publishers Association.

Skinner, B.F. (1968). *The teaching machine.* New York: Appleton-Century Croft.

Soe, K., Koki, S., & Chang, J. (2000). Effect of computer-assisted instruction (CAI) on reading achievement: A meta-analysis. Honolulu: Pacific Resources for Education and Learning. Available from http://www.prel.org/products/Products/Effect-CAI.pdf

Streibel, M. (1991). A critical analysis of the use of computers in education. In Denis Hlynka & J. C. Belland (Eds.), *Paradigms regained: The uses of illuminative, semiotic and post-modern criticism as modes of inquiry in educational technology* (pp. 283-334). Englewood Cliffs, NJ: Educational Technology Publications.

Tenderbuttons: Gertrude Stein online. Retrieved May 20, 2003, from http://tenderbuttons.com/gsonline/alice.html

The future of children. (2001). *Journal Issue Sheds Light on How Computers Affect Children at School and at Home.* Washington, DC: The David & Lucile Packard Foundation. Available from http://www.futureofchildren.org/newsletter2861/newsletter_show.htm?doc_id=57430

Willis, J. (1984). Educational computing: Current status and future directions. *Computers in the Schools, 1*(1), 3-12.

Cleborne D. Maddux

Twenty Years of Research in Information Technology in Education: Assessing Our Progress

SUMMARY. The twentieth anniversary of *Computers in the Schools* is an occasion to reflect on the state of the art in information technology in education. Computers are probably no longer in danger of being abandoned by schools; and, in fact, computers have gained so much cultural momentum that educators could probably not intentionally *prevent* their continued integration into schooling. On the other hand, they have not brought about the revolution in education that was hoped for when the field first began. This article explores some of the reasons why computers have not yet fulfilled their considerable educational promise, and why research has so little to do with what goes on in schools. The article goes on to identify some of the things that research has taught us about information technology in education, and to explore some possible solutions to our considerable problems. *[Article copies available for a fee from The Haworth Document Delivery Service: 1-800-HAWORTH. E-mail address: <docdelivery@haworthpress.com> Website: <http://www.HaworthPress.com> © 2003 by The Haworth Press, Inc. All rights reserved.]*

CLEBORNE D. MADDUX is Associate Editor for Research, *Computers in the Schools*, and Professor, University of Nevada, Reno, Department of Counseling and Educational Psychology, Reno, NV 89557 (E-mail: maddux@unr.edu).

[Haworth co-indexing entry note]: "Twenty Years of Research in Information Technology in Education: Assessing Our Progress." Maddux, Cleborne D. Co-published simultaneously in *Computers in the Schools* (The Haworth Press, Inc.) Vol. 20, No. 1/2, 2003, pp. 35-48; and: *Technology in Education: A Twenty-Year Retrospective* (ed: D. LaMont Johnson, and Cleborne D. Maddux) The Haworth Press, Inc., 2003, pp. 35-48. Single or multiple copies of this article are available for a fee from The Haworth Document Delivery Service [1-800-HAWORTH, 9:00 a.m. - 5:00 p.m. (EST). E-mail address: docdelivery@haworthpress.com].

10.1300/J025v20n01_03

KEYWORDS. Information technology in education, research quality in education, fads in information technology in education, problems in information technology in education, qualitative research, educational research

INTRODUCTION

Writing an article for the twentieth anniversary of *Computers in the Schools* is a sobering task. It is a reminder that we are beginning the third decade of widespread interest in using computers in education. While 20 years of activity is certainly not a long period of time in the history of academic endeavor, neither is it the mark of a brand new area of interest that has yet to prove itself more than a passing fad. On the contrary, for the first time it is probably safe to say that computers are here to stay, both in the culture at large and in schools. In fact, as I pointed out in a recent article in this journal, educators could probably not *stop* computers from continuing to find their way into schools, even if we tried to do so. For me, that alone makes the 20-year mark an important milestone, an event deserving of notice, and comment.

I am not sure exactly at what point computers in education were no longer at risk of abandonment. It happened gradually and without fanfare sometime in the last 10 years, probably in the last five years. At least, it didn't seem to me to be the case just 10 years ago on the tenth anniversary of this journal. At that time, it still seemed very much in doubt whether or not computers in schools would revolutionize education or end up gathering dust in school closets alongside yellowing stacks of programmed learning workbooks and discarded teaching machines.

What I am trying to say is that the state of affairs on this twentieth anniversary engenders both good and bad news. The good news is information technology in education is alive and well, growing and evolving, and no longer at risk of abandonment. The bad news is that the hoped-for revolution in education has not yet begun, and might never occur at all. In fact, in a field marked by one fantastic development after another, the most fantastic of all may be that anything so ubiquitous and so powerful as information technology has had so little impact on teachers, students, and schools.

THE MINIMAL EFFECT
OF INFORMATION TECHNOLOGY ON SCHOOLING

This fact, although startling, is not new to anyone who has followed events in schools for the last 20 years. For that entire time, article after article and report after report have concluded that the effect of information technology on teaching and learning has been disappointingly minimal. I have made that point myself, in articles that have appeared in this journal and others.

The natural question on this 20th anniversary is one we have been asking ourselves periodically for the last 20 years: Why has information technology failed so completely at living up to its considerable educational potential?

It has taken me more than 30 years as an educator to realize that few, if any, important questions in education have simple answers, and few, if any, educational problems have single causes. This problem is no exception. I can think of a number of factors contributing to the minimal impact of information technology on educational practice. Many of these are related to a truism I avoided admitting for years: the fact that education, like all areas of public policy, is profoundly influenced by political, social, and economic factors, and only superficially by scientific (or even logical) considerations. As a young professional, steeped in the importance of educational research and cloaked in lofty idealism, that was a difficult realization for me to accept. I left teacher training secure in the belief that I would find educational practice based firmly on educational research, and teachers, principals, and school board members eager consumers of the latest educational research results.

Anyone who has worked in a school would marvel at the naiveté of such an expectation. Every teacher knows research results have little to do with what goes on in schools.

The Time Factor

There are many reasons why research lacks strong influence in education. An important factor is that educators do not have time to locate and read research. Teachers face students for the entire workday. Principals, who seldom take even a single class in research or statistics, spend an ever-increasing amount of time on school public relations, discipline problems, and budgetary matters. School board members, even if they are inclined to pay attention to research (and most are not), have their hands full responding to a never-ending succession of "one-issue" community pressure groups while working at their own full-time jobs.

The Education Subculture

While lack of time is unquestionably a factor in weakening the influence of research on educational practice, it is not the whole story. After all, other professionals, such as those working in medicine and engineering are also busy, yet find time for reading and implementing research results. I suspect that the difference has much to do with variations in professional subcultures. Physicians and engineers leave training fully convinced of the critical importance of staying current on the latest research. Educators, on the other hand, are indifferent, and sometimes even hostile, toward the very notion of educational research.

This problem is one that can be laid directly on the doorsteps of those of us in higher education. We have simply failed to convince our undergraduate students and many of our master's-level students of the importance of research. There are multiple causes for this failure.

Deficient Preparation in Research and Statistics

Unlike premedical students and engineering undergraduates, teachers-in-training are usually not required to take even one research or statistics course, and many, if not most, education master's programs also lack such a requirement. In those rare programs in which a course is required, it is all too often taught, not as a practical tool, but as some kind of mathematical *trial by fire*, with every equation tediously derived on the board by an instructor who has little or no experience as a real researcher and who takes pride in the number of failing grades that are issued each semester (Maddux, 2001). Thus, teachers enter the field, and even obtain advanced degrees, without the knowledge needed to be competent consumers of research, much less to conduct their own research. Negative attitudes toward research, already established partly through curricular neglect in undergraduate training, are reinforced as students move into student teaching and encounter cooperating teachers who have passed through the same educational programs and themselves have no expertise in, or respect for, research.

The False Dichotomy of Theory versus Method

Negative attitudes toward research are also an unintentional side effect in colleges that encourage students to think in terms of "methods courses" and "theory courses." This artificial dichotomy implies that theory has no relation to practice, and thus has no practical value. Because research is the way theory is generated and tested, this further denigrates both theory and research in the minds of students. Then, too, "methods courses" in such institutions are all too often based on the infamous "make it and take it" strategy, in which the emphasis is on constructing simple visual display materials for use in the classroom. This atheoretical, crafts orientation to teaching can cause students to conclude that good teaching requires little more than competence with scissors, paste, and construction paper. It is probably inevitable that research will be seen as irrelevant when undue emphasis is placed on producing an attractive bulletin board.

THE QUANTITY AND QUALITY OF RESEARCH ON INFORMATION TECHNOLOGY IN EDUCATION

Of course, any discussion of reasons for the minimal impact of research on educational practice should also consider the quantity and quality of existing research. Certainly, an evaluative approach to the body of research on information technology in education seems appropriate for this 20th anniversary volume. Just how good is our research base, and what have we found out empirically about information technology and its uses in teaching and learning?

There is definitely an impressively large body of research that has been conducted and published over the last 20 years. At least a dozen journals are dedicated to the general topic of information technology in education, and many others deal with specialized, or discipline-specific applications. Most are devoted, wholly or in part, to research. A World Wide Web search in Google (http://www.google.com) using the search string "research" and "information technology in education" produced nearly 6,000 hits, while "research" and "computers in education" produced 18,500 pages.

Research Stages

Of course, quality is much more difficult to evaluate. As I look back over the last 20 years, I think I recognize several phases or stages through which research in this field has passed. In fact, in 1993 I published, in an AACE monograph, an article identifying my perceptions of research stages from the 1970s to that point (Maddux, 1993). At that time, I thought there had been two distinct research stages, and I identified a third that I believed was just beginning.

Stage One. Stage One began in the middle to late seventies amid much discussion of the importance of *computer literacy*. Research was crude and seldom experimental. The literature consisted mostly of position papers, anecdotal reports, descriptive research, informal case studies, needs assessments, and reports of surveys. Because computer software was scarce in both amount and kind, programming in the BASIC language was often an important component of school computer literacy programs. Surveys of teachers, administrators, parents, and others revealed strong concern with providing more children with access to computing for longer periods of time. In short, Stage One research and practice were distinguished by a strong, unstated assumption *that mere exposure to computers would result in general educational benefits.*

Stage Two. Stage Two began in the middle to late eighties, when it became apparent to many educators that the computer literacy movement was ill advised for a number of reasons. At the time, one of the arguments for requiring programming of all students was vocational in nature. Many early school computing advocates had argued that children should be taught to program computers because jobs of the future would require it. However, it became clear that the need for programmers was leveling off (at about 20,000 jobs according to Kelman [1984]) and it would thus make little sense to create a curriculum to make programmers of the nation's 40 million school children.

Research, while still simplistic in concept, improved considerably in Stage Two. Many more studies employing experimental and control groups were published, and most investigators abandoned designs intended to demonstrate general educational benefits as a result of exposure to computers. The best research during Stage Two focused on specific school computing applications and attempted to assess their effects on a variety of dependent variables.

The problem with the bulk of the research in Stage Two was that much of it still focused on simple exposure to computers, *since it ignored teacher and learner variables.* Research hypotheses tended to resemble the following:

> *IF LEARNERS* (AT ANY LEVEL, ANY AGE, ANY GENDER, ANY GRADE, ANY IQ, ETC.) *ARE TAUGHT* [some computer application] (FOR ANY LENGTH OF TIME, USING ANY METHOD, BY ANY TEACHER, ETC.), *THEY WILL IMPROVE MORE IN* [some cognitive or performance variable] *THAN AN EXPERIMENTAL GROUP WHO ARE TAUGHT TRADITIONALLY* [whatever that is]. (Maddux, 1993, p. 16)

These designs were simplistic, but at least they began to include control groups and focus on specific dependent variables, rather than on general educational benefits.

Stage Three. Stage Three was, I thought, just beginning at the time of the 1993 article on research stages. Stage Three research, I suggested, would focus on *specific applications in the context of learner/treatment interactions.* At the time, I listed a few hypothetical research topics I thought illustrative of the type of research that would use this new, more complex, and more productive approach. Then, as now, I believed that the Logo programming language was highly promising as a vehicle to teach improved problem-solving skills. Therefore, the examples I used were Logo-oriented:

1. How successful are students at mastering Logo at different ages and ability levels using discovery teaching methods? In other words, we should seek to determine how learner variables interact with teaching methods as they relate to Logo mastery.
2. How do different teaching methodologies compare in effectiveness when applied to the turtle graphics parts of the language and when applied to the list processing parts?
3. What kinds of misunderstandings are common to learning disabled and non-learning disabled students when structured vs. discovery teaching is employed?
4. There is also the question of whether teaching programming can result in improved problem-solving skills that will transfer to other problem domains. We know that transfer is not automatic, and we now have some clues about how to facilitate transfer. . . . An important question is: What are the best ways to do this with varying types of students and for transfer to varying problem domains? (Maddux, 1993, p. 19)

I concluded that an approach focusing on learner/treatment interactions would be the hallmark of future research as we moved into Stage Three.

WHY DID STAGE THREE NEVER ARRIVE?

In looking back at that optimistic prediction today, I can only wonder what went wrong. While the period since 1993 has produced a number of excellent studies, I find the current overall quality of research in information technology in education to be somewhat disappointing. For the last 10 years, we seem to have been stuck somewhere between Stage Two and Stage Three, with a great many studies still fruitlessly pitting computer approaches against non-computer approaches without consideration of critical learner/treatment interactions and often without sufficient description of the "traditional method" used by control groups. In fact, a recent article by Lowe (2001-2002) analyzed and attempted to synthesize the results from five meta-analyses that covered a total of 247 studies "conducted to compare computer-based education (CBE) to traditional classroom education" (p. 163). Lowe concluded that these five meta-analyses showed that CBE has a positive effect on learning when compared to traditional instruction. Although she does not directly refer to the problem of unaddressed learner/treatment interactions, she cautions that

> The positive effects of CBE may be the uncontrolled effects of instructional method or content differences between treatments that were compared. . . . Unless a design can hold all the variables constant except CBE compared to traditional classroom instruction, these results have limited validity. (p. 169)

I agree, and I cannot help but marvel that so many researchers continue to pursue such a sterile and simplistic research paradigm. Why has this occurred?

The Problem of Fads in Education

Again, there are probably multiple causes. However, I believe one powerful reason is the tendency for professionals in the field of information technology in education to be unduly influenced by fad and fashion. Education in general has always been driven by caprice. However, it seems to me that, since the early 1990s (when, probably not coincidentally, we failed to conclusively emerge from Stage Two), many of us in information technology in education have set an entirely new standard for excess in this regard.

Actually, fleeting enthusiasms have always driven the field. In Stage One, however, such fads consisted primarily of specific technological innovations, which were then arriving at breakneck speed. With Stage Two, some temporary "hot topics" were technological and some conceptual, but all burst upon the scene; consumed a huge amount of time, energy, and enthusiasm (to say nothing of print and paper); and just as quickly as they had arrived, most faded from view. A short list of some of these early vagaries includes computer literacy, equity, the student-to-computer ratio, authoring systems, BASIC programming, Logo programming, and expert systems.

I do not, by the way, mean to imply that all or even many of these fads were somehow unworthy of serious attention. On the contrary, many, such as concern about equity and excitement about the Logo programming language, were then, and today remain, important topics that should be receiving much more attention than they are presently receiving from researchers and practitioners alike. I believe our field the lesser for its too-hasty abandonment.

Therein lies the rub with fashion in general, and fashion in education in particular. Achievement of fad status almost always sounds the death knell for an idea or an innovation, especially in education, where innovations are not adopted as a result of successful research. Instead, practitioners who do not read or value research find out about new practices primarily by word of mouth from other teachers, through the popular media, or from an educational materials salesperson. Information gained from such sources tends to be biased and potential advantages highly exaggerated. Thus, expectations for the innovation are unrealistically high. When they fail to prove to be the panaceas they were predicted to be, a backlash against them tends to result in complete abandonment. Needless to say, such a destructive pendulum cycle of unrealistic expectations followed by disappointment and abandonment creates a roller coaster of ideas and emotions and often results in "the baby being thrown out with the bath water," as has been the case with the Logo programming language (at least in the United States) and a number of other promising innovations.

What has this pendulum cycle to do with the quality of research in information technology in education? Excellent research does not occur in a vacuum. It has been said that scientists stand on the shoulders of their predecessors. An important body of research builds slowly, where new research is based on earlier studies, that guide researchers on what to include and what to avoid. Researchers, however, can be diverted by fads because grant and publishing opportunities tend to favor topics that are currently in vogue. When short-lived fads dominate a field, there is no time for a critical body of early literature to be produced on a specific topic and to lead to more complex, creative, and sophisticated questions and designs. Interest in new innovations can come so quickly that none are ever properly and thoroughly researched before being replaced with something newer.

Since 1993, the fads have increased both in strength and in number. Only a few representative ones include e-mail and the Internet, the World Wide Web, cooperative learning, postmodernism, feminist pedagogy, Neo-Marxism, qualitative research, constructivism, partnerships with business and industry, wireless networks, distance education, handheld computing, and most recently, WebQuests.

E-mail, the Internet, and the Web are so powerful and pervasive that they can be considered a fad only in the sense that interest is intense and expectations are unrealistically high. However, the interest is unlikely to be temporary, so perhaps they should not be included in a list of fads. However, the point is that there have been so many "hot topics" of late that there has been no time to develop a competent body of research on any one topic. E-mail, the Internet, and the Web, although in a class by themselves, have certainly contributed to that dilemma.

The Problem of Extremism and Qualitative Research

There is another of the above topics that seems to me to deserve a place of its own, especially in terms of the destructive nature of its influence on research in education in general, and on research in our field in particular. That topic is *qualitative research*.

Widespread interest in qualitative research began to emerge in our field in the early 1990s and has recently reached a fever pitch. While there is nothing really new about qualitative research, and while it is a completely legitimate form of inquiry for certain research questions in certain educational domains, extremists who view it as a panacea have taken its advocacy to a level that is near religious in fervor.

Like feminist pedagogy and Neo-Marxism, extremist advocacy of qualitative research in education seems to have emerged most recently from a collection of diverse counter-culture movements sometimes given the appropriately contradictory term of *postmodernism* by some of its devotees. The extremists to whom I refer are unabashedly and openly antiscientific in their attitudes, but they have gained a surprising following in education, particularly among higher education faculty in information technology in education. The more extreme of these individuals take the position that science and the scientific method have nothing to offer education, and they maintain that traditional, quantitative research should be totally abandoned in favor of qualitative methodologies. Kauffman (1999) has commented on postmodern/deconstructivist philosophy as follows: "We should not underestimate the popularity of nonscientific and aggressively *anti*scientific beliefs today. Nor should we dismiss the danger of such sentiments and frames of mind for education" (p. 249).

Of course, there are some excellent examples of qualitative research that have been published in education in the last few years. However, I have read every research manuscript submitted to this journal over the last 20 years, and I serve as a referee for a number of other journals devoted to information technology in education. In the last 10 years, I believe I have seen a troubling increase in the number of incompetent and incomprehensible manuscripts submitted under the rubric of qualitative research. The situation has reached such a deplorable level that I believe it is time for us to tell the emperor the truth about his new clothes.

Calling an article "qualitative" does not excuse sloppy thinking, poor writing, or a total lack of structure or advance planning. I believe it is imperative that we put a stop to the idea that a qualitative study excuses the writer from any need to be clear, thorough, and succinct, or that political correctness requires us to be accepting or even welcoming of manuscripts that do not demonstrate basic literacy.

I believe there are two different types of manuscripts that currently make up most of the qualitative submissions to our journals. The first group tends to be written by a small number of authors and their manuscripts are highly professional, literate, thorough, and deserving of publication. These authors usually regard qualitative and quantitative strategies as equally legitimate, and while they may have a personal preference for qualitative designs, they read, appreciate, and understand quantitative studies. The second group, which is deplorably large and growing, is authored by individuals who have embraced qualitative research because they believe it releases them from rigor or discipline of any kind in their thinking, writing, or research methodology. Many of these individuals suffer from mathematics anxiety, and embrace the idea of qualitative research only because they believe it means they can continue to humor their mathematics anxiety and ignore the need to master the basic arithmetic and number concepts necessary to use statistics as a tool in quantitative research.

I have no quarrel at all with the first group. It is the second group that is making an unfortunate contribution to the poor quality of research in our field. It is especially deplorable that many recent doctoral degree recipients openly admit they have no training or interest in quantitative design. I have actually heard that position expressed during interviews for faculty positions at my own institution. I have no way of knowing for sure, but suspect that dogmatism of this degree is unlikely to be characteristic of those individuals who are producing some of the few good qualitative studies I have seen recently. I suspect instead that these are the types of individuals who seem to believe that poor qualitative research is superior to good quantitative research, and who produce the incredibly poor manuscripts to which I have been referring in this article.

This deplorable state of affairs has inevitably begun to have an effect on the quality of theses and dissertations. I have recently attended a number of doctoral dissertation proposal meetings during which students have proposed studies they have characterized as qualitative in nature. A few of these have been interesting and well planned and have led to informative and competent manuscripts. However, others have been completely unplanned, unstructured to the point of chaos, and the student has emerged from the meeting with the committee's approval to proceed with instructions so vague and ill-defined that they amount to *carte blanche* to do whatever the student pleases. If such students ever finish their degrees, I cannot help but wonder if they will have the research tools they will need to prosper as professors, or more importantly, to help us improve the quality of research in our field.

There is a strong indication that such attitudes toward doctoral-level research is spreading across the country. At a recent international conference, I was surprised to hear one of the pioneers in our field, and an individual for whom I have had the greatest respect, announce in a formal presentation that he believed that a doctoral dissertation in information technology in education could quite appropriately be a play, a poem, a statue, a novel, or anything that enhances the well-being of oppressed minority groups. He went on to assert that quantitative research and the scientific method have been completely unsuccessful and unproductive in education. I do not believe that such attitudes are likely to ensure the success of future generations of scholars in our field.

A MORE OPTIMISTIC NOTE

While I find some of the above trends to be disheartening, the news is not all bad. Although the quality of research in information technology in education does leave something to be desired, the same could probably be said of most fields of inquiry, especially those as recently established as the field of information technology in education. With all of our problems, research and practice in our field have taught us some important things in the last 20 years. Here are only a very few of the valuable lessons we have learned from research on information technology in education:

We know that mere exposure to computers is not automatically educationally beneficial. The value of integrating technology lies in *how*, not *whether*, it is used.

We know that, while most teachers believe that information technology can improve teaching and learning, most say they have not been given the time and training they need to learn to use it well.

We know that teachers believe they do not have sufficient technical or pedagogical support to help them integrate information technology into their teaching.

We know that the most common use of computers in schools is for supplementary activities, enrichment, or rewards.

We know that most educational software is of the drill-and-practice variety.

We know that use of technology can improve student attitudes toward learning.

We know that students tend to write more and have better attitudes toward writing when they use word processing, and small improvements have been found in quality of writing.

We know that while 80% of households with incomes over $75,000 per year own computers, only about 16% of households with incomes between $10,000 and $15,000 have computers.

We know that learning tends to improve more when computers are located in classrooms than when the same number of machines are placed in a school lab.

We know that experts in early childhood education emphasize the importance of insuring that experiences with computers are not substituted for social experiences with peers and the teacher or active play in a language-rich environment.

We know that the Logo programming language, when properly taught, can be used to improve problem-solving skills and metacognitive processing.

We know that there is a gender difference in access and use of computers in classrooms and in homes.

We know that, while good teachers very frequently find ways to use the Internet in teaching without formal help, beneficial student use of the Internet usually requires formal institutional help and support and good Internet access at school for large numbers of students.

We know that integrated learning systems have shown slightly positive effects on learning, especially in the acquisition of basic mathematical skills, but such positive effects are greater when assessed with research supplied by vendors than with research obtained independently.

There are many excellent research reviews available, and I will not make an attempt to summarize all the research findings in our field in this short paper. A recently published review I would like to recommend, however, is by Parr (2002), who provides the following excellent conclusions:

The overall conclusion is that the level of effectiveness of educational technology is influenced by features of the software, the specific student population and also the level of access to technology and features of the educational context, particularly how the educator or educational body organizes for its use. . . . The main implications . . . are in terms of conceptualizing what principles of system design make for the most productive system-learner-teacher interactions.

This is exactly the point I attempted to make in 1993 and earlier in this paper—that research in information technology in education would be greatly improved if researchers paid more attention to critical learner/treatment interactions.

CONCLUSIONS

Information technology in education is no longer in danger of abandonment. However, the educational potential of this technology has not been fully realized, and its impact has been modest, at best. One reason for its minimal effect on teaching and learning is that school practices are not based upon what we have learned from research. Research results are not highly valued by practitioners and policymakers for a variety of reasons. One of these is that undergraduate degrees and many master's degrees in education usually do not require research or statistics courses, and the education subculture thus does not regard theory and research as practical necessities. Then, too, when statistics or research courses are required, they are sometimes taught by instructors with little or no real research experience who are unable to show students the practical value of what they are learning. The artificial dichotomy of "research" versus "theory" courses also contributes to a devaluing of research and theory, as do education courses if they are excessively methodological and atheoretical in their approach.

The solution to these problems would require that undergraduate and master's programs revise their curricula to include research and statistics courses taught by experienced and productive educational researchers who teach their courses not as abstract mathematical exercises but as practical tools. Then, too, all courses should include both methodology and theory, with students shown how theory and research can be used productively in day-to-day and minute-to-minute teaching situations.

The quality of research in information technology in education is also partly to blame for its minimal effect on practice. Stage One research was based on the assumption that mere exposure to computers would result in general educational benefits. Stage Two research improved, and researchers began looking at the effects of specific technological applications on specific learning variables. Stage Three research was never fully implemented, but would have further improved research practices to include consideration of critical learner/treatment interactions. One reason that Stage Three designs did not become common is that information technology has been beset by a succession of short-lived fads that have prevented the kind of sustained, long-term research interest in specific topics that is needed for a high-quality body of studies to be produced.

There is little that we can do about this problem, except to resist the temptation to "jump on the bandwagon" of every new development, to concentrate our research activity on a manageable number of topics, and to encourage our students to do the same. We can also take every opportunity to caution against the kind of unrealistically positive expectations that tend to attach themselves to each new fad, and that tend to result in rapid disillusionment and abandonment of even our most promising new developments. We should always remember that it is a mistake to promise more than we can deliver.

Another factor in the arrested progress of research is the extent to which we are endorsing, or at least accepting, an extreme position with regard to qualitative research. Qualitative designs are valuable research tools, but are neither a panacea nor a replacement for all other types of research strategies. We must demand that our graduate students master as many different research tools as possible, and we must require that published research and research done as part of the requirements for graduate degrees maintain a high standard of quality. Calling a study qualitative does not excuse the author from requirements to be clear, thorough, and succinct, and we should be firm in making that point in our roles as graduate advisers, journal referees, and teachers.

I have sometimes been accused of being a pessimist. Although that accusation is not without some justification, and although this article has concentrated on what I believe are problems in our field, I am generally optimistic about information technology in education in general and research in the field in particular. Although I believe our problems are serious, I know they are solvable. While the quality of research is not as good as it could be, recent misunderstandings about qualitative designs notwithstanding, research quality is improving and will continue to do so.

Computers in the Schools will continue to publish good research of any type, and I believe we will continue to have no difficulty obtaining a sufficient quantity to fill our issues. In the meantime, I think it is important for us to discuss some of the issues outlined in this article. We are all "in this together"; and, while we will certainly disagree on many details of how our field can be advanced, we are all interested in the same goal–using information technology to help improve teaching and learning.

REFERENCES

Kauffman, J.M. (1999). Commentary: Today's special education and its messages for tomorrow. *The Journal of Special Education, 32*, 244-254.

Kelman, P. (1984). Computer literacy: A critical re-examination. *Computers in the Schools, 1*(2), 3-18.

Lowe, J. (2001-2002). Computer-based education: Is it a panacea? *Journal of Research on Technology in Education, 34*(2), 163-171.

Maddux, C.D. (1993). Past and future stages in educational computing research. In H. Waxman & G. Bright (Eds.), *Approaches to research on teacher education and technology* (pp. 11-22). Charlottesville, VA: Association for the Advancement of Computing in Education.

Maddux, C.D. (2001). Computers, statistics, and the culture of university mathematics education. *Computers in the Schools, 17*(1/2), 9-15.

Parr, J.M. (2002). *A review of the literature on computer-assisted learning, particularly integrated learning systems, and outcomes with respect to literacy and numeracy: A report to the New Zealand Ministry of Education.* Auckland, New Zealand: The University of Auckland. Retrieved June 2, 2001, from the World Wide Web: http://www.minedu.govt.nz/web/document/document_page.cfm?id=5499&p=1003.1024

Dwight W. Allen

The Effects of Technology on Educational Theory and Practice: A 20-Year Perspective

SUMMARY. In this article, the author takes the position that technology really has changed education and society in some dramatic ways. He celebrates some of the advances in education brought about by the advent of the World Wide Web, but also expresses regret for the fact that the potential of present-day technology has not been fully taken advantage of, and that its power is not universally available. *[Article copies available for a fee from The Haworth Document Delivery Service: 1-800-HAWORTH. E-mail address: <docdelivery@haworthpress.com> Website: <http://www.HaworthPress.com> © 2003 by The Haworth Press, Inc. All rights reserved.]*

KEYWORDS. Technologies, information technology, knowledge, teachers, audio, copyright, intellectual property

INTRODUCTION

It has been said that when Thomas Edison invented the 16mm projector he predicted that eventually all teachers would have to do would be to turn it on in

DWIGHT W. ALLEN is Eminent Professor of Educational Reform, Old Dominion University, Norfolk, VA 23529 (E-mail: dwallen@odu.edu).

[Haworth co-indexing entry note]: "The Effects of Technology on Educational Theory and Practice: A 20-Year Perspective." Allen, Dwight W. Co-published simultaneously in *Computers in the Schools* (The Haworth Press, Inc.) Vol. 20, No. 1/2, 2003, pp. 49-57; and: *Technology in Education: A Twenty-Year Retrospective* (ed: D. LaMont Johnson, and Cleborne D. Maddux) The Haworth Press, Inc., 2003, pp. 49-57. Single or multiple copies of this article are available for a fee from The Haworth Document Delivery Service [1-800-HAWORTH, 9:00 a.m. - 5:00 p.m. (EST). E-mail address: docdelivery@haworthpress.com].

http://www.haworthpress.com/store/product.asp?sku=J025
© 2003 by The Haworth Press, Inc. All rights reserved.
10.1300/J025v20n01_04

the morning and turn it off at the end of the school day. Ever since we have been trying to turn on various technologies to solve the problems (or, more accurately, manage the process) of education. There have been a succession of candidates for the magic bullet of change for the educational process, a litany of the history of educational technology: film, audio wire, audiotape, radio, television, the computer, and now the Internet. Along the way, we have had a supporting cast of lesser technologies: ditto and mimeograph machines, the overhead projector, photocopiers, laser disks, CD-ROMS and DVDs, to mention a few.

Not to be ignored are the ever-changing technologies of the society around us and the transformation of our life space. Fundamental technologies such as lighting, heating, air-conditioning, refrigeration, and the microwave oven are paralleled by the total metamorphosis of transportation and communication, and the resultant emergence of an interdependent global economy, destined to become a global civilization.

IT (Information Technology) changes the needs of education as well as its potential processes. This is so obvious that it is often not directly faced. Typing classes were once the province of aspiring secretaries–almost all female. Keyboard skills are now ubiquitous and most students learn them on their own, much like learning to use a telephone. The vast libraries of the great institutions of society, with their massive physical presence, once symbolized the precious nature of knowledge and its special availability–to the privileged. Knowledge collections infinitely more vast can now be accessed from any desktop. If anything, knowledge has become even more precious. The challenge of education has been transformed from making knowledge available and facilitating its simple mastery, to understanding issues of its categorization, aggregation, and evaluation, including its accuracy, credibility, and reliability, its relevance and priority for use.

It is often the case that the analyses of the effects of technology on education are viewed narrowly within the classroom and within the school itself. Technology outside the classroom and school affects student performance in school. For example, students often come to school with advanced keyboard skills gained from home computer use. Students with access to multiple sources of information on the Internet dramatically alter the potential for student research. Teacher knowledge and activity are fundamentally changed with home computer access, television viewing habits, travel, and distance education opportunities. Schools are no longer limited in the same way by weather (availability of air conditioning) and propinquity (extensive bus transport is ubiquitous). Unfortunately, schools still proceed from the premise of stability: continuity of students, curriculum, and social context, though none are now true. Technology has changed the starting point for students in the classroom and continues to dramatically expand the options for teaching and learning in and out of the classroom.

Ultimately, technology will force us to acknowledge the global context of education, the multicultural nature of society, and the continued transformation of requirements and opportunities–personal, professional, and institutional. But today's early 21st century schools are more the bastions of the past than the progenitors of the future, as they struggle to master an ever-changing panoply of technologies, which even now transform the educational environment in sporadic and dramatic ways.

The World Wide Web

It is difficult to imagine that the first Web site in the United States was put up just over 10 years ago at Stanford University (http://www.slac.stanford.edu). The Web has significantly changed the world of education already, and the changes have just begun. Teachers are still not systematically trained to exploit the use of search engines. Many elementary teachers, for example, have never learned that Google, one of the premier search engines, can search 400,000,000 images to find pictures of their choosing in less than a second with the click of a tab on the home page. Teachers needing an answer for a student question about a Chinese bawu (a Chinese musical instrument)–or who just want to know what it looks like–can find 60 images in less than half a second. Although there are numerous copyright issues in the use of both text and images, we need to find ways to make access easy, comfortable, and legal. It is interesting that encyclopedias–even online encyclopedias–are made virtually obsolete by search engines able to access the database of more than two billion Web sites in less than a second (see Lessig, 2001). The World Wide Web has transformed the central issue of education from having enough information to being buried under information with varying levels of credibility and trying to make sense out of it.

Audio and Radio

Radio education got lost in the frenzy of television instruction in recent decades. However, it remains an inexpensive and powerful educational tool, vastly underexploited, particularly for populations with little or no access to the classroom–and there are more than 100,000,000 kids who will never see the inside of a classroom in the world today. It is also a powerful enrichment tool, particularly when coupled with reproduction audio technologies such as MP3, which allow learners tremendous flexibility of when and where they learn.

We haven't even begun to examine the potential for vast increases in the way we use and allocate the broadcast spectrum. Many scholars now argue that the principle of "allocating" exclusive use of spectrum bands to individual organizations is obsolete and that a much greater use could be made through alternative allocations.

ISSUES

Support Staff–Role of Teachers in IT

As we learn to use the full potential of various new technologies, it will become more and more evident that our concept of the self-contained teacher is obsolete. We need a new concept of the teacher as a part of his or her staff. One of these staff members may be a technologist with or without expertise and experience in teaching. For teachers to have staff support in technology, administrative tasks, and semi-professional tasks, without enormous increases in funding, it will require rethinking the way schools are organized. Much larger groups of students will be under the direction of a master teacher. Class size will increase dramatically, but several adults with differing roles will be there to support instruction. When this happens, teachers will have much greater confidence in the use of new instructional methods that fully integrate technology.

Student Tech Staff

One of the realities of the information age is that it becomes an ordinary expectation for students to know more than their teachers. Technology is a prime example. Many students have become fascinated with technology and have high levels of mastery. Teachers must be taught to take advantage of these student skills and not to be threatened by them. Schools are just beginning to learn how to tap into these new-found resources. A few master teachers have done this, in an informal way in their classrooms, for years with excellent results. Some schools are now beginning to organize student "tech teams" to provide technical support for teachers in more formal ways.

A specific example of the problems of getting the necessary change of mind may serve to highlight the problems of dramatically integrating new instructional designs in the school. The potential is great, but the barriers are significant. For example, in one program it was proposed to provide "advanced tech support" students with pagers. When teachers required help, they could "beep" student support staff who would likely be in other classes. Students would decide whether their current classroom activities would allow them to be absent and respond when they felt their absence would not interfere with their learning. Student judgment would be validated by their maintaining the same level of performance in the class as before, with "B" being the default grade requirement. If any grade went down, students would lose their pagers. The advantages of this arrangement are substantial. Individual student initiative, decision-making, and responsibility are enhanced and teachers gain access to more real-time tech support as needed, with minimal financial implications. But the barriers are usually perceived to be greater. Teachers are extremely reluctant to have students come and go from their classes, even when they maintain a high level of performance. "Seat time" is still important to most teachers, even when there is great evidence that responsibility and engagement are higher correlates of learning. There are administrative problems with students "roaming the halls" during class time. Everyone would have to learn new responses–trial and error is necessary and should be expected. The present mindset in schools is to dismiss such proposals out of hand as having too many potential problems. Until we gain a different, more open mindset, which encourages trial and error, and accepts risk, educational technology will be limited in its uses and effects.

Copyright and Intellectual Property

As classroom use of instructional software and more traditional mediated materials increases, it is increasingly difficult for teachers to know the limits of copyright protection. Fair use is becoming more restricted as ease of use becomes greater. This is one of the current paradoxes of the information age. As a society, we are caught between the new low cost of information and the need to find ways to protect intellectual property rights. Creativity should be rewarded, but at the same time we have to find ways to make important learning technology available at reasonable cost with universal access. Current approaches of copyright and copy protection are patently inadequate, but a better system has yet to emerge. We must be creative in finding ways to unlock the potential of inexpensive access to information for the benefit of humanity.

Research Issues

IT provides many new research opportunities. One of the most powerful educational technologies just emerging is Data-Driven Education (DDE). As it becomes possible to design curriculum that assumes universal online use of computers, the ability to track student progress in real time can transform both the instructional and the assessment processes. There are many research initiatives underway to exploit this new potential. The author has had the opportunity to work with the M.I.N.D. (Musical Intelligence Neural Development) Institute as it implements its MST Math STAR Integration curriculum for elementary school classes. Student progress has been tracked "mouse click by mouse click," giving developers (and assessors) completely new tools with which to modify and improve the curriculum while recording student progress at levels and increments never before possible. Professor Mark Bodner of the University of California at Los Angeles has taken leadership in DDE in the Math STAR program, working with Matthew Peterson, the originator of STAR, to incorporate increasingly sophisticated feedback loops for the students with real-time access for curriculum developers. With DDE there is no need for separate assessment. An unprecedented level of assessment is embedded in the instruction. The results are highly correlated with other standardized measurements of achievement.

Uneven Access

We are still immobilized by the uneven availability of information technology. Clearly, colleges of education should be at the forefront of the introduction and use of technology, but this has not been the case. Until the effective intervention of the U.S. Department of Education with its PT3 program (Preparing Tomorrow's Teachers to Use Technology), colleges of education were consistently behind the leading public schools in their adoption, use, and training for technology. Even now, the job has just begun and the future of the PT3 program is uncertain. It is unlikely that individual state initiatives being proposed can create the same critical mass of response. It has all moved too quickly to be anticipated by traditional planning models. Now schools must be built to accommodate technology not invented at the time of architectural planning. While some schools are still waiting for funds to "wire" their school districts, wireless technology makes such wiring plans obsolete. Additionally, when colleges and universities write technology-training grants, the equipment specified for training and use will often be obsolete at the time of funding and implementation.

Even without factoring in the constant flow of new technologies making equipment and training obsolete, colleges of education are challenged by the fact that the teachers they train will go into widely disparate settings, ranging from more advanced technology than the college which trained them to schools with little or no instructional use of technology. Thirty years ago, when I was dean of education at the University of Massachusetts, Amherst, I told entering students that the choice was "to train teachers for schools that didn't exist, or for schools that shouldn't exist." The same is even truer today.

Society is quick to blame teachers and teacher trainers for the ills of education, and certainly there is need for more accountability in the profession. But until society provides a predictable level of instructional tools–in this case technology–and the budgets to maintain and replace technology as needed, with training time and programs for teachers to consistently update their skills, meaningful accountability is beyond reach (see the proposal for a national Internet in-service program for all teachers: "American Schools: The $100 Billion Challenge," Allen & Cosby, 2000).

New Assessment Options

DDE is only one of many new assessment options made possible by technology. Paradoxically, the development of new assessment procedures has lagged behind other uses of educational technology. Online testing and assessment protocols are still relatively underdeveloped, but they offer exciting new options of immediate feedback, randomization, item analysis, student-initiated and validated questions, and peer editing. There is promise of many new options on the near horizon, including automatic grading of essay answers, and increasingly sophisticated electronic portfolios that can be indexed to educational standards as desired. It is ironic that new technologies offer the promise of more individualized, interactive, and personalized assessment options.

Teacher-Written Programs

Online databases of teacher-generated lesson plans have sprouted like mushrooms. Literally thousands of lesson plans are available, free, for teachers to review, adapt, and use. It's a matter of developing new habits of mind: conditioning ourselves to search out, explore, and modify existing plans; and to give credit for ideas and inputs that shaped the final lessons that are taught. We have yet to develop reasonable protocols for citing sources for materials taken from the Web and combined and synthesized for individual teacher use. Teachers are still relatively unsophisticated in both the access and use of Web-posted lesson plans. Teacher education programs are still not geared up to use these and other Web resources systematically.

Standardization and Individualization

Inherent curiosity is a human characteristic, and, paradoxically, the current processes of education tend to dampen it rather than develop and channel it. The result of "2 + 2" is about the same in Missoula, Montana, as it is in Tyler, Texas. Though our national heritage of individualism has served us well, it has also blinded us to sensible commonalities. Our goal in education, as well as in society as a whole, should be unity in diversity. We must learn to assert without apology those skills that students should and must share in common to be successful citizens of the 21st century, while we remain equally committed to nurturing individual initiative, of teachers, students, parents, schools, communities, and regions. Let us find better ways to share what we know even as we find better ways to provide opportunities for individual initiative at all levels of education. Technology can help us. It can help track individual progress. It can give "report cards" to schools and communities as to the relative success of their educational programs. It can make us more efficient in what we do in common so we have time and resources to go beyond what is common. Educational technology has given us new ways to think of standardization and even more ways to encourage individual initiative with an unprecedented diversity of resources available to each student and teacher.

Trial-and-Error Learning

We have always been trial-and-error beings. We learn from mistakes, feedback, and multiple trials. But somehow the formal system of education has forgotten this basic reality and has placed unreasonable value on one-trial learning. Technology, properly configured, can encourage multiple trials, multiple approaches, and reward the "right kind" of mistakes–mistakes from which we learn and rise to new levels of performance.

It is simply not possible to learn to ride a bicycle without falling off. In China, even now, students, afraid to make mistakes in pronunciation, can study English for ten years without being able to speak even a sentence. For mistakes to be useful and to contribute to learning, they must be accompanied by feedback. In the traditional learning setting it is difficult to provide individualized, focused, real-time feedback. We're not there yet, but new technologies have given us a glimpse of what is possible. For example, new testing protocols are being developed to make it possible to retest concepts immediately, which have been confusing. First, immediate feedback, not only on success or failure, but to provide links to supplemental instructional materials can be given automatically without instructor intervention. Parallel test items can be administered as many times as needed to gain success. Previously identified weaknesses in learning can be rehearsed and retested periodically. Sophisticated instructional design will make possible alternatives never before considered, exploiting important but often-neglected brain-based learning principles, such as trial-and-error learning.

Synchronous and Asynchronous Courses

Schooling has long been defined as a face-to-face encounter between teacher and students. At first, technology enhanced and provided more choices for face-to-face instruction. But, with the advent of different delivery systems that do not require a "classroom" presence either for teacher or student, new options have become available–all of which are still in the beginning stages of implementation. Live television eliminated barriers of space, and taped presentations also eliminated the barrier of time. However, both of these technologies assume passive learning. With the addition of telephone bridges, the Internet and discussion rooms, two-way interactivity and connectivity have become increasingly possible and should soon become the norm. Until now, most asynchronous and distance courses have been measured against the effectiveness of face-to-face instruction. Hybrid models are beginning to emerge, and it is easily predicted that soon some of the tasks of teaching and learning can be more effectively taught in a mediated environment that may be asynchronous in time and space.

Universal Access

There is no doubt of the success of educational technology in selected applications. But it still offers mostly an enrichment or add-on to basic traditional programs. Many experts are predicting that the next major step forward in the use of technology in education will come when we have universal access to whatever technology is being employed. It is very difficult to assign a Web-search to students when it is known that some students can access the Web at home and others will be limited to access in the study hall or library. Schools are still struggling to find resources to acquire common-use technologies and most often do not have funding to maintain and replace these. A dramatic increase in sustained technology funding for schools will be required before we can take the next important step of universal access.

SYNERGISM–THE VISION OF THE FUTURE

As we consider where we've been, where we are, and contemplate where we are going in education, we SHOULD take note of the exciting reality of multiple futures which all of us in education CAN help to create. Some of these alternatives will depend on the development of new technologies; some, the refinement and dissemination of current technologies; and, in many cases, simply an awareness of the numerous, yet untapped potentials of existing technologies. Often finances will be a barrier, but even more often, the principal barrier will be a lack of vision of what is truly possible. I believe that 95% of all children can learn 95% of the curriculum we are committed to teach if only we can find the time, the patience, and the vision to use what we know while striving to learn more. If we succeed, education will be truly transformed in the decades ahead in much more fundamental ways than it has in past decades, with all the excitement and opportunities by technologies undreamed of two decades ago, but ordinary in our time.

REFERENCES

Allen, D., & Cosby, W. (2000). *American schools: The $100 billion challenge*. New York: Time Warner.

Lessig, L. (2001). *The future of ideas*. New York: Random House.

Glen Bull
Randy Bell
Sara Kajder

The Role of "Computers in the Schools" Revisited

SUMMARY. The 20th anniversary of *Computers in the Schools* seems an appropriate time to take stock of the effects of computers in the schools. The past, present, and potential future effects on K-12 education are reviewed in this article. Three eras are considered–characterized by initial theoretical foundations, current practice, and future transformations–with an emphasis on the coming transformational era, in which the authors believe multisubject, personal portable computers will become nearly universally available. Educators need to begin planning now for the effects of ubiquitous computing and consider ways in which universal access to computing might permit reconceptualization of the school curriculum. The kinds of educational software available to schools will substantially affect how computers are used. An open source software

GLEN BULL is Ward Distinguished Professor of Education, University of Virginia, Curry School of Education, Charlottesville, VA 22904-4279 (E-mail: gbull@Virginia.edu).

RANDY BELL is Assistant Professor, University of Virginia, Curry School of Education, Department of Curriculum Instruction & Special Education, Charlottesville, VA 22904-4273 (E-mail: rlb6f@Virginia.edu).

SARA KAJDER is a graduate student, University of Virginia, Curry School of Education, Charlottesville, VA 22904-4275 (E-mail: sbk8q@Virginia.edu).

[Haworth co-indexing entry note]: The Role of "Computers in the Schools" Revisited." Bull, Glen, Randy Bell, and Sara Kajder. Co-published simultaneously in *Computers in the Schools* (The Haworth Press, Inc.) Vol. 20, No. 1/2, 2003, pp. 59-76; and: *Technology in Education: A Twenty-Year Retrospective* (ed: D. LaMont Johnson, and Cleborne D. Maddux) The Haworth Press, Inc., 2003, pp. 59-76. Single or multiple copies of this article are available for a fee from The Haworth Document Delivery Service [1-800-HAWORTH, 9:00 a.m. - 5:00 p.m. (EST). E-mail address: docdelivery@haworthpress.com].

10.1300/J025v20n01_05

development model is described that can potentially empower teachers with the capability to adapt and modify programs according to local needs. A call for an international dialog on the intersecting trends of ubiquitous computing and the open source educational model is issued. *[Article copies available for a fee from The Haworth Document Delivery Service: 1-800-HAWORTH. E-mail address: <docdelivery@haworthpress.com> Website: <http://www.HaworthPress.com> © 2003 by The Haworth Press, Inc. All rights reserved.]*

KEYWORDS. Open source software, handheld computers, educational software, instructional technology, software development, graphing calculators, digital microscopes, portable computers

The first personal computer, the Altair 8800, was sold as a hobbyist kit, but by 1977 the Apple II, the Radio Shack TRS-80, and the Commodore PET were available as full-fledged assembled microcomputers. By the early 1980s, when *Computers in the Schools* was founded, microcomputers were beginning to enter the schools in appreciable numbers.

The 20th anniversary of *Computers in the Schools* provides a suitable time to take stock. The effects of computers in schools thus far have been minor in comparison with their potential future impact. We are currently midway through a half-century transition period that can be divided into three eras–theory, practice, and transformation (see Table 1). Each of the three eras is examined, and possible futures for computers in the schools are suggested in this review.

ORIGINS: THEORETICAL UNDERPINNINGS

As microcomputers were finding their way into schools for the first time, there was considerable theoretical discussion regarding best use. Just prior to establishment of the journal *Computers in the Schools*, a book of readings titled *The Computer in the School* (Taylor, 1980) was published. Its subtitle,

TABLE 1. Three Eras of Computers in the Schools

Era	Focus	Activities
Early	Theoretical Exploration	"Tutor, Tool, Tutee" Paradigm Established
Intermediate	Applied Implementation	Networks Developed, Multimedia Created
Universal Access	Transformation	Social and Educational Systems Change

"Tutor, Tool, Tutee," suggested three ways in which computers might be used in schools.

The word *tutor* referred to the computer as a teacher. The word *tool* referred to productivity software such as word processors, spreadsheets, and graphical applications. The meaning of the word *tutee* is less apparent, but refers to a reversal of the role of computer as teacher and child as learner. In this paradigm, the child becomes the tutor by programming the computer (which fills the role of learner or "tutee"). Arthur Luehrmann (1980) argued for development of universal expertise in programming the computer ("computer literacy"), suggesting that programming is, in effect, "teaching the computer."

Luerhmann believed that every student should master computing science as a new content area and use this knowledge, for example, to explore geometry through development of graphical plots and displays, to secure and analyze information in the social sciences from a database query system, and to develop general algorithm-based problem-solving skills. These curricular objectives are all consistent with current reform documents in the respective content areas.

APPLIED PRACTICE AND EXPLORATION

The IBM PC was introduced in 1982, followed by the Macintosh in 1984. Dozens of computer vendors and operating systems were winnowed down to two primary computing platforms, represented by the Microsoft operating system on an Intel microprocessor, and the Macintosh operating system on a Motorola microprocessor. As computers entered schools in greater numbers, the dialog shifted from a theoretical discourse to discussion of mechanics and logistical issues.

Throughout the 1980s *multimedia* and *multimedia computers* were ongoing topics of academic study, with more than one journal established to address this topic. The term *multimedia computer* is rarely heard today, just as the term *talking movie* is seldom employed. It is assumed that films will have associated soundtracks and that computers will have the capacity to process and display sounds and images. The ubiquity of MP3 music files that are transforming the music industry, constituting a fair percentage of Internet traffic, attests to the multimedia capacity of today's computers.

Similarly in the 1990s the emphasis shifted to networking and the Internet. Hundreds of articles and conference presentations were devoted to effective ways to wire schools and interconnect them. The emphasis is now shifting from wired networking to wireless network access. A mechanical focus on technical advances in computing is an unavoidable stage in the evolution of school computing and is likely to continue for another decade at least.

TRANSFORMATION: UNIVERSAL ACCESS

At some point in the future, near-universal access will be attained. This has already occurred at the college level. A Pew *Internet & American Life Project* study reports that almost all college students (85%) own their own computers (Jones, 2002). This has changed both academic and social habits at that level. For example, the majority of college students now use the Internet more than the library for research:

> For most college students the Internet is a functional tool, one that has greatly changed the way they interact with others and with information as they go about their studies. . . . They use the Internet to communicate with professors and classmates, to do research, and to access library materials. (Jones, 2002, online)

In contrast, despite the billions invested in K-12 school computers each year, the average child in a K-12 school has limited access to a computer in school. A recent survey found that half of all teachers report that their students have access to a computer for only 15 minutes per week (Norris, Soloway, & Sullivan, 2002). This is hardly sufficient to transform learning in any appreciable way, under any imaginable scenario. However, within the foreseeable future, and possibly within the decade, the majority of students will have access to portable, wireless computing devices.

At some point in the near future, most likely before the 30th anniversary of *Computers in the Schools*, a tipping point will arrive (Bull, Garofalo, & Harris, 2002). The tipping point can be defined as the time that almost every student has access to a portable computing device 24 hours a day. This tipping point has arrived almost unnoticed in one subject area, high school mathematics. High school mathematics at the level of pre-calculus and above is predicated upon use of a portable computing device such as the TI-83 graphing calculator.

A Single-Subject Device–The Graphing Calculator

Surveys by vendors suggest that more than 70% of all high school students in the United States routinely employ graphing calculators in their mathematics classes. Their ubiquity is suggested by the fact that they are now required for the Advanced Placement (AP) calculus test. The graphing calculator is a portable, programmable handheld computer designed for mathematics instruction. It has a screen on which graphs and plots can be displayed, and a keyboard with specialized mathematics functions (see Figure 1).

The graphing calculator is of interest for two reasons. First, it was created specifically for the educational market, designed to address the high school and middle school mathematics curriculum. Second, the majority of students in algebra and above now have access to this tool in their classes. Since it is the

FIGURE 1. The TI-83 Graphing Calculator

only computer (albeit specialized) that is widely available in any content area, its use is notable.

Transition to a Multisubject Device

The graphing calculator is a single-subject device, useful primarily in mathematics class. However, its success in that content area has spurred efforts of vendors to develop a comparable multisubject device. General-purpose hand-held computers are now available for about the same price as a graphing calculator. Once the functionality of a graphing calculator is transferred to a handheld computer, mathematics students can begin to acquire general-purpose Personal Digital Assistants in place of single-purpose devices, opening the door to use in all content areas.

There will inevitably come a day–probably within the next decade–in which K-12 students each have access to a personal portable computer. The exact form and capability of this all-subject computing device cannot yet be predicted with certainty, but it is likely to be about the size and shape of a paperback book or a notebook. It must be small enough to be portable, but offer sufficient onscreen real estate to allow efficient visual scanning of text by the reader. Alan Kay's *dynabook*, proposed two decades ago as a theoretical construct, is as good a model as any. Alan Kay described the dynabook as "a portable interactive personal computer, as accessible as a book" (Goldberg & Kay, 1976, online).

TEACHING AND LEARNING

The majority of K-12 students are likely to have access to the equivalent of a dynabook well before the 30th anniversary of *Computers in the Schools*. By the time every student has access to a personal portable computer, patterns of use may be irrevocably set—just as freeways irrevocably changed cities before anyone considered the implications. Therefore, it is important to consider implications for schools and schooling sooner rather than later. Generally speaking, there are two philosophical approaches to use of technology in schools.

1. One approach is to employ the technology to deliver the existing content more efficiently.
2. An alternate approach is to employ the innovation to reconceptualize aspects of the existing curriculum.

Approaches that emphasize *efficient delivery of the existing content* tend to be associated with centralized control of the curriculum. Randy Pausch, a professor in the Human-Computer Interaction Institute at Carnegie Mellon, observed that the cost of creating an entire curriculum virtually mandates a centralized approach:

> Mass-produced textbooks provided for the standardization of curriculum, shifting power from the individual teacher to the centralized authors and purchasing boards. Currently, the most powerful forces in American education are the textbook selection committees of Texas and California. So technology is important when it shifts the social power regarding who makes what decisions about education, as well as in the actual education itself. (Pausch, 2002, p. 56)

Unforeseen consequences occur when new technologies supplant prior ones:

> Printed textbooks will disappear in favor of electronic books, and economically *force a nationwide textbook market* . . . electronic books will simply become cheaper than paper textbooks. This will further centralize the decision-making, and in order for the profit motive to work, there will need to be national standards for e-books that require royalties to be paid on a per-student basis for all content. So e-books will move power from the states to the federal government. (Pausch, 2002, p. 56)

Approaches that involve *reconceptualization of the curriculum* often are grassroots endeavors, or in some instances, originate from reform movements external to the school system. Everett Rogers classic work, *Diffusion of Innovation* (1995), reviews thousands of academic studies in science, medicine, agriculture, business, and education. Rogers concluded that successful technological innovation is difficult in every profession and that there are often unintended consequences despite the best of intentions.

The U.S. Secretary of Education, Rod Paige, asserted that education differs from other professions in regard to adoption of technological innovations:

Education is the only business still debating the usefulness of technology. . . . Many schools have simply applied technology on top of traditional teaching practices rather than reinventing themselves around the possibilities technology allows. The result is marginal–if any–improvement. (Paige, 2002, p. 4)

However, businesses are free to innovate individually, while schools must work within an overlapping framework of state, local, and national standards.

The two approaches of *centralized, efficient delivery of the existing curriculum* and *innovative reconceptualization* of the curriculum are sometimes presented as dichotomous, but that need not necessarily be the case. The more plausible scenario is that the curriculum will be revised in instances in which innovation is most clearly advantageous, rather than overturned in its entirety in a single sweeping movement (Rogers, 1995).

Efficient Delivery of Existing Content

Alfred Bork described tutorial learning as "conversational interaction between a skilled tutor and one or a very small group of students. Unlike the classroom, learning proceeds at an individualized pace until the student succeeds at learning, mastery learning" (Bork, in press). He summarizes the potential of such an approach as follows:

We need ways of learning that allow us to give individualized attention to each student, adapting learning to the student, both in pace and in the learning material presented. We need careful individual attention to each learning problem each student has, as soon as possible after the problem develops. We need to work for each student in the zone of proximal development. We need every student to succeed. . . . This is just what computers make possible. (Alfred Bork, personal communication, September 2002)

Cost is a significant disadvantage of this approach. Bork, who leads one of the more experienced research groups in this area, estimates that development of an entire course in this manner would cost five million dollars (but notes that the high cost could be amortized across many users, potentially even across different countries and cultures). At present almost no full-scale computer-based tutorials that cover an entire course are available, in part as a result of design and content issues required to develop such materials, and in part due to the expense.

A less ambitious (but less expensive) approach is to leverage existing texts, adding value by providing interactive capability. This approach does not replace the teacher, as Bork envisions, but provides teachers with all of the former capabilities of the printed text, plus additional ones offered by electronic media. Explore Learning (www.ExploreLearning.com), for example, is developing electronic texts for commercial publishers that build upon the existing text, and add interactive capabilities.

The potential effects are currently being studied in a number of classrooms in which the teacher has the ability to project live textbooks electronically, and/or in which every student does have a portable, wireless computing device. We are currently observing the changing role of teachers and learners who have these capabilities in classrooms in Walton Middle School in Virginia, and many others around the globe are pursuing similar studies.

Reconceptualization of the Curriculum

In some cases technology makes it possible to go beyond the existing curriculum and address content that would not otherwise be accessible. The graphing calculator is an interesting case study because students have near universal access in many higher-level mathematics classes at the secondary level.

Thus far, some teachers simply use the graphing calculator for teaching existing content, albeit more efficiently. For example, graphing calculators allow mathematics students to explore and integrate multiple representations of data—numeric, graphical, and algebraic—on a single handheld computational device. The graphing calculator removes the computational overhead associated with construction of this data by hand.

Other teachers use the graphing calculator as an opportunity to revise and update the curriculum, introducing new content. Many applications are not feasible in the classroom at all without the aid of a graphing calculator, due to the time that would be required to perform the requisite analyses and associated computations. Graphing calculators allow students to visualize relationships that might not be otherwise apparent. As a consequence, students have the opportunity to make connections between real-world events and associated mathematical descriptions.

MODELS OF EDUCATIONAL SOFTWARE DEVELOPMENT

After K-12 students have universal access to computing hardware, the focus can shift to software utilization. The types of educational software available to schools will substantially affect how computers are used in those schools. Software development and dissemination have proven to be complex, multifaceted processes that warrant some consideration.

Tight top-down coordination has traditionally been considered requisite for large-scale software development initiatives (Brooks, 1975). A centralized approach to development is often accompanied by a proprietary marketing strategy. The overwhelming majority of educational software is now developed under a proprietary model. Commercial shrink-wrapped software applications are licensed rather than sold to the user. In almost all instances, the underlying code is proprietary, and the end user does not have the right to view the underlying code or modify it.

The Proprietary Model

The proprietary nature of the code, which reserves all rights to the owner, is designed to protect the investment that the developer has made. This issue was most famously addressed in an open letter by Bill Gates to the emerging microcomputer community in 1976 shown in Figure 2.

The Uniform Computer Information Transactions Act (UCITA) is the ultimate expression of the view first articulated by Bill Gates in 1976. One of the primary objectives of UCITA is to give shrink-wrap licenses force of law. The provisions of UCITA have been adopted by two states (Virginia and Maryland) and are on the legislative agenda in others. The basic provisions reflect

FIGURE 2. An Open Letter to Hobbyists

AN OPEN LETTER TO HOBBYISTS

by William Henry Gates III

February 3, 1976

To me, the most critical thing in the hobby market right now is the lack of good software courses, books and software itself. . . . Almost a year ago, Paul Allen and myself, expecting the hobby market to expand, hired Monte Davidoff and developed Altair BASIC.

The feedback we have gotten from the hundreds of people who say they are using BASIC has all been positive. Two surprising things are apparent, however: (1) Most of these "users" never bought BASIC (less than 10% of all Altair owners have bought BASIC), and (2) The amount of royalties we have received from sales to hobbyists makes the time spent on Altair BASIC worth less than $2 an hour. . . . Why is this? As the majority of hobbyists must be aware, most of you steal your software. . . . One thing you do is prevent good software from being written. Who can afford to do professional work for nothing? What hobbyist can put 3-man years into programming, finding all bugs, documenting his product and distribute for free?

I would appreciate letters from any one who wants to pay up, or has a suggestion or comment. Nothing would please me more than being able to hire ten programmers and deluge the hobby market with good software.

Bill Gates

---

the concerns of software vendors. For example, UCITA in its basic form contains provisions that would allow vendors to prohibit criticism of their software by purchasers, even in a published review, permit vendors to change the terms of the licensing agreement by posting a notice on the corporate Web site, and include time bombs and back-door traps permitting the vendor to disable or remove the software from the purchaser's machine if the vendor deems that licensing terms have been violated (www.infoworld.com/articles/uc/xml/00/08/21/000821ucissues.xml).

The Open Source Model

Until 1992 the proprietary model was the primary commercial method for development and distribution of software. The open source movement suggested an alternative model, succinctly described by Eric Raymond (2001) in his seminal work, *The Cathedral and the Bazaar* (www.tuxedo.org/~esr/writings/cathedral-bazaar/).

The cathedral model is a top-down corporate model, characterized by large groups of programmers working in coordinated, well-disciplined teams. This was the primary commercial model for large-scale software development until 1992. In that year Linus Torvalds demonstrated that the Internet could be used as a collaborative vehicle for volunteer teams of programmers. Torvalds used the GNU software developed by Richard Stallman as a foundation for GNU/Linux. Today the basic protocol of the World Wide Web itself, established by Tim Berners-Lee, is open source, as is the most widely used Web server, Apache (so-called because it contains many "patches" contributed by many different volunteers around the world).

The original General Public License (GPL) developed by the Free Software Foundation formalized a legal definition of "open code." A GPL license specifies that software distributed under GPL must provide access to the underlying source code, and allow users to modify and adapt the program to address individual needs. Further, GPL grants the right to redistribute revised versions of the code, either gratis or for a fee, but in such cases the derivative work also falls under GPL (www.fsf.org/copyleft/gpl.html). There are a number of other open code licenses inspired by GPL that vary in their legal details, but GPL established the framework for the underlying concept (Lessig, 2002, p. 59).

In 2002 IBM, the world's largest computing corporation, adopted open source as the model for its entire line of servers, from the largest mainframe to the smallest workstation (www.ibm.com/linux/). This answered the question of whether the open source approach could constitute a viable model in business.

PROPRIETARY EDUCATIONAL MODELS

The practical implication of proprietary software for the educational community is that it, out of necessity, is designed for mass consumption. For the most part educational software cannot be customized to meet the needs of individual schools or teachers. To protect the rights of the developer, the code is inaccessible to the user and cannot be revised or modified.

Teachers typically use textbooks as a resource, adapting them and supplementing them with other materials. Proprietary licenses make this more difficult to do in the case of software and electronic media. There are other issues that may dictate consideration of non-proprietary approaches in education. A proprietary license, by design, allows the vendor to withdraw it from the market. Teachers who adapt their curriculum often find that an application is no longer available.

For example, Intel established a consumer division that developed a number of applications well-suited for educational use. Among other applications, the corporation developed an inexpensive digital microscope (the IntelPlay QX3) for the consumer market that was well- suited for classroom use as well. The software included with the microscope made it possible for science classes to acquire time-lapse images of microscopic events such as crystals growing, beans sprouting, etc.

This software created opportunities to reconceptualize topics in middle-school science class. Teachers developed complementary lesson plans and supplementary resources to support the Intel digital microscope application. Intel subsequently withdrew the product from the market due to changes in economics. Teachers who wish to adopt these field-tested applications now find that the QX3 is no longer commercially available. No other comparably priced digital microscope has replaced it as yet, but even if another firm develops a comparable product, there is no assurance this offering will not suffer a similar fate.

Technology changes rapidly, making new bells and whistles attractive, requiring software developers to continuously develop new versions on new media, while at the same time supporting the schools whose technology lags behind. Intel and other vendors certainly have the legal right to withdraw any software application from the market at any time. They, after all, invested the funding to develop the products. However, teachers, in an echo of Bill Gates' open letter to the end user, might address the following query to vendors regarding the practice of withdrawing applications from the market in this way:

> One thing you do is prevent good supplementary educational materials from being written. What teacher can put hundreds of hours into development of lesson plans, supplementary materials, and resources, field testing them in pilot tests in classrooms, if the software for which it is designed may be withdrawn from the market at any moment?

Hundreds of educational software applications used by teachers who came to depend upon them are no longer available. This occurs for a variety of reasons. The software industry is volatile, and companies come and go with surprising rapidity. When this occurs, the software often falls into a legal limbo. In other instances, vendors simply judge that distribution and support of an educational product does not generate sufficient revenues to justify its continuation.

When intellectual property is instantiated in traditional educational media (e.g., print curriculum), development cost is a one time expense amortized against a very long and low-cost product lifespan. But in software development, there is an ongoing expense required to allow a product to meaningfully outlive hardware generations that have only 16-month life cycles. Alfred Bork noted in a personal communication (September 2002) that he invested years developing the IBM *Scientific Reasoning Series* software, created "to help students think as scientists might think." Yet this software, developed in 1984, is no longer available because it was not possible to secure the funding required for ongoing maintenance and updates. Many other educational software developers have emphasized this same point.

The revenue model for even exemplary educational software can be problematic. *The Geometer's Sketchpad* is an instance of exemplary mathematics software that can transform the way in which high school geometry is taught. It is demonstrably effective and has garnered numerous awards and endorsements. The CEO of the firm that developed *The Geometer's Sketchpad*, Steve Rasmussen, reports that "the revenue stream from sales–while sufficient at any point to maintain and support present-generation software on present-generation hardware–is insufficient to support either a serious ongoing research and development project or migration of existing technologies to new hardware architectures that come online" (S. Rasmussen, personal communication, September 2002).

In this instance, the firm has supported a significant portion of its long-term product research efforts through National Science Foundation grants and other forms of sponsored research. This case raises an important question: If the revenue stream associated with even exemplary software cannot fund its full research costs, what is the research and development model for less popular educational software? The open source model offers a potential methodology that warrants examination.

OPEN SOURCE EDUCATIONAL MODELS

There will always be a need for proprietary educational software vendors. Only the electronic equivalents of the media conglomerates have the resources to develop, distribute, and warranty an entire curriculum. School boards will always want assurance that a curriculum is warranteed, whether it is distributed via print media or electronically.

However, there are a number of instances in which open source applications may be a viable complement to proprietary development. The *Society for In-*

formation Technology and Teacher Education (SITE) has established an academic partnership with Red Hat, Inc., a leading open source developer, to explore this question. The *Open Source Education Initiative* (OSEI) was founded as a joint endeavor to investigate the viability and potential of the open source model in education. This initiative is explicitly aiming at the development of K-12 centered projects within both the realms of the humanities and the sciences.

In one realm, the digital microscopy project is an OSEI pilot undertaking designed to study open source educational models. This project involves development of the open source equivalent of the Intel digital microscope software that can be loaded onto digital cameras and adapted to *any* optical microscope, as well as to telescopes and binoculars. The project has two potential educational benefits:

1. It will allow educators who cannot obtain the discontinued QX3 to use the materials and resources developed for use with a digital microscope.
2. Because the software is open, it will allow educators to work with volunteer programmers to modify, adapt, and customize the software to address their own educational needs.

In a related exploration, the *Poetry Forge* (www.poetryforge.org) is a project designed as a springboard for exploration of the use and development of open source writing tools within the K-12 setting. The *Poetry Forge* offers multiple classroom-tested tools with short (three- to five-line) scripts that can be revised by teachers to address their curricular needs. The overarching vision is to inspire and challenge teacher communities to adapt and change the software to meet their individual classroom goals and needs.

We would like to acknowledge that these prototypical initiatives rest upon the foundation of a rich heritage of work by the Logo community. E. Paul Goldenberg developed a series of explorations in language with Logo, while a teacher at Lincoln-Sudbury Regional High School in Massachusetts (Goldenberg & Feurzeig, 1987). His early work in this area served as the ongoing inspiration for a series of columns on language and learning in the *Logo Exchange* journal throughout the 1980s (Bull & Cochran, 1989).

Similarly, in science, works such as Hurley's *Logo Physics* (1985) explored use of programming as an investigatory and problem-solving tool, an effort that continues through the present at sites such as the Epistomology and Learning Group in the MIT Media Laboratory (http://el.www.media.mit.edu/groups/el/). However, although the extended Logo community established a rich conceptual framework linking programming to a broad spectrum of content areas, this vision proved difficult to sustain on a widespread basis in K-12 schools. An open source educational initiative is likely to face many of the same issues, as well as other issues unique to the open source community.

OPEN SOURCE EDUCATIONAL ISSUES

There are significant questions regarding potential use of open source software in education. A key issue is that most teachers are not programmers and are not likely to become programmers under any foreseeable model. This raises the question of whether volunteer programmers distributed across the Internet might potentially work productively with teachers and students who are the end users. How best can we support the work of K-12 teachers so that they can become empowered, informed users, and creators of interactive, curricular tools? Steve Rasmussen comments,

> Open Source projects have good track records of allowing interested and able participants in a product's ecosystem to evolve its technology into new platforms and media incrementally following technology fashion and user interest. One of the challenges in making Open Source fly as a model for educational software development will be in aligning the developer community's (usually high-end, cutting-edge) interest with the educational community's (usually low-end, cost-delimited) deployment realities. (S. Rasmussen, personal communication, September 2002)

Another critical issue is validating and warranting educational content. There is already a considerable amount of open source educational software available, the majority of which has been developed as volunteer contributions by engineers and programmers. Almost none of this material is usable in the classroom, for several reasons. It rarely is aligned with educational requirements and standards. In some instances, the material is factually incorrect. Worse yet, no mechanisms exist for screening and validating such content.

The community that the open source movement engenders has proven to be a key factor in its success. The community established within the *Poetry Forge* is essentially "manufactured," provided within the context of the resources that the greater Web site provides. The community within the digital microscopy project will be one of end users and those curious about its further development. How can these communities be nurtured and sustained so that each develops its own life, not prodded and spurred by the original creators? Where pride of the produced code added the generative energy behind the business open source community, what is the force that will be needed to propel such efforts within the K-12 communities?

COMING FULL CIRCLE

Publication of *The Computer in the School: Tutor, Tool, Tutee* occurred at a time when there were few computers in the schools. The twentieth anniversary of *Computers in the Schools* seems an opportune time to revisit this paradigm.

Arthur Luehrmann first presented the paper "Should the Computer Teach the Student, or Vice-Versa?" at a Boston conference in 1972. This paper advocated programming as a basic skill for all citizens. We asked him to reflect on his thesis, and received the following summation of outcomes 30 years later.

> I hadn't reread this little parable in ages–probably not since Bob Taylor republished it in *The Computer in the School: Tutor, Tool, Tutee* in 1980. . . . And how have things turned out? That's easy. Out of Taylor's trichotomy, teaching tool use is just about the only impact that computers have had on schools.
>
> The computer as tutee (programming) is limited to a tiny fraction of students aiming for careers in computer science. The days are gone when the central focus of the typical classroom with computers (few as they were) was to solve problems by writing simple programs in BASIC or Logo.
>
> This saddens me. Seymour Papert and I argued a lot about BASIC vs. Logo as a suitable language, but we were in firm agreement that learning the syntax of a particular programming language was far less important than being able to express an understanding of a problem or an idea by means of a simple program. My freshmen at Dartmouth College, for example, could show their understanding of Newton's Laws of Motion by writing 10- or 20-line programs to calculate and plot orbits. (Luehrmann, 2002)

Applications such as *The Geometer's Sketchpad* have inherited the instructional space once occupied by activities such those described by Luehrmann. The *Sketchpad* includes a specialized programming language that can be used to create simulations in just the manner that Luehrmann describes. Similarly, the TI-83 graphing calculator includes a scripting language that teachers and students have used to create hundreds of programs shared across the Internet.

These capabilities combined with open source educational initiatives could potentially fulfill Luehrmann's original vision. Multimedia programs such as Macromedia *Flash* permit teachers and students initially to achieve powerful effects without the benefit of programming, and later leverage this expertise as they begin to incorporate short scripts into their projects. Educational models for explicitly encouraging the transition to novice programmer are needed, however.

This is a critical point within the development of the *Poetry Forge* project. At the simplest level of use, the Web site provides teachers with tools that can be immediately integrated into classroom instruction. Students and teachers can utilize poetry tools to create a three-line poem exploring metaphor or a two-stanza "found poem" which examines more complex language structures and devices.

The more sophisticated uses challenge teachers and students to customize the tools. These short scripts, currently available in *NetLogo* (a modern-day successor to Papert's Logo) and in *ActionScript* (for those already using

Macromedia *Flash*), allow teachers and students both to create and adapt tools that meet their individual goals and programs of study. Leading teachers to this stage of ownership of the authoring process is what transforms the *Poetry Forge* from a Web site offering sound educational software to an *open source forge* that houses and supports the collaborative contributions and tools of a fuller community.

Whether such open source educational experiments are sustainable on any widespread educational scale remains to be seen. However, no one conceived that an open source model was feasible for development of an operating system until release of GNU/Linux proved it to be so in the 1990s. This suggests that when events reach a tipping point, an idea can diffuse at a rapid rate once proof of concept is achieved.

CONCLUSIONS

The original Altair had only 256 bytes of memory. The first microcomputers used in schools–the Apple II, the Radio Shack TRS-80, and the Commodore PET–had only 4 kilobytes of memory when first introduced in 1977. The memory of today's microcomputers is measured in megabytes and gigabytes, and their capabilities are vastly greater than the initial prototypes first used in schools. However, the central philosophical issues remain the same.

One watershed event for technology in schools will occur when each student has a personal portable computing device. At that point substantial revisions in the way in which schools do business can occur. There are two possible paths.

In one path, efficiencies will be achieved through electronic distribution of curriculum materials previously disseminated via print. This alone will be a significant achievement, permitting the social studies curriculum to be current and freshly updated, the mathematics curriculum to incorporate interactive electronic equations in place of static printed fonts, the English curriculum to address new voices and critical perspectives, and the science curriculum to include dynamic media and materials. The interdisciplinary possibilities also increase as a result. A further and more dramatic extension of this path would be development of interactive tutorial software that replaces the teacher, allowing students to learn at their own pace. This latter vision is so difficult to achieve that proof of concept has yet to be established after more than 30 years of advances in hardware and software, but could significantly change how the world learns.

Another path could more nearly reflect the vision of Luerhmann and Papert, allowing teachers and students to assume ownership of materials, modifying and adapting them to address individual learning needs. This is the less probable path, requiring a fairly substantial leap. The chief difficulty is that in practice it requires a highly gifted teacher, and hence is difficult to scale and sustain. However, even if only a few (perhaps less than a percent) of teachers and students ultimately participate in adaptation of education software in this manner, the body of materials created will be potentially available to all schools if they are released under an open source license. Assurance of quality of content is an important unresolved issue in this scenario.

A key issue at stake is locus of control. Centrally developed and distributed materials will remain centrally controlled. Open source materials potentially place the locus of control in the hands of the learner. An open discussion of the potential choices will ensure that educators have the requisite understanding of the inherent potential when every student gains access to the 21st century equivalent of Alan Kay's dyanabook.

ACKNOWLEDGMENTS

Our thanks to Arthur Luehrmann, who was kind enough to review a draft of this article, commenting,

> I am less optimistic than you about significant numbers of teachers participating in open-source development of educational software. It takes powerful incentives to make things happen, and with the present structure of K-12 schools, I don't see incentives for real change of any significance. However, preparing future teachers to play a more creative role is a big step in the right direction.

Alfred Bork, a pioneer in development of tutorial software, helpfully reviewed drafts of the article, concluding,

> I think we are still far from the most effective use of computers in learning, in practice. Studies repeatedly show, when they are done by outside professional evaluators, that so far computers have only a minor effect on learning today. . . . The vast majority of teachers and students do not have the time or interest to adapt existing materials to their needs. We need ways of learning that allow us to give individualized attention to each student, adapting learning to the student, both in pace and in the learning material presented. This is just what computers make possible.

Thanks also to Brian Harvey, a pioneer in the Logo community, who contributed substantive suggestions. We are indebted to Steve Rasmussen, CEO of Key Curriculum Press, for insight into practical issues associated with development and distribution of educational software in schools.

REFERENCES

Berners-Lee, T. (1999). *Weaving the Web: The original design and ultimate destiny of the World Wide Web*. San Francisco: Harper.

Bork, A. (in press). *A new lifelong learning system for the world*.

Brooks, F. (1975). *The mythical man month*. New York: Addison-Wesley.

Bull, G., Bull, G., Cochran, P. S., & Bell, R. (2002). Learner-based tools revisited. *Learning and Leading with Technology, 30*(2), 10-17.

Bull, G., Bull, G., Garofalo, J., & Harris, J. (2002). Grand challenges: The coming technological tipping point. *Learning and Leading with Technology, 29*(8), 6-12.

Bull, G., & Cochran, P. (1989). Listful thinking. In D. Harper (Ed.), *Logo: Theory and practice* (pp. 219-277). Pacific Grove, CA: Brooks/Cole.

Bull, G., & Cochran, P. S. (1991). Learner-based tools. *The Computing Teacher, 18*(7), 50-53.

GNU General Public License. (1991). Boston: Free Software Foundation, Inc. Retrieved from <www.gnu.org/copyleft/gpl.html> October 22, 2002.

Goldberg, A., & Kay, A. (1976). *Personal dynamic media.* Xerox Palo Alto Research Center, Learning Research Group. Retrieved from <www.dolphinharbor.org/dh/documents/pdm.zip> October 22, 2002.

Goldenberg, P. E., & Feurzeig, W. (1987). *Exploring language with Logo.* Boston: MIT Press.

Hurley, J. (1985). *Logo physics.* New York: Thompson Publishing.

Jones, S. (2002, September 15). *The Internet goes to college: How students are living in the future with today's technology* [Online]. Pew Internet and American Life Project. Available: <www.pewinternet.org/reports/toc.asp?Report=71>.

Lessig, L. (2001). *The future of ideas: The fate of the commons in a connected world.* New York: Random House.

Luehrmann, A. (1980). "Should the computer teach the student, or vice-versa?" In R. Taylor (Ed.), *The computer in the school: Tutor, tool, tutee* (pp. 129-135). New York: Teachers College Press.

Luehrmann, A. (2002, October 22). Should the computer teach the student . . .–30 years later. *Contemporary Issues in Technology and Teacher Education* [Online serial], *2*(3). Retrieved from <www.citejournal.org/vol2/iss3/seminal/article2.cfm>.

Norris, C., Soloway, E., & Sullivan, T. (2002). Examining 25 years of technology in U.S. education. *Communications of the ACM, 45*(8), 15-17.

Paige, R. (2002, September 17). Preface. In *2020 visions, transforming education and training through advanced technologies.* U.S. Department of Commerce Technology Administration. Retrieved from <www.ta.doc.gov/reports/TechPolicy/2020Visions.pdf>.

Papert, S. (1980). *Mindstorms: Children, computers, and powerful ideas.* New York: Basic Books.

Pausch, R. (2002, September 17). A curmudgeon's vision for technology in education. In *2020 visions, transforming education and training through advanced technologies.* U.S. Department of Commerce Technology Administration. Retrieved from <www.ta.doc.gov/reports/TechPolicy/2020Visions.pdf>.

Raymond, E. (2001). *The cathedral and the bazaar.* New York: O'Reilly & Associates, Inc. Retrieved from <www.tuxedo.org/~esr/writings/cathedral-bazaar/>.

Rogers, E. (1995). *Diffusion of innovation* (4th ed.). New York: Free Press.

Taylor, R. (Ed.) (1980). *The computer in the school: Tutor, tool, tutee.* New York: Teachers College Press.

Taylor, R. (2002, October 22). A digital world in the school: An update to "The Computer in the School." Retrieved from <www.c5.cl/ieinvestiga/actas/ribie2000/charlas/taylor.htm>.

Nancy Wentworth
Rodney Earle

Trends in Computer Uses as Reported in *Computers in the Schools*

SUMMARY. A study of the articles from *Computers in the Schools* reveals the evolution of the uses of computers in the classroom and the ways in which the integration of technology in education has influenced classroom learning environments. These articles help describe the impact this evolution has had on the education of teachers and define the experiences teachers will need to have as they learn to teach with computers. *[Article copies available for a fee from The Haworth Document Delivery Service: 1-800-HAWORTH. E-mail address: <docdelivery@haworthpress.com> Website: <http://www.HaworthPress. com> © 2003 by The Haworth Press, Inc. All rights reserved.]*

KEYWORDS. Computers, integration, technology, learning environments, programming instruction, teacher education

As *Computers in the Schools* celebrates 20 years of publication, it is appropriate to review the uses of computers in education as reported in articles pub-

NANCY WENTWORTH is Associate Professor, Brigham Young University, Department of Teacher Education, Provo, UT 84602 (E-mail: nancy_wentworth@byu.edu). RODNEY EARLE is Professor, Department of Teacher Education, Brigham Young University, Provo, UT 84602 (E-mail: rodney_earle@byu.edu).

[Haworth co-indexing entry note]: "Trends in Computer Uses as Reported in *Computers in the Schools*." Wentworth, Nancy, and Rodney Earle. Co-published simultaneously in *Computers in the Schools* (The Haworth Press, Inc.) Vol. 20, No. 1/2, 2003, pp. 77-90; and: *Technology in Education: A Twenty-Year Retrospective* (ed: D. LaMont Johnson, and Cleborne D. Maddux) The Haworth Press, Inc., 2003, pp. 77-90. Single or multiple copies of this article are available for a fee from The Haworth Document Delivery Service [1-800-HAWORTH, 9:00 a.m. - 5:00 p.m. (EST). E-mail address: docdelivery@haworthpress.com].

lished in this journal. In the early history of the integration of computers in education their uses were described as (a) tutor or computer-aided instruction (CAI), (b) tool (word-processing, spreadsheet, and database skills), and (c) tutee (the computer being programmed by the student) (Taylor, 1980). More recently computers have been described as the hope for creating new learning environments (Carroll, 2000). The role of the teacher may be very different when comparing the early uses of computers with the learning environments described by Carroll where teachers take on the role of a guide and co-learner with students. Teachers will need additional experiences in their education to help them understand teaching with computers in these new learning environments.

A study of the articles from *Computers in the Schools* reveals the evolution of the uses of computers in the classroom and the ways in which the integration of technology in education has influenced classroom learning environments. These articles help describe the impact this evolution has had on the education of teachers and define the experiences teachers will need to have as they learn to teach with computers. The role of the teacher in classrooms where computers are used is revealed. A review of the articles in the past two decades of issues starting in 1984 will be presented along with a comparison of the articles to the early descriptions of computer uses in the classroom.

SUMMARY OF ARTICLES
IN *COMPUTERS IN THE SCHOOLS*

In order to code the articles in *Computers in the Schools* we copied and read all tables of content. We initially used the categories of tutor, tool, and tutee defined by Taylor (1980) to code the articles. As we test-coded a few issues, however, we found that many articles did not fall into those categories. We both found several articles dealing with the attitudes of students and teachers toward computers. One of us used "attitudes" as the code for these articles, the other used "social issues." We also found articles describing the impact of computers on test scores, which we both coded as "assessment." We agreed on the code of "research" for articles that addressed attitudes toward computers and for articles that addressed the impact of computers on test scores. If, however, an article specifically addressed the use of the computer as tutor, tool, or tutee, it was coded into that specific category rather than the "research" category. Several other categories emerged but to a limited degree. A few articles were coded as as "teacher education" or "teacher training." Others were coded as "hardware," "games," and "multimedia." After the test-coding we agreed on four main categories: computer uses, research, teacher education, and other. We also used three secondary codes for computer uses: tutor, tool, and tutee.

With the codes well-defined, we began to code all articles, using both the titles of the articles as well as the abstracts. When we compared our coding, in most cases the codes were identical. When the coding was different, we discussed why. In some cases the article was recorded in two codes. In most cases, however, we were able to agree on the same code for the article.

Figure 1 shows a percentage breakdown of the coding of articles published in *Computers in the Schools* between 1984 and 2002. Articles coded as "computer uses" included those describing the use of computers as tutor, tool, and tutee (programming) and comprised 47% of all articles. The "research" code made up 37% of the articles and included topics on attitudes about computers, gender issues related to computers, cost of computers in education, and evaluation of student learning. Articles on the training of teachers and building leadership in technology instruction were coded as "teacher education" (8%) and first appeared in 1991, the year the Society for Information Technology and Teacher Education (SITE) (originally called STATE) had its first conference. The mission of this new organization included the "development and dissemination of knowledge about teacher education and technology . . . and the embodiment of a vision . . . that computers and related technology will bring about fundamental changes in education" (Johnson & Maddux, 1991). After 1996 teacher education articles became quite common and were some of the articles that shared a double code because they were often about attitudes ("research" code) or the use of the computer in the classroom ("computer use" code). The "other" category (8%) included articles on hardware advances, distance education, special education issues, and administration issues.

FIGURE 1. Percentages of Articles in *Computers in the Schools*

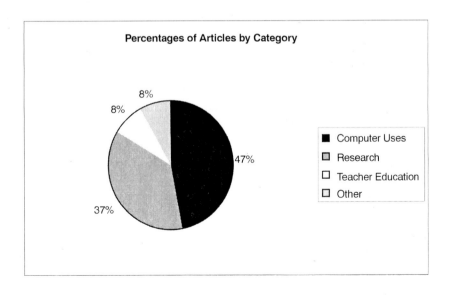

The "computer uses" category was coded into the three additional categories from Taylor (1980): tutor, tool, and tutee. A brief description of each category is given to aid in the readers' understanding of each, followed by the results of coding the articles in *Computers in the Schools*.

COMPUTER USES CATEGORIES

Tutor: Computer-Aided Instruction

Computer-aided instruction (CAI) is a process-product model of computer use in education in which students use drill-and-practice programs. Students often "shoot" or "eat" or in some way capture correct answers. Tutorials, another form of computer Skinnerian learning, improve simple drill-and-practice programs by monitoring right and wrong student responses. If the student inputs a predetermined number of incorrect answers, the program returns to a previous learning screen for tutoring or more simplified problems. Alfred Bork (1980, 1988) believed that with well-designed CAI computers could replace teachers and that open universities could exist where students would work in scattered locations at computer terminals. Patrick Suppes (1985), another advocate of CAI, described drill-and-practice and tutorial programs as a way to free teachers for more personal interactions with students in specialized technical courses, math and science, foreign language, and basic skills. Corcoran (1989) described software that could be used to develop critical and analytical math skills and link mathematics with daily living skills. Janey (1989) discussed issues of educational equity connected with the use of CAI for remedial, compensatory, and special education for minority students.

Educators have had a variety of concerns about the value of CAI and tutorial implementation of computers. Machine-driven drill and practice could stifle independent thinking and creativity (Sardello, 1985). Drill-and-practice programs might become tools for the mindless force of acquisition of facts because correct answers and process are reinforced more often than conceptual understanding (Simpson, 1983). Students exposed to machines might become unable to deal with human interactions (Bradtmueller, 1984; Dreyfus & Dreyfus, 1984). Vernon (1983) addressed questions related to CAI in schools and concluded that (a) students receiving CAI learned more than non-CAI students, (b) CAI did not stifle independent thinking and creativity, (c) CAI promoted social skills, and (d) CAI did not decrease learning initiative. Eubanks (1988) found no significant differences on a competency mathematics test between students receiving computer lab drill in basic arithmetic problems and students in traditional classrooms.

CAI programs have most often been evaluated in terms of student improvement of mathematics achievement scores (Reglin, 1990), and most achievement test scores reflected a superficial understanding of mathematical concepts.

While "good" CAI may include interaction with the student, it seldom requires the student to think about the concepts being drilled. Right answers reached with simple symbol manipulation were all that was measured. Concept understanding was not measured or encouraged.

Tool

A second computer implementation in the classroom was a tool to enhance learning in traditional subject areas. Word processing allows students to make rough draft revisions in written assignments for subjects such as English and history. Databases are available in history, sciences, literature, and so forth, that allow students to search out information in several different formats and relationships. Spreadsheets allow students to create formulas in mathematics as they practice problem solving (Hoeffner, 1990; Verderber, 1990; Wood, 1990). Luehrmann (1980), a proponent of using computers as tools across subject areas, stated that not to give a student instruction in how he/she might use the computer was the chief failure of the CAI effort. He mentioned editing text (word processing), searching databases, creating graphical information, processing musical information, all as powerful uses of a computer.

Brown, Collins, and Duguid (1989) stated that knowledge is like a tool: Both "can only be understood through use, and using them entails both changing the user's view of the world and adopting the belief system of the culture in which they are used" (p. 33). Different understanding of the use of the tool will develop from different uses, just as carpenters and cabinetmakers use chisels in different ways, and physicists and engineers use mathematics in different ways. The computer becomes less mystical when practical applications of the tool are presented to the students. The practical applications of many subjects become more apparent when coupled with the computer used as a tool. Students will assume responsibility for their own learning, develop interest in their work, and become lifelong learners (Tse, 1989). Instruction across areas using computers as a tool provides students with ways to improve their own work and their understanding of several subject areas.

While word processing, spreadsheets, and databases were the early technology tools integrated into education, new tools have been developed to enhance learning. Presentation software, including HyperStudio and PowerPoint, content-specific tools, including Geometor's Sketchpad, Geographic Information System (GIS), and the Internet for research and communication are additional tools for instruction. Each of these tools has had little if any opposition. Word processing has been shown to improve writing skill (Grejda, 1991). Computer spreadsheets are readily adaptable for problem solving, can enhance the user's insight into the development and use of algorithms and models, can free students from being hampered by laborious manipulations of numbers, and can allow students to see the progression of calculations on the screen as they are generated (Masalski, 1990). Spreadsheets and CD-ROMs are used in science classrooms to enhance inquiry learning (Lawrenz & Thornton, 1992; O'Bannon, 1997). Hyper-media and the Internet have been used to encourage problem solving in many classrooms and content areas (Brucklacher & Gimbert, 1999; Maddux, 1996; Reed & Wells, 1997). Computers as tools have been a major focus in teacher education courses as well (Wiburg, 1991; Willis, 1997).

Tutee: Programming

A third educational use of the computer has been the teaching of programming, the student instructing the computer to perform a set of instructions. In this environment the computer is the tutee. Programming as a part of education must be evaluated at two levels, the importance of learning a computer language (how a computer "thinks") and the experiences the student has teaching the computer. The value of programming is not the mastery level of the language but the thinking processes involved (Salomon & Perkins, 1987). It is not hard to make the case that all students do not need to learn a computer language. Most students will never need to program a computer outside of a classroom, but advocates of programming instruction claim the importance of cognitive growth in the student. The problem-solving experiences in programming include the skill of designing a program, implementing it, testing it for bugs, and seeing the final project in operation (Casey, 1997; Lafer & Markert, 1994). Few projects in a standard curriculum allow the students the chance to see a project through from start to finish on such an individual level.

Seymour Papert, a primary spokesperson for programming instruction, argued that the computer as tutee represents a valuable environment for the growth of cognitive skills (1980, 1984, 1985, 1984, 1987). His Logo programming language gives the control of learning to the students and allows them to learn how to think. Other advocates of programming describe additional benefits from programming. Nickerson (1980) claimed that through programming students learn task specification, sequencing, anticipation, hypothesis generation and testing, language precision, thoroughness, avoidance of unnecessary complexity, and consideration of alternate representations. In BASIC programming, students are required to decompose complex problems into subprograms and that programming increases problem-solving tasks, including use of analogy, working backward, and top-down design. These are all higher order thinking aspects that may be taught when the computer is used as the tutee.

As computers and programming classes became more common in classrooms, research on their effectiveness in problem solving and achievement scores increased. (Riebar, 1986; Schaefer & Sprigle, 1988). Many, Lockard, and Abrams (1988) reported a modest support for the efficacy of Logo in developing reasoning skills in seventh- and eighth-graders, especially for girls. When compared with CAI, Clements (1986) found that programming had positive effects on classification and serration, metacomponents, the originality and elaboration subscales of the Torrance creativity measures, and a measure of children's abilities to give directions. Clements recognized the importance of the Logo "environment" on the cognitive and creative growth of students.

Not all research has shown the cognitive growth predicted by programming instruction. Empirical evidence that the activities of programming increase higher order thinking is "thin and inconclusive" (Patterson & Smith, 1986; Shaw, 1986). Johanson (1988) reviewed computer programming using Logo, BASIC, and Pascal as tools for developing problem-solving skills and higher level thinking skills, concluding that expectations have not been met and that there is more failure in curriculum and weakness in teacher preparation than in the usefulness of programming. Logo was shown to be the most promising environment for cognitive growth in students (Lafer & Markert, 1994). Reed, Palumbo, and Stolar (1988) found that the value of programming instruction in promoting problem-solving skills depends on the method of instruction and not on the language used. However, Thompson and Wang (1988) found that students were able to transfer mathematical concepts from a programming environment to a traditional learning environment.

Bitter and Frederick (1989) reported that technology in the classroom has affected not only teaching practices but the kinds of skills taught. Burns and Hagerman (1989) concluded that programming increases students' ideas about themselves as learners. McCoy (1990) reported success in problem-solving instruction in mathematics through computer programming, including increased skill in planning, logical thinking, and variable understanding. Programming was reported to be a factor in significant gains in reflectivity and divergent thinking, and superior performance on metacognitive ability measures and ability to describe directions (Cathcart, 1990; Clements & Gullo, 1984; Mayer & Fay, 1987). Clements and Battista (1990) indicated that the Logo environment enriched children's mathematics conceptualization. Cognitive development, achievement in mathematics, and achievement in programming all share a common factor, that students who do well in one area are likely to do well in the other two areas (Turner & Land, 1988). Oprea (1988) reported that students having programming instruction scored significantly higher than control groups on generalizations and understanding of variables.

TUTOR, TOOLS, AND TUTEE
IN *COMPUTERS IN THE SCHOOLS*

The "computer uses" category was coded into the three categories previously described: tutor, tool, or tutee (shown in Figure 2). Each bar represents 100% of the articles published that year that were coded in the "computer uses" category, with each shade of gray representing one of the three categories. A study of the evolution of these articles will give insight into the integration of technology in education and the impact on teacher education.

FIGURE 2. Computer Uses by Year and Category

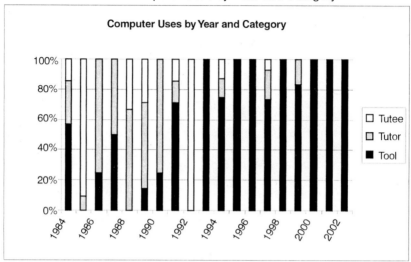

Early in the history of *Computers in the Schools* the articles were fairly balanced between the three categories. If any category of computer use was dominant it was the computer as a tutor. Typical titles include "Computing and Information: Steering Student Learning" (Hoelscher, 1986) and "Designing Feedback for CBI: Matching Feedback to the Learner and Learner Outcomes" (Sales, 1988). These articles supported the use of computers that would direct the learning of students and, to some extent, replace teachers in the learning process. Programming was also written about quite often as indicated by the bar for 1985 and 1992. Most of these articles were about the use of Logo in the classroom or a comparison of more than one programming language. Articles coded in this category include "BASIC, Logo, and Pilot: A Comparison of Three Computer Languages" (Maddux & Cummings, 1985) and "Authentic Learning Situations and the Potential of Lego TC Logo" (Lafer & Markert, 1994). In these articles the focus was not on the role of the teacher as much as the problem solving that students experienced as they programmed the computer.

As early as 1993 "tools" began to dominate the articles published in *Computers in the Schools*. Typical articles include "A Transfer of Data Base Skills from the Classroom to the Real World" (Ennis, 1993), "Spreadsheets as Generators of New Meanings in Middle School Algebra" (Abramovich & Nabors, 1997) and "WebQuests: Can They Be Used to Improve Thinking Skills in Students?" (Vidoni & Maddux, 2002). By the year 2000 all of the articles that were about computer uses in the schools were describing computers as tools, not as tutor or tutee. Publishing tools, spreadsheets, databases, the Internet, and communication tools were the most common tools integrated into the curriculum. The Internet as a tool for learning and instruction was featured in 17 articles published between 1996 and 2002. These tools seemed to be creating new learning environments as described in articles on interdisciplinary instruction (Dutt-Doner, Wilmer, Stevens, & Hartmann, 2000), collaborative learning (Reed & Wells, 1997), authentic learning (Lafer, 1997), and problem solving (Pelton & Pelton, 1998). The role of the teacher was changing in these new learning environments, and this had an impact on teacher education programs. These programs began to provide pre-service teachers experiences with computers as tools and with the new learning environments. The pre-service teachers began to learn to integrate technology into curriculum. The changes in pre-service programs began to be reported in articles on teacher preparation in *Computers in the Schools.*

IMPLICATION OF COMPUTER USES
ON TEACHER EDUCATION

Carroll (2000) presented to the Preparing Tomorrow's Teachers to Use Technology (PT3) conference the ways in which technology would create new learning environments. He said that technology-enhanced units could be more student-centered and collaborative, that the learning should be more active and more problem-based. The role of the teacher in a classroom using computers as tools was changing, and the articles in *Computers in the Schools* described these changes. Carey (1993) discussed the changing roles of teachers from director to facilitator as technology created interactive learning environments. Cates (1995) addressed the need to plan for change in teacher education as technology had an impact on restructuring education. Hunt (1995) reported on the need to help pre-service teachers learn to revise curriculum to include information technology, especially while in their field experiences.

Figure 3 shows the increase of articles in *Computers in the Schools* on teacher education. This increase seems to parallel the growth of the use of computers as a tool. As the interest in computers as tools grew, so did the need for teacher education on using of computers in the new learning environments. This was not as true when the focus of computers in the classroom was shared with programming and computer-aided instruction. Pre-service teachers were not likely to be teaching programming in a traditional curriculum classroom. Programming was often a stand-alone class in the mathematics or business department. CAI was thought to be a possible replacement for teachers so that training them to use technology in the classroom was not needed. The role of the teacher in a strong CAI classroom was more of a manager and processor of scores than of an instructor.

FIGURE 3. Number of Teacher Education Articles Each Year

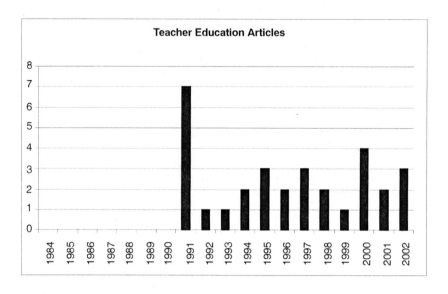

CONCLUSION

Articles published in *Computers in the Schools* provide evidence of the evolution of computer integration in education, whether tutor, tool, or tutee–and the impact these have had on teacher education. The evidence that articles on computers as tutor and tutee have diminished over time and articles on computers as tools for instruction have increased supports Carroll's (2000) vision of the impact of technology on education. Articles on computers as tools reflect the creation of new learning environments. Technology-enhanced classrooms were shown to be more student-centered and collaborative. Learning was shown to be more active and more problem-based. Articles reviewing spreadsheets, databases, word processing, CD-ROMs, and the Internet as tools show that these applications help create environments in which students use information in ways never available in a computer-free classroom. These uses of computers enhance instruction with inquiry learning. The new learning environments require changes in the role of the teacher in the classroom.

The need to have teacher education programs that help teachers use the new tools became important. Programs began to expose pre-service teachers to computers as tools for networking, collaboration, and multimedia presentations. Pre-service programs began to include the development of curriculum that integrated these new technologies as pre-service teachers began to think differently about the teaching and learning process. Teacher education programs began to address the need to use different models of instruction, including lessons that are more learner-centered. Pre-service teachers were encouraged to become more of a facilitator and guide in the classroom. The increase in the number of articles on teacher education in *Computers in the Schools* reflects the impact of computers as tools in the classroom. These trends have been carefully reflected in the articles published in *Computers in the Schools* over the past 20 years.

REFERENCES

Abramovich, S., & Nabors, W. (1997). Spreadsheets as generators of new meanings in middle school algebra. *Computers in the Schools, 13*(1-2), 13-25.

Bitter, G. G., & Frederick, H. (1989). Techniques and technology in secondary school mathematics. *NASSP Bulletin, 73*(519), 22-28.

Bork, A. (1988). Scientific reasoning via the computer. *Science Teacher, 55*(5), 79.

Bork, A. (1980). Interactive learning. In R. P. Taylor (Ed.), *The computer in the school: Tutor, tool, tutee*. New York: Teachers College Press.

Bradtmueller, W. (1984). Perception of the use of high technology in the teaching of reading: Microcomputer use in teaching reading. *Journal of the Association for the Study of Perception, 19*(2), 12-19.

Brown, J. S., Collins, A., & Duguid, O. (1989, January-February). Situated cognition and the culture of learning. *Educational Researcher, 18*(1) 24-35.

Brucklacher, B., & Gimbert, B. (1999). Role playing software and WebQuests–What's possible with cooperative learning and computers. *Computers in the Schools, 15* (2), 37-68.

Burns, B., & Hagerman, A. (1989). Computer experience, self-concept, and problem solving: The effects of Logo on children's ideas of themselves as learners. *Journal of Educational Computing Research, 5*(2), 199-212.

Carey, D. M. (1993). Teacher roles and technology integration: Moving from teacher as director to teacher as facilitator. *Computers in the Schools, 9*(2-3), 105-18.

Carroll, T. G. (2000). If we didn't have the schools we have today would we build the schools we have today? *Contemporary Issues in Technology and Teacher Education, 1*(1), online journal. Retrieved July 10, 2002, from <www.citejournal.org/vol1/iss1/currentissues/general/article1.htm>.

Casey, P. (1997). Computer programming: A medium for teaching problem solving. *Computers in the Schools, 13*(1-2), 41-51.

Cates, W. M. (1995). The technology of educational restructuring: Planning for change in teacher education. *Computers in the Schools, 11*(4), 65-83.

Cathcart, G. W. (1990). Effects of Logo instruction on cognitive style. *Journal of Educational Computing Research, 6*(2), 231-242.

Clements, D. H. (1986). Effects of Logo and CAI environments on cognition and creativity. *Journal of Educational Psychology, 78*(4), 309-318.

Clements, D. H., & Battista, M. T. (1990). The effects of Logo on children's conceptualization of angle and polygons. *Journal for Research in Mathematics Education, 21*(5), 356-371.

Clements, D. H., & Gullo, D. F. (1984). Effects of computer programming on young children's cognition. *Journal of Educational Psychology, 76*(6), 1051-1085.

Corcoran, A. (1989). Software that helps develop critical and analytical math skills. *Electronic Learning, 9*(1), 50-52.

Dreyfus, H. L., & Dreyfus, S. D. (1984). Putting computers in their proper place: Analysis verses intuition in the classroom. *Columbia Teachers College Record, 85*(4), 496-523.

Dutt-Doner, K., Wilmer, M., Stevens, C., & Hartmann, L. (2000). Actively engaging learners in interdisciplinary curriculum through the integration of technology. *Computers in the Schools, 16*(3-4), 151-166.

Ennis, D. L. (1993). A transfer of data base skills from the classroom to the real world. *Computers in the Schools, 9*(2-3), 55-63.

Eubanks, C. (1988). A comparison of the performance on the New York state regents competency test in mathematics of remedial high school students receiving computer-assisted instruction and students not receiving computer-assisted instruction. *Graduate Research in Urban Education and Related Disciplines, 19*(1-2), 52-66.

Grejda, L., & Hannafin, M. (1991). The influence of word processing on revisions of fifth graders. *Computers in the Schools, 8*(4), 89-102.

Hoeffner, K. (1990). Teaching mathematics with technology: Problem solving with spreadsheets. *Arithmetic Teacher, 38*(3), 52-56.

Hoelscher, K. (1986). Computers and information: Steering student learning. *Computers in the Schools, 3*(1), 23-34.

Hunt, N. (1995). Bringing technology into the pre-service teaching field experience. *Computers in the Schools, 11*(3), 37-48.

Janey, C. B. (1989). Technology in the classroom: A chance for equity? *Equity and Choice, 5*(3), 32-35.

Johanson, R. P. (1988). Computers, cognition and curriculum: Retrospect and prospect. *Journal of Educational Computing Research, 4*(1), 1-30.

Johnson, D. L., & Maddux, C. D. (1991). The birth and nurturing of a new discipline. *Computers in the Schools, 8*(1-3), 5-14.

Lafer, S. (1997). Audience, elegance and learning via the Internet. *Computers in the Schools, 13*(1-2), 89-97.

Lafer, S., & Markert, A. (1994). Authentic learning situations and the potential of Lego TC Logo. *Computers in the Schools, 11*(1), 79-94.

Lawrenz, R., & Thornton, E. (1992). Trends in K-12 computer uses in Minnesota science classes. *Computers in the Schools, 9*(1), 39-47.

Luehrmann, A. (1980). Should the computer teach the student or vice-versa? In R. P. Taylor (Ed.), *The computer in the school: Tutor, tool, tutee* (pp. 129-136). New York: Teachers College Press.

Maddux, C. D. (1996). The state of the art in web-based learning. *Computers in the Schools, 12*(4), 75-102.

Maddux, C. D., & Cummings, R. E. (1985). BASIC, Logo, and Pilot: A comparison of three computer languages. *Computers in the Schools, 2*(2-3), 139-63.

Many, W. A., Lockard, M., & Abrams, P. D. (1988). The effect of learning to program in Logo on reasoning skills of junior high school students. *Journal of Educational Computing Research, 4*(2), 203-213.

Masalski, W. J. (1990). *How to use the spreadsheet as a tool in the secondary school mathematics classroom.* Reston, VA: National Council of Teachers of Mathematics.

Mayer, R. E., & Fay, A. L. (1987). A chain of cognitive changes with learning to program Logo. *Journal of Educational Psychology, 79,* 269-279.

McCoy, L. P. (1990). Literature relating critical skills for problem solving in mathematics and in computer programming. *School Science and Mathematics, 90*(1), 48-60.

Nickerson, R. S. (1980). Computer programming as a vehicle for teaching thinking skills. *Thinking: The Journal of Philosophy for Children, 4*(3), 4.

O'Bannon, B. (1997). CD-ROM integration peaks student interest in inquiry. *Computers in the Schools, 13*(2-3), 127-34.

Oprea, J. M. (1988). Computer programming and mathematical thinking. *Journal of Mathematical Behavior, 7*(2), 175-190.

Papert, S. (1987). Computer criticism vs. technocentric thinking. *Educational Researcher, 16*(1), 22-30.

Papert, S. (1985). Different visions of Logo. *Computers in the Schools, 2*(2-3), 3-8.

Papert, S. (1984). Tomorrow's classrooms. In M. Yazdani (Ed.), *New horizons in educational computing.* Chichester, England: Wiley, John and Sons, Inc.

Papert, S. (1980). *Mindstorms: Children, computers, and powerful ideas.* New York: Basic Books, Inc.

Patterson, J. H., & Smith, M. S. (1986). The role of computer in higher-order thinking in microcomputer and education. In J. A. Culbertson & L. L. Cunningham (Eds.), *Microcomputers and education* (pp. 81-108). Chicago: University of Chicago Press.

Pelton, L. F., & Pelton, T. W. (1998). Using WWW, usenets, and e-mail to manage a mathematics pre-service technology course. *Computers in the Schools, 14*(3-4), 79-93.

Reed, W., Palumbo, D., & Stolar, A. (1988). The comparative effects of BASIC and Logo instruction on problem-solving skills. *Computers in the Schools, 4*(3-4), 105-117.

Reed, W. M., & Wells, J. G. (1997). Merging the Internet and hypermedia in the English language arts. *Computers in the Schools, 13*(3-4), 75-102.

Reglin, G. L. (1990). CAI effects on mathematics and achievement and academic self-concept seminar. *Journal of Educational Technology Systems, 10*(1), 43-48.

Riebar, L. P. (1986, January). The effect of Logo on young children. Paper presented at the annual convention of the Association for Educational Communications and Technology, Las Vegas, NV.

Sales, G. C. (1988). Designing feedback for CBI: Matching feedback to the learner and learner outcomes. *Computers in the Schools, 5*(1-2), 225-239.

Salomon, G., & Perkins, D. N. (1987). Transfer of cognitive skills from programming: When and how? *Journal of Educational Computing Research, 3*(2), 149-169.

Sardello, R. J. (1985). The technological threat to education. In D. Sloan (Ed.), *The computer in education: A critical perspective* (pp. 93-101). New York: Teachers College Press.

Schaefer, L., & Sprigle, J. E. (1988). Gender differences in the use of the Logo programming language. *Journal of Educational Computing Research, 4*(1), 49-55.

Shaw, D. G. (1986). Effects of learning to program a computer in BASIC or Logo on problem-solving abilities. *AEDS Journal, 19*(2/3), 176-189.

Simpson, B. (1983). Heading for the ha-ha. *British Journal of Educational Technology, 14*(1), 19-26.

Suppes, P. (1985). Computer-assisted instruction: Possibilities and problems. *NASSP Bulletin, 69*(480), 30-34.

Taylor, R. P. (1980). *The computer in the school: Tutor, tool, tutee.* New York: Teachers College Press.

Thompson, A. D., & Wang, H. C. (1988). Effects of Logo microworld on student ability to transfer a concept. *Journal of Educational Computing Research, 4*(3), 335-347.

Tse, M. S. (1989, July). The use of computers in early childhood education: A growing concern. Paper presented at the International Conference on Early Education and Development, Hong Kong.

Turner, S. V., & Land, M. L. (1988). Cognitive effects of a Logo-enriched mathematics program for middle school students. *Journal of Educational Computing Research, 4*(4), 443-452.

Verderber, N. L. (1990). Spreadsheets and problem solving with Apple Works in mathematics teaching. *Journal of Computers in Mathematics and Science Teaching, 9*(3), 45-51.

Vernon, L. (1983). For parents particularly: Parents consider computers the challenge of the '80s. *Childhood Education, 59*(4), 267-270.

Vidoni, K. L., & Maddux, C. D. (2002). WebQuests: Can they be used to improve thinking skills in students? *Computers in the Schools, 19*(1-2).

Wiburg, K. (1991). Teaching teachers about technology. *Computers in the Schools, 8* (1-3), 115-29.

Willis, E. (1997). Technology: Integrated into, not added onto, the curriculum experience in pre-service teacher education. *Computers in the Schools, 13*(1-2), 141-153.

Wood, J. B. (1990). Utilizing the spreadsheet and charting capabilities of Microsoft Works in the mathematics classroom. *Journal of Computers in Mathematics and Science Teaching, 9*(3), 65-71.

Leping Liu
Norma Velasquez-Bryant

An Information Technology Integration System and Its Life Cycle: What Is Missing?

SUMMARY. In celebration of *Computers in the Schools'* 20th anniversary, we take a look back at the evolution of technology integration in education over the past two decades. In this retrospective analysis we have identified four critical components in a typical integration life cycle that contribute to the failure to integrate information technology: (a) a missing link, (b) a misguided direction, (c) an area of weakness, and (d) a major dilemma. Also, in this paper we propose a new conceptual framework that represents both a macro- and micro-perspective of technology integration. The new conceptual framework consists of a three-dimensional ITD (Information, Technology, Instructional Design) information technology integration system that is associated with two other integration models. The first model–the Information Technology Integration Life Cycle–examines the macro-processes of integration over time (years). The second model–the Information Technology Integration Design Model–examines the micro-processes in any single case of integration. *[Article copies available for a fee from The Haworth Document Delivery Service: 1-800-HAWORTH. E-mail*

LEPING LIU is Assistant Professor, University of Nevada, Reno, Counseling and Educational Psychology, Reno, NV 89557 (E-mail: liu@unr.edu).
NORMA VELASQUEZ-BRYANT is Program Evaluator/Data Analyst, University of Nevada, Reno, Research & Educational Planning Center, Reno, NV 89557 (E-mail: normah@unr.edu).

[Haworth co-indexing entry note]: "An Information Technology Integration System and Its Life Cycle: What Is Missing?" Liu, Leping, and Norma Velasquez-Bryant. Co-published simultaneously in *Computers in the Schools* (The Haworth Press, Inc.) Vol. 20, No. 1/2, 2003, pp. 91-104; and: *Technology in Education: A Twenty-Year Retrospective* (ed: D. LaMont Johnson, and Cleborne D. Maddux) The Haworth Press, Inc., 2003, pp. 91-104. Single or multiple copies of this article are available for a fee from The Haworth Document Delivery Service [1-800-HAWORTH, 9:00 a.m. - 5:00 p.m. (EST). E-mail address: docdelivery@haworthpress.com].

*address: <docdelivery@haworthpress.com> Website: <http://www.HaworthPress.
com> © 2003 by The Haworth Press, Inc. All rights reserved.]*

KEYWORDS. Information technology, instructional design, technology integration, integration model, technology life cycle, education

In celebration of *Computers in the Schools'* 20th anniversary, we take a look back at the evolution of technology integration in education over the past two decades. In this retrospective analysis we have identified four critical components in a typical integration life cycle that contribute to the failure to integrate information technology: (a) a missing link, (b) a misguided direction, (c) an area of weakness, and (d) a major dilemma. Also, in this paper we propose a new conceptual framework that represents both a macro- and micro-perspective of technology integration. The new conceptual framework consists of a three-dimensional ITD (Information, Technology, Instructional Design) information technology integration system that is associated with two other integration models. The first model–the Information Technology Integration Life Cycle–examines the macro-processes of integration over time (years). The second model–the Information Technology Integration Design Model–examines the micro-processes in any single case of integration.

Using this new conceptual framework, it is our hope that we can more clearly (a) explain the characteristics of technology integration and its life cycle, (b) detail the missing link, (c) prevent advancement in a misguided direction, (d) examine any weak areas, and (e) alleviate the negative effects of a major dilemma. In addition, it is our intent to provide educators with a better understanding of the characteristics necessary for successful technology integration.

DEVELOPMENT OF THE THREE-DIMENSIONAL ITD INTEGRATION SYSTEM

A literature review of the past 20 years provided a comprehensive view of technology integration. The result of this review was a merging of the uses of information and technology into a system that follows the rules, theories, and models of instructional design. In the ITD system shown in Figure 1, the first dimension–*information (I)*–represents the learning or teaching content, and any supporting resources and materials. The second dimension–*technology (T)*–represents the hardware and software tools that can be used appropriately to support or enhance learning and teaching. The third dimension–*instructional design (D)*–represents a set of rules for instructional design.

Assumptions of the ITD Integration System

As shown in Figure 1, each of the three dimensions points in a different direction, and each has different functions, emphases, and issues that contribute to learning. What we want to demonstrate, however, is that no single dimension will produce effective learning outcomes independently (without interaction with the other two). We will explore the nature of technology integration through three major assumptions of the ITD system:

1. Technology-based learning will never occur in any single dimension.
2. Technology-based learning will never occur in any combination of just two dimensions.
3. Technology-based learning only occurs as the result of the *integration* of all three components: Information (I), Technology (T), and Instructional Design (D).

Why Not Single Dimension?

If we start from the development of a lesson plan using a particular technology to teach a certain topic, we discover that the three dimensions should not be viewed separately. First, *information* (learning content) requires a series of decisions to be made about content to determine: (a) the type of content, facts,

FIGURE 1. The Three-Dimensional ITD Information Technology Integration System

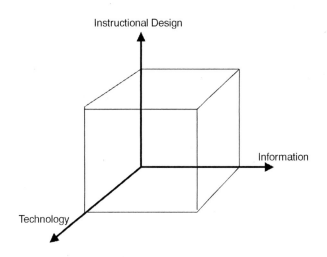

concepts, or generalizations (Eggen, Kauchak, & Harder, 1979); (b) the order required to present the content according to levels of difficulty and generality (Ausubel, 1963); and (c) the scope, focus, and sequence of the content in a lesson unit (Gunter, Estes, & Schwab, 1999). However, keep in mind that these are not simple content issues. All content decisions must be based on an analysis of the characteristics of the learners and learning goals, outcomes, and objectives–all of which are considerations in instructional design (Kemp, Morrison, & Ross, 1998; Smith & Ragan, 1993). It is also important to note that information itself does not function independently in the ITD system; it must interact with the other two dimensions (technology and instructional design) if learning is to occur.

Second, before *technology* (any hardware or software used in learning or teaching) can be adopted, decisions must be made as to (a) what particular hardware or software to use, (b) how to use a particular technology to promote learning in specific areas or topics, and (c) how to use a particular technology in different learning environments or with students who have different learning styles (Johnson & Liu, 2000). Again, these decisions must be based on an analysis of learning content, learner characteristics, and instructional–all of which are considerations in instructional design (Gunter, Estes, & Schwab, 1999). Technology itself is a static tool; it won't produce learning outcomes without merging learning content and instructional components.

The third dimension, *instructional design*, includes the major components of and the phases of instructional development. According to Kemp, Morrison and Ross (1998), there are four fundamental elements in instructional design: learners, objectives, methods, and evaluation. Additionally, the process of instructional development consists of four major phases (Gunter, Estes, & Schwab, 1999; Smith & Ragan, 1993):

1.   Planning instruction–analyzing content, learners, and tasks;
2.   Designing instruction–determining the strategies for lessons (declarative knowledge, concept, rules, problem solving, cognitive strategy, attitude change, motivation, and interest), methods of delivery (with a series of design models), and evaluation plans;
3.   Implementing instruction–using the designed methods and procedures; and
4.   Evaluating instruction–conducting formative and summative evaluations for revision and improvement of instruction.

The third dimension is very important and the design in each phase has a strong theoretical foundation consisting of a series of cognitive learning theories (Driscoll, 2000; Smith & Ragan, 1993). The ITD system won't work without the addition of *information* and *technology* into the framework of *instructional design*. As shown in Figure 2, if each of the three dimensions points in a different direction, it is neither a learning system nor a technology integration system.

FIGURE 2. Single Dimensions of the ITD Integration System

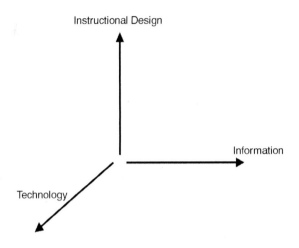

Why Not Two Dimensions?

We propose that technology-based learning won't occur in any combination of just two dimensions in the system. As shown in Figure 3, there are three different combinations of two-dimensional (2-D) models:

1. information–instructional design (I-D)
2. technology–instructional design (T-D)
3. information–technology (I-T)

The first 2-D model, I-D, merges learning content into instructional design, which has typically worked well for traditional classroom instruction. However, the design is not merged with the use of technology; hence, it does not result in a technology-based learning experience. Next, the second 2-D model, T-D, focuses on only technology and the instructional design procedure. This is also an "empty" dimension; no appropriate decisions about instruction or use of technology can be made without first understanding and analyzing learning content. Finally, the third 2-D model, I-T, emphasizes only the learning content and available technology.

If we wanted to build a house, we not only need the proper tools and materials, but we must follow the design of the house. It is with this same logic that we stipulate that technology tools and learning content cannot be simply combined together to produce learning outcomes–the rules or models of instruc-

FIGURE 3. The Different Two-Dimensional Components of the ITD Integration System

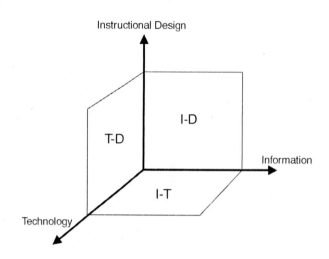

tional design must be applied to develop a successful unit of teaching and learning.

The Three-Dimensional ITD Integration System

By contrast, when we look at the ITD three-dimensional integration system in Figure 1, we see that it logically merges all three components–*information, technology*, and *instructional design*–into one unit, compensating for the missing component of integration in each dimension or combination of two. Furthermore, it illustrates theoretically and practically a structure that exhibits what does and does not work, what is missing, and what should be the future direction in the field.

We view the processes of technology integration as a system, observing that any system development has a life cycle, and that each phase in the life cycle is implemented through different design models (Burch, 1992, p.152). Typically, technology integration has been considered in a case- or project-oriented approach. If the system-oriented approach is used to conduct future work, the focus of technology integration should logically move to the next level–the *design* of the integration.

We believe that the ITD integration system exhibits the nature of technology integration and that the integration-design component is missing because educators were not aware of it. The ITD technology integration system does have a life cycle and each phase of that life cycle should reflect the true nature of integration. We emphasize the design dimension to ensure a complete life cycle that reflects that true nature.

LIFE CYCLE OF THE INFORMATION TECHNOLOGY INTEGRATION SYSTEM

The "Proposed" Life Cycle

There are two underlying properties of the ITD information technology integration system used in the design model; it is a dynamic system and has a developmental life cycle, and it is implemented through design models. According to our system, the life cycle of information technology integration includes four major phases:

Phase 1: Planning integration
Phase 2: Designing integration
Phase 3: Implementing integration
Phase 4: Evaluating integration

The underlying theoretical foundation for the proposed integration life cycle is that of instructional design. In the integration life cycle (a) phase one determines the needs, and analyzes learning goals, outcomes, content, learner characteristics, and available technology tools; (b) phase two matches the needs with instruction and learning strategies, including decisions regarding both content and appropriate use of technology; (c) phase three implements the design of instruction and learning, which produces the learning outcomes; and (d) phase four evaluates the procedures and outcomes, making recommendations to revise the plans or designs–resulting in a new cycle. We propose this life cycle based on the three-dimensional ITD integration system, learning theories and instructional design models, and system development theories (Burch, 1992; Driscoll, 2000; Gunter, Estes, & Schwab, 1999; Smith & Ragan, 1993). We use this life cycle to examine the macro-processes of the integration over a period of years.

The "Typical" Life Cycle of the Past

Interestingly, a review of literature over the past two decades shows a different life cycle structure, with most of the literature focusing on four different major phases:

Phase 1: Current technologies and how to use them
Phase 2: Theoretical foundations of using the technologies
Phase 3: Classroom practice
Phase 4: Assessment of the impact of the technologies

This structure represents the typical life cycle in the past. Although technology has been used in the field of education for the past 20 years or so, it is still not clear to what extent technology *has been* integrated into teaching and learning.

In the typical life cycle, phase one introduces available technology, including new technology and how to use it, such as (a) Logo or BASIC programming, (b) educational software, (c) multimedia authoring programs, (d) telecommunications and the Internet, (d) the use of the World Wide Web (WWW) as a resource, and, more recently, (6) the use of the WWW as an instructional delivery tool (Taylor, Smith, & Riley, 1984). Phase two of the typical life cycle provides traditional theoretical foundations, ranging from the various learning theories, information processing systems, and cognitive learning, to the different approaches of instruction and learning. Phase three introduces teachers' practices in the classroom, from exploring the use of technology to the methodology of teaching students using technology. Phase four focuses on the assessment of the effectiveness of technology-based learning compared with non-technology-based learning, including distributions of computers in schools, attitudes toward technology, and proficiency levels.

Based on our literature review and on an examination of the typical integration life cycle, we have identified and will discuss a missing link, a misguided direction, an area of weakness, and a dilemma in the typical integration life cycle.

The Missing Link

The missing link in the four phases of the typical life cycle is the *design* component for technology integration. Although most classroom practices have explored the use of technologies, these practices were generally based on the I-T dimension of the three-dimensional ITD system shown in Figure 3, where technology was simply added to the learning processes without careful design of the instruction component. As previously discussed, any combination of two dimensions without inclusion of the third will not produce successful technology-based learning. What is very surprising is the fact that in the macro-process of technology integration over the past 20 years, true nature of technology integration–the merging of the three components (ITD)–was ignored. It is believed that educators are very familiar with instructional design theories, components, procedures, and models, and that they have employed instructional design principles in traditional classroom teaching for years. What then caused this missing link in the technology-based learning context? There are numerous possibilities, but if we start with the typical life cycle itself, the answer becomes obvious–in certain places the life cycle points in the wrong direction.

A Misguided Direction

Using the typical life cycle and the literature review, we identified six life cycles that occurred during the past 20 years. Interestingly, each life cycle started with the use of new technology–for example, the use of (a) Logo and BASIC programming in the early 80s, (b) educational software in the mid 80s, (c) multimedia authoring programs in the late 80s, (d) telecommunications and the Internet in the early 90s, (e) the WWW as a resource in the mid 90s, and (f) the WWW as an instructional delivery tool in the late 90s and early 2000s. It is important to keep in mind that the purpose of technology integration is to achieve learning goals and enhance learning–not to use fancy technology tools. Theoretically, the integration life cycle should start with identifying learning needs or with revising the integration plan and design. It should not start merely from the appearance of new technology–this "misguided direction" is the cause of an incomplete life cycle.

In fact, it appears that just when teachers are about to reach the core integration design, usually after many successful practice attempts, new technology and/or new trends of using technology are released. Unfortunately, it is very easy to be attracted to and sidetracked by new technology and new trends. Thus, once again, time is spent on learning to use the new technology, exploring its theoretical foundations, trying to use it in the classroom, and finding better ways of using it. In this manner, the faulty life cycle is repeated over and over again with the same missing link, and subsequently, resulting in an incomplete life cycle. Intuitively, we realize this is occurring–yet, why do we let it happen repeatedly? Perhaps the solution can be found in the identification of a major dilemma.

The Dilemma

Whenever new technology or a new method of using technology is released, there is a tendency for consumers to try to immediately adopt it. Therein lies the dilemma–many feel that, if they don't adopt the newest technology, they will lag behind the "cutting edge." Unfortunately, this translates into an incomplete integration process.

Educators who get caught in this dilemma should instead try to focus on their goals. We propose that if educators accept our three-dimensional ITD information technology integration system, they will be able to determine where the new technology fits into the system and how it can be used effectively. In fact, if a well-developed integration design model was provided to educators, they would think of the integration design when they started using a new technology. Consequently, they would not have to experience an isolated practice period before they reached the point of integration design; they could practice and design the integration simultaneously.

An Area of Weakness

Assessment results provide a broad range of information on the effectiveness of technology integration. However, the information is usually too broad for educators, especially K-12 teachers, to gain a clear perspective of the major components involved in technology integration. Most teachers tend to look at and learn from specific successful cases. While this is not technically incorrect, it does limit them from exploring the full potential and true nature of technology integration.

To add to the problem in assessing technology integration, it typically requires three to five years for a user to move from entry-level technology usage to proficient levels of fully integrating technology into the curriculum (Anderson, 2000; Johnson, Maddux, & Liu, 1997, 2000; Liu, Johnson, Maddux, & Henderson, 2001; Roblyer, Castine, & King, 1988). Because technology evolves so rapidly, it is difficult to develop a standardized form of assessment for determining a level of technology integration and effectiveness.

INFORMATION TECHNOLOGY
INTEGRATION *DESIGN* MODEL

The development of an integration design model is not an easy task. In fact, it might take a lifetime of study to test, revise, and retest the model. In this paper, our proposed information technology integration design model is based on the four phases of our recommended integration life cycle: Planning, Design, Implementation, and Evaluation. Again, the core of this model is the merging of the three components–*Information, Technology,* and *Instructional Design* (see Table 1).

This integration design model describes the micro-processes of technology integration that can be used in any single case. As shown in Table 1, first, planning integration includes defining different types of objectives (cognitive, affective, and psychomotor), analyzing content (facts, concepts, or generalizations), assessing learner needs (previous knowledge, special needs, and technology skills), and evaluating available technologies (types of the technology, access to the technology) (Gunter, Estes, & Schwab, 1999).

Second, in the phase of designing integration, learning objectives, learning content, and learner needs are matched to the instructional strategies. Instructional strategies include those for direct instruction, concept attainment, concept development, inquiry, cause and effect, vocabulary acquisition, resolution of conflict, cooperative learning, and so on (Gunter, Estes, & Schwab, 1999). Also, during this phase, the use of appropriate technologies is designed to

TABLE 1. Information Technology Integration Design Model

Integration Design	Information	Technology
Planning	• Define learning goals, objectives, and learning outcomes • Analyze content • Determine evaluation strategies • Assess learners' previous knowledge, learning styles, and special needs	• Evaluate available technologies • Select the technologies • Assess the access to technologies • Examine learners' computer skills
Design	• Match objectives and needs to instruction strategies • Determine models of instruction to different content • Determine models of instruction to different learning styles	• Match objectives and needs to the use of technology • Match content to the use of technology • Match instructional strategies to the use of technology • Develop the procedures and instructions for using the technology
Implementation	• Implement the designed methodology • Promote learning-treatment interaction	
Evaluation	• Evaluate learning procedures and outcomes • Make recommendations to revise the plan and design	

match the learning objectives and instructional strategies. The technologies can be used as information resource or tools to deliver instruction and can be used to acquire and review knowledge or assess learning outcomes (Johnson & Liu, 2000), according to the learning objectives and instructional strategies.

Third, in the phase of implementation, learning-treatment interaction takes place, and the designed methodology is implemented and examined. And last, the evaluation of the integration takes place during and after the implementation of the design. Learning procedures and outcomes will be evaluated via formative and summative evaluations.

IMPLICATIONS FOR RESEARCH

Findings from the typical real world integration life cycle and further directions for technology integration we recommended in this paper (the three-dimensional integration design) are consistent with the three research stages proposed by Maddux (1993):

Stage One: Exposure to computers
Stage Two: Computer education
Stage Three: Learning-treatment interaction

The first two research stages are parallel with the first phase of the typical technology integration life cycle–exploring available technologies and learning to use them. As Maddux discusses in his article in this issue, research in the area of instructional technology should move to research of Stage Three–discovering the learning-treatment interaction. This major issue of instructional design and integration design is the missing link we identified in the past 20 years of technology integration. This might explain why few studies have been conducted in this area; that is, what is missing in practice is also missing in research. Correspondingly, as we suggested, when technology integration moves to the next level–the *design* of integration–learning-treatment interaction occurs in the phase of implementation of integration design (as shown in Table 1). Research and integration practice are parallel areas in the field of educational information technology and should move forward simultaneously.

CONCLUSION

We have identified four critical areas that have contributed to the failure to integrate technology in a typical integration life cycle: the missing link (the exclusion of integration design), the tendency for educators to be misguided by the appearance of new technology, the dilemma of not being on the cutting edge when new technology does appear, and the difficulty in developing an assessment tool for determining a level of technology integration and effectiveness.

As we have outlined our three-dimensional ITD system of technology integration, our recommended four-phase life cycle, as well as the integration design model, which together formulate the new conceptual framework of technology integration (see Figure 4), we hope that we have provided educators with new direction and a concrete system for integrating technology. We also hope that our system will provide them with a structural tool for their practice and research. With continual practice, we believe the ITD integration system, proposed life cycle and integration design model will be continually examined, revised, and used to guide the start of another life cycle with a clear focus on integration design.

FIGURE 4. The Conceptual Framework of Information Technology Integration

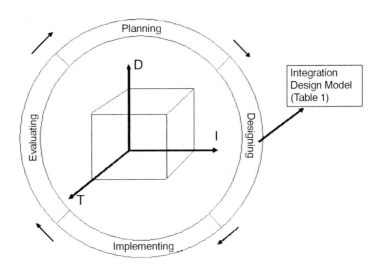

REFERENCES

Anderson, M. A. (2000, November/December). Assessing teacher technology skills. *Multimedia Schools, 7*(6), 25-27.

Ausubel, E. (1963). *The psychology of meaningful verbal learning.* New York: Grune & Stratton.

Burch, J. G. (1992). *Systems analysis, design, and implementation.* Boston: Boyd & Fraser.

Driscoll, M. P. (2000). *Psychology of learning for instruction* (2nd ed.). Boston: Allyn & Bacon.

Eggen, P. D., Kauchak, D. P., & Harder, R. J. (1979). *Strategies for teachers.* Englewood Cliffs, NJ: Prentice Hall.

Gunter, M. A., Estes, T. H., & Schwab, J. (1999). *Instruction: A models approach* (3rd ed.). Boston: Allyn & Bacon.

Johnson, D. L., & Liu, L. (2000). First steps toward a statistically generated information technology integration model. *Computers in the Schools, 16*(2), 3-12.

Johnson, D. L., Maddux, C. D., & Liu, L. (Eds.). (1997). *Using technology in the classroom.* New York: The Haworth Press.

Johnson, D. L., Maddux, C. D., & Liu, L. (Eds.). (2000). *Integration of technology into the classroom.* New York: The Haworth Press.

Kemp, J. E., Morrison, G., & Ross, S. M. (1998). *Designing effective instructions* (2nd ed.). Upper Saddle River, NJ: Merrill.

Liu, L., Johnson, D. L., Maddux, C. D., & Henderson, N. J. (Eds.). (2001). *Evaluation and assessment in educational information technology.* New York: The Haworth Press.

Maddux, C. D. (1993). Past and future stages in educational computing research. In H. C. Waxman, G. W. Bright, C. D. Maddux, & M. D. Waggoner (Eds.), *Approaches to research on teacher education and technology* (pp. 11-22). Charlottesville, VA: Society for Technology and Teacher Education.

Roblyer, M. D., Castine, W. H., & King, F. J. (Eds.). (1988). *Assessing the impact of computer-based instruction.* New York: The Haworth Press.

Smith, P. L., & Ragan, T. J. (1993). *Instructional design.* Upper Saddle River, NJ: Merrill.

Taylor, V. L., Smith, D. D., & Riley, M. T. (1984). A pre-math computer program for children: Validation of its effectiveness. *Computers in the Schools, 1*(3), 49-60.

Paul F. Merrill

Entering Skills of Students Enrolling in an Educational Technology Course

SUMMARY. The purpose of this paper is to document the diverse entering skills of teacher education students enrolling in an educational technology course and to suggest an approach to addressing that diversity. *[Article copies available for a fee from The Haworth Document Delivery Service: 1-800-HAWORTH. E-mail address: <docdelivery@haworthpress.com> Website: <http://www.HaworthPress.com> © 2003 by The Haworth Press, Inc. All rights reserved.]*

KEYWORDS. Technology skills, proficiency level, technology integration, self-instructional modules

As we look back over the last twenty years, one thing that many of us did not anticipate is that we would still be offering a required basic skills course as part of our teacher education curriculum. Even in the early years, we discussed the expectation that our students would soon be coming to the university with basic skills in hand and that we would no longer need to require a basic skills course. However, that expectation does not seem to have materialized.

Today what we seem to find is an increasing diversity in the entering skills of our students. Byrum (2001) has observed that this student skill diversity

PAUL F. MERRILL is Professor, Brigham Young University, Instructional Psychology & Technology, Provo, UT 84602 (E-mail: Paul_Merrill@byu.edu).

[Haworth co-indexing entry note]: "Entering Skills of Students Enrolling in an Educational Technology Course." Merrill, Paul F. Co-published simultaneously in *Computers in the Schools* (The Haworth Press, Inc.) Vol. 20, No. 1/2, 2003, pp. 105-111; and: *Technology in Education: A Twenty-Year Retrospective* (ed: D. LaMont Johnson, and Cleborne D. Maddux) The Haworth Press, Inc., 2003, pp. 105-111. Single or multiple copies of this article are available for a fee from The Haworth Document Delivery Service [1-800-HAWORTH, 9:00 a.m. - 5:00 p.m. (EST). E-mail address: docdelivery@haworthpress.com].

ranges all the way from computer novice to skilled professional. Sisk (2001) suggests that today's students arrive with much higher levels of technology skills than their counterparts just a few years ago. Although both of these statements are probably true, the skill level of many entering students does not appear to be as high as we would have anticipated.

The purpose of this paper is to document the diverse entering skills of teacher education students enrolling in an educational technology course and to suggest an approach to addressing that diversity.

METHOD

Subjects

Two hundred and eighteen students enrolled in IP&T 286, Technology in Teaching, during the winter 2002 semester at Brigham Young University participated in this study. Typically, most of the students enrolled in this class are female and are majoring in elementary education. Students generally take this class during their sophomore year prior to beginning the bulk of their teacher education curriculum. Brigham Young University is a private, church-sponsored university and draws students from every state in the United States and many other countries. This particular sample consisted of students from 34 states and three other countries (Canada, Belgium, and France). Fifty-one students came from Utah, 39 from California, 18 from Washington, 12 each from Texas and Arizona, 10 from Colorado, 8 each from Idaho and Nevada, 5 each from Oregon and Virginia, 4 each from Tennessee, New York, and Georgia, 3 each from Montana and Ohio, 2 each from Florida, Maryland, Michigan, New Mexico, Pennsylvania, and 1 each from Illinois, Iowa, Louisiana, Maine, Minnesota, Missouri, North Dakota, New Hampshire, Nebraska, South Carolina, South Dakota, Wisconsin, and Wyoming.

Instrument

A survey questionnaire titled "Technology Skills Prior to Enrolling in IP&T 286" was prepared by the author for use in this study. The questionnaire asked the students to record the city and state where they graduated from high school and respond to 16 Likert-type items. The following instructions were presented on the questionnaire:

> This is a survey to access your perception of your level of proficiency in several technology skills prior to enrolling in IP&T 286, Technology in Teaching. Please rate your proficiency in the following skills prior to enrollment in IP&T 286 by circling the appropriate number associated with the following scale:

1–no proficiency; 2–limited proficiency; 3–functional proficiency; 4–skilled proficiency; 5–advanced proficiency

The following 16 skills were included on the questionnaire: word processing, spreadsheet, database management, computer graphics, desktop publishing, e-mail, Internet navigation, Internet searching, digital video recording, digital video editing, Web page creation, HyperStudio, computer programming, technology integration, electronic portfolios, and electronic presentations. Each skill was listed on a separate line followed by the numbers 1-5.

Procedures

The questionnaire, "Technology Skills Prior to Enrolling in IP&T 286," was distributed at the beginning of class to all students enrolled in three different sections of IP&T 286, Technology in Teaching, during the last week of the winter 2002 semester. Students were informed that their responses to the questionnaire would be appreciated and would be helpful in revising the curriculum for the course. However, they were not required to complete the questionnaire, and they were informed that their responses would have no affect on their grade for the course. They were asked not to write their names on the questionnaire to insure that their responses would be confidential. They were given the opportunity to ask questions of clarification if needed. No questions were asked. They were given 10 minutes to complete the questionnaire. All of the students submitted the questionnaire, although one student did not fill in the information concerning the city and state where he/she graduated from high school.

The questionnaire was administered at the end of the semester rather than at the beginning to insure that the students understood the meaning of the skills listed in the questionnaire.

DATA ANALYSIS

Student responses to the questionnaire were transcribed into an Excel spreadsheet. The data were sorted by state and city to determine where students had graduated from high school. Excel formulas were then used to determine the percentage response frequency for each of the 16 Likert items. The mean and standard deviation for each item were also calculated using Excel formulas.

RESULTS

The results from the question regarding the city and state where the students graduated from high school were reported previously in the Subjects section.

Table 1 presents the distribution of student responses, means, and standard deviations for each of the 16 Likert items. The items listed in Table 1 have been sorted in descending order based on the mean response to the items.

As can be seen from Table 1, the mean proficiency level prior to enrolling in the Technology in Teaching course was reported by the students to be between skilled and advanced proficiency for e-mail, Internet navigation, Internet searching, and word processing. Reported mean proficiency then drops to functional proficiency for computer graphics and then to between limited and

TABLE 1. Distribution of Student Responses, Means, and Standard Deviations by Skill

Skill	Percentage Response Frequencies					Means	*SD*
	No	Limited	Functional	Skilled	Advanced		
E-mail	1	0	11	29	59	4.46	.76
Internet Navigation	1	1	14	34	49	4.29	.85
Internet Searching	1	1	18	33	46	4.23	.85
Word Processing	2	2	14	53	29	4.06	.82
Computer Graphics	7	25	32	24	12	3.10	1.12
Spreadsheet	14	30	37	16	4	2.66	1.02
Desktop Publishing	28	23	26	14	9	2.52	1.27
Electronic Presentation	36	25	20	13	6	2.29	1.25
Database Management	27	34	28	9	1	2.23	.98
Technology Integration	39	32	18	7	4	2.06	1.10
Electronic Portfolios	52	26	12	6	3	1.81	1.06
Digital Video Recording	65	20	10	4	1	1.56	.91
Web Page Creation	75	12	6	3	3	1.46	.95
Computer Programming	73	16	7	3	0	1.42	.80
Digital Video Editing	78	12	6	3	1	1.39	.84
HyperStudio	78	12	6	4	0	1.38	.80

functional proficiency for spreadsheets, desktop publishing, electronic presentations, database management, and technology integration. The reported mean proficiency was between no to limited proficiency for electronic portfolios, digital video recording, Web page creation, computer programming, digital video editing, and HyperStudio.

DISCUSSION

Although the data from this survey were collected from students enrolled in only one university, the students graduated from high schools across 34 different states and three other countries. Therefore, I feel confident that other universities and colleges would find similar results.

Self-report data are always suspect, but the data seem to make sense. It is not surprising that students would feel comfortable with their e-mail, Internet searching, Internet navigation, and word-processing skills before enrolling in a university technology in teaching course. The ordering of the proficiency levels with the other skills is also not surprising. Although the data are not surprising, it is quite interesting and informative. For example, although most students reported that they were quite skilled in using the Internet and word-processing software, there were a few that reported no proficiency in these areas. What provisions should we make in our curriculum for such students?

The finding that a majority of the students reported no or limited proficiency in 10 out of the 16 skills listed in the questionnaire is noteworthy. Another very important observation is the wide disparity between proficiency levels across students. There were students at every level of proficiency for all but three skills. How do we address these widely varying entering skills?

Byrum (2001) has suggested several different strategies for dealing with this student skill diversity:

1. Have students with advanced skills teach or assist those students who might be struggling.
2. Allow advanced students to test out of the course. This might be done through the use of some kind of performance test or submission of portfolio items.
3. Allow advanced students to study independently.
4. Provide multiple instructional paths: beginning, intermediate, and advanced. Allow students to progress at their own pace along these various paths.
5. Provide differentiated assignments and allow students to choose skills they would like to acquire.

At Brigham Young University we have chosen to address these changing and varying entering skills of our students by providing a library of self-instructional modules. Most of these modules have been developed by graduate students enrolled in our Instructional Psychology and Technology program. Some have been developed by advanced undergraduate students. Undergraduate students often update modules when new versions of software are released. A few of these modules are computer-based, but most are print-based materials.

After students go through the self-instructional modules, they are asked to complete assignments where they must demonstrate their ability to apply their new skills to develop some educational product such as a newsletter, presentation, or instructional program. Each assignment is reviewed and passed off by a lab proctor. If a product does not meet specified standards, the student is given feedback and asked to make appropriate revisions. If a student enters with adequate proficiency in a required skill, he/she can demonstrate proficiency and choose an alternate module. These self-instructional modules allow us to focus on technology integration and other National Educational Technology Standards (NETS) (International Society for Technology in Education, 2000) in our classroom lectures and discussion periods rather than using class time to teach technical skills.

We are also trying to encourage our methods and subject matter instructors to model technology integration in their own classrooms and to give students assignments that require them to use the technology skills they have previously learned. The self-instructional modules make it possible for students to refresh their skills if necessary when completing these assignments.

Why is there so much diversity in students' entering skills and why do a majority of students still have so many limited technology skills? With the pervasiveness of computers in the schools and in the homes, one would expect that a majority of students would be entering colleges and universities with a greater level of technology skill. Unfortunately, no data were collected in this study to address the question of why so many students have limited technology skills. Nonetheless, some reasoned conjectures are offered that would be worthy of further investigation.

From the data that were collected in this study, it appears that most students are proficient in some skills but not others. It may be that students are skilled in those areas that are most useful to them and that are required of them in many of their classes. Apparently, students are being required to write papers and use the Internet to obtain information for those papers. Thus, word-processing and Internet skill levels are quite high. E-mail proficiency may come more from personal utility than from school use.

The other skills may be lacking because schools are not providing significant opportunities for students to learn and apply those skills in their curriculum. This is probably not only the case in the public schools but also in colleges and universities. It does not do much good to teach many of these skills in our technology courses if students seldom use them after they leave the educational technology classroom. Thus, our continuing challenge is to help college and public school teachers to integrate technology applications into their own instruction.

CONCLUSION

The purpose of this paper was to document the extent of the diversity of entering skills of pre-service elementary education teachers enrolling in an educational technology course and to suggest some ways to address that diversity. The results of a questionnaire administered to 218 students from 34 different states and three other countries revealed that the diversity of students' entering skills is very extensive and ranges from students with no proficiency to students with advanced proficiency in nearly every skill listed in the questionnaire. It was surprising to find some students entering with no e-mail or word-processing proficiency and that a majority of the students had no or limited proficiency in 10 out of the 16 skills listed.

The use of a library of self-instructional modules was suggested as a viable approach to addressing this extensive entering skill diversity. To overcome this diversity we need to do a better job of integrating technology across the curriculum in both the colleges and the public schools.

REFERENCES

Byrum, D. C. (2001, March). Technological diversity: Managing differing technology skills in the edtech course. In W. Bump (Ed.), *Proceedings of the Society for Information Technology and Teacher Education International Conference* (pp. 8-9). (ERIC Document Reproduction Service No. ED457 824).

International Society for Technology in Education (2000). *National educational technology standards for teachers.* Eugene, OR: Author.

Sisk, K. A. (2001, March). Challenges to currency in the educational computing course. In W. Bump (Ed.), *Proceedings of the Society for Information Technology and Teacher Education International Conference* (pp. 50-52). (ERIC Document Reproduction Service No. ED457 824).

Karin M. Wiburg

Technology and the New Meaning
of Educational Equity

SUMMARY. This article investigates the changing meaning of educational equity as a result of the growth of technology, especially computer-mediated networks and learning environments. The work is grounded in an overview of educational equity and access in U.S. history and the changed meaning of access in a digital age. Perhaps the most important point made is the need to broaden our definition of access and equity and to focus on connections between leadership, teaching, and technology. *[Article copies available for a fee from The Haworth Document Delivery Service: 1-800-HAWORTH. E-mail address: <docdelivery@haworthpress.com> Website: <http://www.HaworthPress.com> © 2003 by The Haworth Press, Inc. All rights reserved.]*

KEYWORDS. Digital access, equity, digital divide, diversity, computers, telecommunications, community-based education, technology

What does educational equity mean in a digital age? Despite extensive writing about the multiple dimensions of the digital divide (Swain & Pearson, 2001; Soloman, Allen, & Resta, 2002; Charp, 2001), the most common concep-

KARIN M. WIBURG is Associate Professor of Instructional Information Technology, New Mexico State University, Curriculum & Instruction Department, Las Cruces, NM 88003-8001 (E-mail: kwiburg@nmsu.edu).

[Haworth co-indexing entry note]: "Technology and the New Meaning of Educational Equity." Wiburg, Karin M. Co-published simultaneously in *Computers in the Schools* (The Haworth Press, Inc.) Vol. 20, No. 1/2, 2003, pp. 113-128; and: *Technology in Education: A Twenty-Year Retrospective* (ed: D. LaMont Johnson, and Cleborne D. Maddux) The Haworth Press, Inc., 2003, pp. 113-128. Single or multiple copies of this article are available for a fee from The Haworth Document Delivery Service [1-800-HAWORTH, 9:00 a.m. - 5:00 p.m. (EST). E-mail address: docdelivery@haworthpress.com].

tion remains that the divide is an isolated issue related to access to computers and networks. This is indeed one aspect of the gap between the haves and have nots in a digital era, but it is an overly simplified reflection of deeper issues involving equity and how its meaning has changed as society has moved from an industrial to an information/communication age. This article discusses issues of educational equity within a larger historical and sociopolitical context related to the nature of educational access.

Digital equity is the latest battle in the effort to keep access to education and political representation open to all–to avoid having a technological underclass that contributes to the economic and educational divides that already exist. Educational access in its deepest sense is about the right to learn and to know and the right to an education. It is about who has a right to know and who decides what is important to know. Further, in a digital age it requires understanding the changing nature of how one comes to know. The meanings of knowledge, learning, and literacy, not to mention work, have changed as a result of powerful new computer-mediated tools and networks. Symbolic and visual literacy are increasingly important in the world even as schools continue to focus primarily on print. This article begins with a short summary of the history of educational access, then suggests how technology has changed what students and citizens need to know and be able to do and finally concludes with a revised framework for understanding and creating educational equity.

HISTORY OF EDUCATIONAL ACCESS

The history of educational access in this country starts almost at the beginning of the establishment of the United States. Public policy providing access to a free education began as early as shortly after the landing of the Pilgrims when the people of Massachusetts in 1647 passed the Old Deluder Satan Act. This law required each township to appoint someone to teach any interested children to read and write. It also required that any township with one hundred families establish a grammar school to prepare students to attend a university. The name of the act reflects the purpose of keeping its youth informed–so they would maintain their religious culture. In 1787, under the Northwest Ordinance, townships were created, reserving a portion of each township for a local school. In 1862, the Morrill Act designated one land grant college for each state. The law was intended to ensure a higher education for the working classes and for those who could not afford private colleges.

EDUCATIONAL ACCESS AND STUDENTS OF COLOR

In early American history, free educational options were intended for the children of White families only. After the Civil War, Black children began to attend White schools, although the people in power desired the maintenance of a color line. This lead in 1896 to the *Plessy v. Ferguson* Supreme Court decision that officially established separate Black schools. According to this ruling such schools were to be designed to be separate and equal. It was because of the Plessy case that segregation continued for another 50 years after the Civil War. Smith (1996) described the reality of the separate but equal policy in Virginia. He depicted how White schools were often made of brick while the separate Black schools were little more than tarpaper shacks. The White schools had gymnasiums, infirmaries, and cafeterias while the Black schools were asked to function without those specialized facilities and in very overcrowded conditions.

In 1954, the historic court decision of *Brown v. Board of Education* of Topeka, Kansas, finally overturned the Plessy case by declaring that separate schools are inherently not equal. This case and the cases that followed it which resulted in integration in the public schools were based on the Fourteenth Amendment to the Constitution, which guarantees equal protection and due process to all. The law now supports children of any race attending their neighborhood schools; however, it can be argued that a different kind of segregation continues to exist due to the economic inequities present between neighborhoods and districts.

Children of color who are most likely to live in poor communities are still not receiving equal access to a quality education because of inadequate funding of their neighborhood schools. Darling-Hammond (1997) reports that schools at the 90th percentile of school funding spend nearly 10 times more than schools at the 10th percentile. Poor schools also have the most rapid turnover of teachers and the most difficulty keeping teaching staff (Ingersoll, 2001). Their teachers also receive the least professional development (Darling-Hammond, 1997). They are often without textbooks, paper, furniture, and even adequate bathrooms (Kozol, 1991). Until the economic issues of school funding, including funding for access to technology, are adequately addressed, there will continue to be color and poverty lines.

EDUCATIONAL ACCESS AND LANGUAGE

The United States has always been a country of immigrants representing many languages and cultures. Schools have traditionally been the places where students have learned English. In simpler times, when schools were charged with teaching a smaller, fairly homogeneous body of knowledge and when students speaking other languages lived in communities in which English was the common goal, schools seem to have largely succeeded in helping students gain English. As society demanded that schools teach the complex knowledge and information needed in the 21st century, the complexity of teaching this knowledge while also teaching English has increased. In addition, there are now large groups of children such as those living in the Southwest border area of the United States where the children attending schools continue to live in communities where the dominant language is not English. For example, when the U.S.-Mexican border was moved in 1848 many Mexican children suddenly became U.S. citizens and began to attend U.S. schools in Texas, Arizona, and New Mexico. This was a case of involuntary immigration. These children continued to live in communities in which the Spanish language and culture were dominant. Immigration of linguistically diverse groups is continuing to grow, with Spanish-speaking immigrants being the fastest growing group (Census, 2000). In some states, like New Mexico, Hispanic students are now the majority. The United States is rapidly becoming a bilingual (Spanish/English) rather than an English only country. Technology has increased the use of English via the Internet and international commerce. The need to know English is becoming increasingly important in terms of having power in the new global economy. While technology has created the need for English it can also help meet this need. There are many ways in which computer-based technologies can be useful in helping students learn English while also learning academic content (Butler-Pascoe & Wiburg, in press).

While debates rage about how best to help students gain English, the bottom line is that all children must have access to a good education. When students are not taught in a language they can understand, they do not have equity of access. For example, the failure of the San Francisco School District to provide English language instruction to 1,800 Chinese children or to provide them with other access to learning resulted in the famous *Lau v. Nichols* Supreme Court case. This case established the rule that equal treatment may not be equitable. For example, if a student who does not speak English is in a class in which the teacher provides information only in English, the student is not receiving equal treatment in terms of getting an education.

EDUCATIONAL ACCESS AND SPECIAL EDUCATION

Individuals with special needs have also had to fight similar battles for equity. In 1975, the passage of Public Law 94-142 stipulated that all children must receive a free and appropriate public education regardless of their degree of disability. In 1990 this law was reauthorized as the Individuals with Disabilities Education Act (IDEA). The 1997 amendments to IDEA focused specifically on students who experience overt personal disjunction in the general education classroom. These students comprise 10% to 12% of the nation's student population. Roughly 5.6 million students receive IDEA services (IdeaData, 2001).

In addition to the powerful potential of technology to assist language learning, it has also provided educational access to children with special needs. Without this assistive technology many of these students would not have had access to a good education. For example, with new technologies a child can type using a special mouthpiece in order to communicate in class or access resources on the Web. Special text-to-speech devices also offer access to electronic educational resources that would not be usable without assistive technology. A student may, with the help of technology, control the speed of his or her reading or use special devices to access information even when she or he may have visual or hearing impairments.

In summary, technology can play a powerful role in ensuring access to educational resources for underserved students. The following section builds a case for how educational equity is now closely tied to the capacity of new telecommunications tools and computers and to the ability of educational providers to use the power of computer-mediated learning.

EDUCATIONAL ACCESS TO COMMUNICATION

With the invention of electricity, new forms of transportation, telephones, and eventually computers and networks, access to information and knowledge changed in fundamental ways throughout the 20th century and that change has only accelerated in the 21st century. Since the 1930s the government has made efforts to ensure access to communication tools. In 1934, as telephones became commonly available, the U.S. Congress passed the Communications Act of 1934 to ensure that the pricing of telephone service was economical enough that all Americans could have access to this service. In addition, the Federal Communication Commission (FCC), created as part of Franklin Roosevelt's New Deal, was designed to provide a rapid and efficient national and worldwide access to wire and radio communication services. The pricing structures created as a result of this act and the 1996 Revised Act, while helpful, have still not made telecommunications available to all U.S. citizens, and the goal of universal access has not yet been achieved. Service is still prohibitively expensive in some parts of the county, such as in rural America and on some American Indian reservations.

Access to telephone lines is the foundation on which the development of the Internet rests. Even with newer wireless and satellite systems, equity will continue to be an issue. Without phone and/or cable access many students in rural and poor schools and on Indian reservations with poor electricity and phone service can literally not be hooked up to the vast information and educational resources now available on the Internet. Phone companies are not always willing to spend resources to provide telephone connections in communities that have no commercial infrastructure.

In 1993, Clinton established the National Information Infrastructure Initiative (NII, 2002). Clinton's agenda under the NII Initiative included the goal of making information resources available to all at affordable prices by extending the universal service concept. Then he announced that he wanted the best schools, teachers, and courses available to all students without regard to geography, distance, resources, or disability (NII, 2002). In order to assist poor schools in obtaining access to telecommunications services, Congress passed the Telecommunications Act of 1996 that provided discounted rates on goods and services to poor districts. This popular program became know as the E-rate and has had a significant effect in helping many poorer districts obtain access to the Internet in their schools and classrooms. The E-rate, however, is limited to schools and libraries and cannot be used to acquire resources for other community organizations.

COMMUNITY-BASED EDUCATION AND DIGITAL ACCESS

While the need still remains great for more equitable digital access, both community organizations and libraries have begun to work toward increasing public access. The Community Technology Centers (CTCNet, 2001) are a national, nonprofit membership organization of more than 600 independent community technology centers where people get free or low-cost access to computers and computer-related technology. CTC envisions a society in which all people are equitably empowered by technology skills and usage. Their mission statement is very clear.

> CTCNet shares with Playing To Win, its founding organization, a recognition that, in an increasingly technologically dominated society, people who are socially and/or economically disadvantaged will become further disadvantaged if they lack access to computers and computer-related technologies. CTCNet brings together agencies and programs that provide opportunities whereby people of all ages who typically lack access to computers and related technologies can learn to use these technologies in an environment that encourages exploration and discovery and, through this experience, develop personal skills and self-confidence.

Kevin Rocap (2003), of the Center for Language Minority Education and Research (CLMER) in California, tells the following story about the origin of Break-Away Technologies, another community technology center initiative:

> During the 1992 "disturbances," or uprisings, in South-Central Los Angeles one African American community leader, Joseph Loeb, watched his community literally go up in flames fueled by anger and historical patterns of neglect. Joseph decided he had to do what he could to make a difference. He quit his job, sold his car, and cleared out his garage to set-up a makeshift computer lab to start teaching computer skills to inner-city children and youth, as a way of providing new skills and hope for an economically brighter future. Joseph and many more committed

members of the community then opened two small community technology centers before the newly formed Break-Away Technologies. This group found a home in a 15,000 square foot facility near Jefferson and Crenshaw in Los Angeles. Break-Away Technologies became an after-school and weekend center for K-12 inner-city children, youth and adults; became a point of training and access for community-based arts, nonprofit and economic development organizations; and initiated a successful CyberSeniors program, with many seniors developing high-tech entrepreneurial skills and becoming mentors to neighborhood youth. (Rocap, 2003, pp. 72-73)

These movements illustrate how educational access is not limited to schools but is most usefully considered in the context of community-based learning needs.

THE PUBLIC LIBRARY

In addition to free access to education, telephony, and other infrastructure items, access to public libraries has been supported by the government since the 1800s. The Library of Congress is required by law to be open to all citizens in order to continue to receive federal funding. During the second half of the 19th century cities began to establish libraries, although at first they were only available to people who could pay the required rental fees. The Boston Public Library was established in 1848 as the first library free to the public and tax-supported. In the late 1800s Andrew Carnegie used his steel fortune to further the status of libraries in most major cities in the United States.

Public libraries have meant a great deal to poor people who have had no other access to free books. Adults could access information that would help them learn new skills and prepare for jobs as well as check out books for themselves and the education of their children. In 1988 the American Association of School Librarians and the Association for Educational Communications and Technology formally expanded their mission from being keepers of texts to purveyors of information. As new media became available, the library expanded to provide electronic recordings, videos, books on tape, and access to computers and the Internet. However, students still need to get to these libraries, and in many rural and urban areas this is not possible. In addition, once in the library, there are often long waiting lines and time limits for those wishing to use the Web.

THE INCREASING CAPACITY OF COMPUTERS

While economics continues to be a key factor in dividing learners and schools that have easy access to powerful computers and networks from those that don't, the problem is compounded by the rapid growth in computing power and the fact that in many schools the computers are simply not new enough to run new software. This technological growth, often referred to as Moore's Law, was named after Gordan Moore, a co-founder of Intel Corporation. Moore predicted that the number of transistors the industry would be able to place on a computer chip would double every year. While originally intended as a rule of thumb in 1965, it has become the guiding principle for the industry to deliver ever-more-powerful semiconductor chips at proportionate decreases in cost. As the power of the computer chip increases, one can buy a computer with twice the power 18 months after the previous purchase, yet pay the same price (Provenzo, Brett, & McCloskey, 1999).

FROM NUMBER CRUNCHERS
TO COMMUNICATIONS TOOLS

When the first electromechanical computer, the ENIAC, was brought into action in 1946, it basically served the initial function of number crunching. The ENIAC's development in the 1940s was partly a response to the needs of the military to decipher enemy codes. This first number-crunching computer was about 1,000 times faster then the previous generation of relay computers. The ENIAC used 18,000 vacuum tubes, about 1,800 square feet of floor space, and consumed about 180,000 watts of electrical power. Ironically, a pocket calculator you can buy at the check-out stand today, for under $5.00, does more than these early computers.

While numbers were the focus of early computers, by the end of the 1970s about 80% of the information processed was text. The major function of computers during this era was data processing, usually done in batches and controlled by the computer operator. As computing power grew, a type of smaller mainframe was developed called a mini-system. Software for running computers was also developed, with the first word-processing software, WordStar, becoming available in the early 1980s.

Bell Laboratories invented the transistor in 1958, and with it came the birth of the microcomputer. Microcomputers put significant computing power in the hands of individuals, causing a redistribution of power from the hands of technical gurus to ordinary people. With the help of two college dropouts, Steve Jobs and Steve Wozniak, microcomputers became available to schools, teachers, and students in the form of the Apple II computer. The computer became both a personal and an educational tool. New software operating systems were also developed to run the new microcomputers. These operating systems helped determine what computers could do and meant huge financial successes as new systems such as the Macintosh and then the Windows system came to dominate the market and the educational applications of computers in schools.

In the 1990s the networks to which computers were connected became as important as the computer itself, and the functions of computers changed from data processors to communication devices. Power no longer came from the computer itself, but from its ability to link to networks of worldwide and local information. Computer operating systems also evolved to include graphical interfaces and broadened the definition of communication to include not only text, but also pictures, video, and sound. Communication via multimedia became affordable, and the educational implications of using multimedia for learning grew. While schools still operate primarily in a print-dominant space, this is not true in society or in the workplace where the ability to manipulate graphical images and symbols is common and necessary.

NEW KNOWLEDGE ENVIRONMENTS

As computer capacity has grown and network resources increased exponentially, the potential of computing in education has changed from glorified typing and teaching machines to systems in which it is now possible to create as well as distribute knowledge. High levels of access allow teachers and students to learn not only in their individual classrooms but also to participate in learning with others in the larger community. These new networks allow easy access to research and content information that is beyond what an individual teacher might be able to deliver. In such environments, new knowledge is created when people from different locations create new ideas together on the computer network. One of the fastest growing educational applications involves telecollaboration (Harris, 2002), a rich array of opportunities for learners to work interactively at a distance using the Web. The computer is no longer just a means for the distribution of curriculum—its function has been expanded to include the creation of knowledge and support for the formation of new communities of learners.

POWERFUL COMPUTERS AND TRADITIONAL TEACHING

The integration of these new learning environments into schools is a challenging task. First of all, reports of the increasing numbers of computers in schools means little unless the computers are capable of running the current multimedia software. In addition, access to the Internet at any reasonable speed is often very difficult. A recent report from the Pew Foundation (Levin & Arafeh, 2002) described the widening gap between Internet-savvy students and their schools as well as between those who have the Internet at home and those who don't: "The gap between those students who have access to the Internet at home is a serious matter to these students. In the classroom, it is apparent to Internet-savvy students when a classmate does not have access to the

Internet. Indeed, students with easy Internet access assert that they have a clear and persistent advantage over their peers with no access" (p. 24).

Second, even when there are computers in classrooms they are not always turned on or used well. In a recent book on digital equity, Fulton and Sibley (in press) described what they consider to be a pedagogical divide. The authors reported the results of a questionnaire distributed at a national educational technology leadership meeting asking participants to list the barriers they believe stand in the way of closing the digital divide in K-12 education. The response most frequently given was the lack of vision and understanding regarding the link between technology and learning. As one educator put it, "There is not a clear understanding of what can be done with technology and what cannot be done. There is not a clear understanding of how technology can be used to support learning. We talk of new ways of learning, but we never define it so that teachers, administrators, legislators, parents and community members can understand" (Soloman, Allen, & Resta, 2002, p. x).

In order for students to have access to computers it is necessary for their teachers to want to use them. There are many reasons for this, not the least of which is the current organization and culture of schooling and the role of teachers in those schools. Larry Cuban has written an interesting history of how teachers have interacted with technological innovations in schools from 1920 to the late 1980s. He began the first chapter of this book with a 1922 quote from Thomas Edison: "I believe that the motion picture is destined to revolutionize our educational system and that in a few years it will supplant largely, if not entirely, the use of textbooks" (Cuban, 1986, p. 9).

Developers from outside the school culture have introduced each new educational technology innovation with similar strong words as to how this new device will fundamentally change education. In reality, many of these innovations have had very little impact on teacher practice. Are the computers and networks available today so fundamentally different from earlier technologies introduced in the schools that changes in practice are sure to follow? Or is the culture of school practice so ingrained that even as businesses and other groups routinely use technology in daily practice, schools are still likely to lag behind?

Cuban's term for how schools and structures shape behavior and practice is *situationally constrained choice* (p. 66). He provided an historical outline of the introduction of film, radio, and instructional television into the schools and demonstrated the remarkably similar and low impact of each invention on actual classroom practice. For example, researchers gave the following reasons in the 1930s for low integration of films into the curriculum:

1. Teachers' lack of skill in using the equipment;
2. Cost of films, equipment, and upkeep;
3. Inaccessibility of equipment, when needed; and
4. Finding and fitting the right films to the class (Cuban, 1986, p. 18).

Cuban concluded that no one was paying attention to the teachers' point of view. Teachers will embrace innovations such as new forms of grouping and chalkboards when the new tools help solve what they consider to be problems. Teachers' needs are anchored in the classroom, an arena largely foreign to researchers and policymakers. He concluded that technologies will be adopted to the extent that they solve classroom problems and when their benefit to the teacher outweighs the cost of learning to use them.

In fact, a new book by Cohen and Hill (2001) on policy and school reform argues that school reform has not been successful because it has not been well connected to the curriculum the teachers are asked to teach, the students they serve, the school within which they work, and the teachers themselves.

At the minimum teachers need professional development on how to do technology integration. Optimally they need an understanding of how technology-mediated learning can expand educational opportunities for all students. One place to start might be with redefining and broadening our understanding of access to include both pedagogy and leadership.

Fulton and Sibley (in press) and Wiburg and Butler (in press), in a new book on addressing digital equity, suggest expanding the idea of digital equity to include four essential components. These ideas are summarized below in order to provide a framework for the discussion and implementation of educational equity in 21st century schools and communities.

ACCESS TO EDUCATION IN A DIGITAL ERA

Educational equity in today's technological age requires more than access to hardware and software, although current computers and access to high-speed networks still remain as one of the four components. The following expands notions of access to include meaningful content, educators who know how to use technology, and, perhaps most important, leaders who have vision related to the educational potential of technology and can implement that knowledge in schools.

1. *Access to up-to-date hardware, software and connectivity.* While access to hardware, networks and programs is a minimum condition for full participation and use of digital resources, the quality of access is also important. North Central Regional Educational Lab (NCREL, 2001) defines *high-performance technology* to be one in which users can take advantage of digital resources interactively and move effortlessly from application to application, routinely using the technology for constructing and managing their own learning. In a practical sense, computers need to be user-friendly and available where teachers and students are working. Accessing and storing materials on school net-

works and the computer systems in schools should include many powerful tools that support learning, research, and group collaboration.

2. *Access to meaningful content.* The Children's Partnership (2001), as part of its work to bridge the digital divide, has done extensive audits of content on the Internet. They believe low-income groups need Web content that includes (a) employment and education information, (b) reading levels that can be understood by limited-literacy users, (c) multiple languages, and (d) ways for underserved users to create content and interact with it so that it is culturally relevant (access level 4). They found significant barriers to usefulness of the Internet for the 22 million Americans that live on under $14,500 per year; for example, 44 million Americans do not have a high enough literacy level to use the Internet. They also found significant language barriers and suggested the greatest need for underserved Americans was useful local information related to jobs and community resources. Such local information is rarely available. Nor do community members, especially in low-income communities and schools, have opportunities to have their voices heard on the Internet. In a democracy the Internet needs to become a two-way communications tool and not just a place where information is delivered by those who have the power to do this.

3. *Access to educators who know how to use digital tools and resources.* While schools were quick to hop on the hardware acquisition bandwagon, they dedicated very small percentages of budgets to training in how to use these resources. The 1995 Office of Technology Assessment (OTA) report, "Teachers & Technology: Making the Connection," raised two important points: (a) that "technology is not central to the teacher preparation experience" and (b) that "most technology instruction . . . is teaching about technology . . . not teaching with technology across the curriculum" (p. 165). This lack of training is true not only at the pre-service level but also in terms of the lack of in-service available for professional development offered in technology integration programs with teaching. The situation, however, is getting better in terms of increased integration of technology in teacher education (Beck & Wynn, 1998). Many credit the Department of Education's current PT3 (Preparing Tomorrow's Teachers to Use Technology) program for increased integration of technology in teacher education institutions and now graduating new teachers who are ready to integrate technology in their classrooms.

However, as mentioned earlier, the culture of education itself works against changes in pedagogy (Stigler & Hiebert, 1999). For many teachers, a significant block to integrating technology in meaningful ways into classroom learning is simply that they don't know how to implement a model of instruction in which different groups of students are doing different things at the same time. Many teachers believe that they must take students to a computer lab so that they can all learn the same software at the same time in the same way. Such technocentric conceptions of computers and computer learning miss the point of using technology for thinking, researching, and problem solving as part of problem-based learning in the content areas. For student learning, an application like PowerPoint is trivial; however, learning how to use the program to communicate the complexity of a problem solution like how to use water resources in a desert community is the real challenge. Using more advanced tools like databases and simulations provides students opportunities to learn content more deeply than they could without the technology. As has been said often before, it is not the technology itself that is important but how you use it.

Until professional development in technology moves beyond a focus on applications to one that centers on building learning communities in schools, we are unlikely to see useful integration. In addition, unless teachers learn to differentiate their uses of technology to better serve the diverse needs of their students, it is also unlikely that we will move far in the use of technology for equity.

4. *Access to systems sustained by leaders with vision.* Fulton and Sibley (in press) describe the need for looking at access. "Digital and networking technologies represent the convergence of vital communication, information, and education resources. Lack of effective access to what we call 'technology' is in fact lack of access to the opportunity to fully participate in American life" (p. 14). Fulton and Sibley continue by suggesting that even the most dedicated teachers are often blocked from high-level access by administrators who do not know how to support the creation of full access. However, they believe there are pockets of hope in recent research that highlights the positive effects of the deeper, more constructivist use of computers that we are suggesting. For example, Wenlingsky (1999) found that those children whose teachers used computers in constructivist ways to teach mathematics (simulations, spreadsheets) scored significantly higher in mathematics achievement than those who used the computers as tutorial and drill-and-practice machines. A powerful synthesis is emerging that connects new theories of how students learn by constructing and sharing knowledge and the capacity of new computer-based technologies to support these types of learning strategies. Access to these best uses, however, will not occur until teachers in classrooms choose to embrace these new methodologies with technology. Nor will teachers even get the opportunity to use these applications unless they are supported by educational leaders and administrators.

As new technologies become available such as the Internet II with its broadband capability for truly interactive information and learning, leaders and policymakers will play a crucial role in determining who gets access to these new information tools and how they are used. Legislative bodies and citizen groups will need help from leaders in education to understand what types of technology and what kinds of training are essential if teachers are to help students gain the skills they need for the 21st century.

CONCLUSION

This article has provided an historical and sociological overview of the meaning of educational equity in the 21st century. It has suggested that the current digital divide is part of other, more familiar divides in education, including access to quality schools and equal educational treatment for all students regardless of color, culture, language, or economic status. At the same time these familiar divides have in some ways deepened as a result of increasing technological power and change. As control over many computer environments has gone from the communities' basements and garages to control by large corporations there is a danger that local communities may lose their presence in the digital world. On the other hand there are causes for hope. Not only has technology helped solidify the power of large corporations, it has also served to empower poor people as in the successful Internet campaign for cheaper AIDS drugs, the communication of injustice in different countries, and in the use of the Internet to support diverse community-based movements. There are numerous examples of how government, the courts, community organizations, and educational groups have committed to providing access to education and information for those who cannot afford it. Such efforts have ranged from early public schools to the current E-rate program. Perhaps the most important point made in this article was the need to broaden our definition of access and equity and particularly to focus on connections between leadership, teaching, and technology. Leaders who understand the deep connections between school culture and organization and what happens in classrooms may be our best hope to tapping the power of technology to provide opportunities for learning for all students.

REFERENCES

American Association of School Librarians & Association for Educational Communications and Technology. (1988). *Information power: Guidelines for school library media programs*. Chicago, IL: Author. Washington, DC: Author.

Beck, J., & Wynn, H. (1998). *Technology in teacher education: Progress along the continuum*. (ERIC Digest. ERIC Document Reproduction Service No. ED424212).

Butler-Pascoe, M.E., & Wiburg, K.M. (in press). *Technology and teaching English language learners*. Boston: Allyn & Bacon.

Charp, S. (2001). Technological horizons in education: Bridging the digital divide. *The Journal 28*(10), 10-12.

Children's Partnership. (2001). Young Americans and the digital future campaign: National fact sheet. Washington, DC: Author.

Coalition to Diversify Computing. (2000). Available from http://www.npaci.edu/Outreach/CDC/news/antonia_stone.htm

Cohen, D. K., & Hill, H. C. (2001). *Learning policy: When state educational reform works*. New Haven: Yale University Press.

CTCNet. (2001). Community technology centers. Retrieved December 14, 2001, from http://www.ctcnet.org/

Cuban, L. (1986). *Teachers and machines: The classroom use of technology since 1920*. New York: Teachers College Press.

Darling-Hammond, L. (1997). *The right to learn*. San Francisco: Jossey-Bass.

Falling through the Net II: New data on the digital divide. (1998). Retrieved July 15, 2001, from www.ntia.doc.gov/itiahome/net2/

Fulton, K., & Sibley, R. (in press). Barriers to digital equity. In G. Soloman, N. Allen, & P. Resta (Eds.), *Toward digital equity: Bridging the divide in education*. Boston: Allyn & Bacon.

Harris, J. (2002). Description of activity structures. Retrieved October 10, 2002, from http://ccwf.cc.utexas.edu/~jbharris/Virtual-Architecture/

IdeaData.org. (2001). Childcount 1999-2000. Washington, DC: Author. Retrieved May 21, 2003, from http://www.ideadata.org/

Ingersoll, R. (2001). Teacher turnover and teacher shortages. *American Educational Research Journal, 38*(4), 499-534.

Kozol, J. (1991). *Savage inequalities*. NY: Crown Publishers.

Levin, D., & Arafeh, S. (2002). *The digital disconnect: The widening gap between Internet-savvy students and their schools*. Prepared by the authors for the Pew Internet and American Life Project, 1100 Connecticut Avenue, NW, Suite 710, Washington, DC 20036.

National information infrastructure. (2002). Retrieved October 10, 2002, from http://www.eff.org/Infra/Govt_docs/nii_task_force.q-a

North Central Regional Educational Lab (NCREL). Retrieved July 15, 2001, from http://www.ncrel.org/sdrs/lwteach1/tsld008.htms

Norton, P., & Wiburg, K. (1998). *Teaching with technology*. Fort Worth, TX: Harcourt-Brace.

Norton, P., & Wiburg, K.M. (2002). *Teaching with technology: Designing opportunities to learn* (2nd ed.). Belmont, CA: Thomson/Wadsworth.

Provenzo, Jr., E. F., Brett, A., & McCloskey, G. (1999). *Computers, curriculum, and cultural change: An introduction for teachers*. Hillsdale, NJ: Lawrence Erlbaum Associates, Inc.

Rocap, K. (2003). *Defining and designing literacy for the 21st century, toward digital equity: Bridging the divide in education*. Boston: Allyn & Bacon.

Smith, R.C. (1996). *They closed their schools: Prince Edward County, Virginia, 1951-1964*. Farmville, VA: Martha E. Forrester Council of Women.

Soloman, G., Allen, N., & Resta, P. (2002). *Toward digital equity: Challenges of bridging the digital divide.* Boston: Allyn & Bacon.

Steigler, J., & Hiebert, J. (1999). *The teaching gap: Best ideas from the world's teachers for improving education in the classroom.* New York: The Free Press (a division of Simon & Schuster).

Swain, C., & Pearson, T. (2001). Bridging the digital divide: A building block for teachers. *Learning and Leading with Technology, 28*(8), 10.

U.S. Census. (2000). Retrieved October 10, 2002, from http://www.census.gov/main/www/cen2000.html

U.S. Census Bureau. (2000, September 26). Poverty: 1999 highlights. Washington, DC: Author. Retrieved July 15, 2001, from http://census.gov/hhes/poverty/poverty99/pov99hi.html

U.S. Department of Commerce. (1993, September). *We the . . . first Americans* [Economics and Statistics Administration, Bureau of the Census, WE-5.] Washington, DC: U.S. Government Printing Office.

Wenglinsky, H. (1998). *Does it compute? The relationship between educational technology and student achievement in mathematics.* Princeton, NJ: Educational Testing Service. Retrieved March 6, 2002, from ftp://ftp.ets.org/pub/res/technology

Wiburg, K., & Butler, J. (in press). Creating educational access. In G. Soloman, N. Allen, & P. Resta (Eds.), *Toward digital equity: Bridging the educational divide.* Boston: Allyn & Bacon.

Tara Jeffs
William F. Morrison
Trinka Messenheimer
Mary G. Rizza
Savilla Banister

A Retrospective Analysis of Technological Advancements in Special Education

SUMMARY. This article investigates the impact that technology and computers have had over the past 20 years in the field of special education. A review of the literature on technology and computers was conducted in the flagship journals in the areas of learning disabilities, mental retardation, deaf/hard of hearing, and gifted/talented. The analysis yielded a va-

TARA JEFFS is Assistant Professor, Bowling Green State University, Division of Intervention Services, Bowling Green, OH 43403 (E-mail: tjeffs@bgnet.bgsu.edu).
WILLIAM F. MORRISON is Assistant Professor, Bowling Green State University, Division of Intervention Services, Bowling Green, OH 43403 (E-mail: fmorris@bgnet.bgsu.edu).
TRINKA MESSENHEIMER is Assistant Professor, Bowling Green State University, Bowling Green, OH 43403 (E-mail: trinka@bgnet.bgsu.edu).
MARY G. RIZZA is Associate Professor, Bowling Green State University, Educational Foundations and Inquiry, Bowling Green, OH 43403 (E-mail: mrizza@bgnet.bgsu.edu).
SAVILLA BANISTER is Assistant Professor, Bowling Green State University, Division of Teaching and Learning, Bowling Green, OH 43403 (E-mail: sbanist@bgnet.bgsu.edu).

[Haworth co-indexing entry note]: "A Retrospective Analysis of Technological Advancements in Special Education." Jeffs, Tara et al. Co-published simultaneously in *Computers in the Schools* (The Haworth Press, Inc.) Vol. 20, No. 1/2, 2003, pp. 129-152; and: *Technology in Education: A Twenty-Year Retrospective* (ed: D. LaMont Johnson, and Cleborne D. Maddux) The Haworth Press, Inc., 2003, pp. 129-152. Single or multiple copies of this article are available for a fee from The Haworth Document Delivery Service [1-800-HAWORTH, 9:00 a.m. - 5:00 p.m. (EST). E-mail address: docdelivery@haworthpress.com].

10.1300/J025v20n01_10

riety of trends that were specific to each subfield. Findings were compared to the general literature in technology and revealed that the literature in each field reflected the general advances in, and availability of, technology over time. *[Article copies available for a fee from The Haworth Document Delivery Service: 1-800-HAWORTH. E-mail address: <docdelivery@haworthpress. com> Website: <http://www.HaworthPress.com> © 2003 by The Haworth Press, Inc. All rights reserved.]*

KEYWORDS. Technology, computers, special education, learning disabilities, mental retardation, deaf, hard of hearing, gifted, talented

INTRODUCTION

Very few innovations have matched the growth of computer use in all areas of education, but the overwhelming changes in technology use in all areas of special education warrant attention. The mid 1970s were especially exciting times for technology innovation. Apple computers released the Apple II series, and computer-based instruction (CBI) emerged as a viable alternative in education. By 1983, IBM was the sole personal computer (PC) manufacturer, and microcomputers gained attention in our society as *Time* magazine named the computer as "Man of the Year" (Blackhurst & Edyburn, 2000).

The growing popularity of microcomputers also became prevalent in the field of special education. A series of federal laws were put into place to support and assure that technology and related services were provided to individuals with disabilities (see Assistive Technology Act, Individuals with Disabilities Education Act, and Americans with Disabilities Act). Blackhurst and Edyburn (2000), however, remind us that technology has played a significant role in the lives of individuals with disabilities, even prior to the innovations seen during the 20th century.

While the infusion of technology into special education programs predates even the invention of the microcomputer, research on the impact of technology is scant in the literature prior to the 1980s. During this early stage of interest in technology as an educational innovation, the main thrust of research was dedicated to how available technologies could be used to address the individual needs of students. Software programs were designed primarily for use as tutorials, to encourage drill and practice, or as enrichment in the form of games and simulations. From the beginning, there was a differentiation in the use of technology, which depended heavily on the exceptionality for which it was used. For example, in the areas that deal with students with disabilities, technology was viewed primarily as assistive, concentrating on facilitating student ability to communicate and promoting academic success. On the other end of the spectrum, technology used with gifted students tended to focus on expanding the users' experience with the content and using software that promoted active engagement, higher order thinking, and abstract reasoning.

Today, many educators view technology as a vehicle for promoting thinking and as a delivery system that allows students to reach beyond the confines of more traditional learning experiences. Even the use of assistive technology for students with special needs has changed and is used to open up exciting possibilities for learning. As a differentiation tool, technology allows students of all ability levels to work within their own style preferences and readiness levels. For example, students who use the Internet as a research tool will find a wide variety of available resources. Teachers may allow some students who have the ability to think abstractly and problem-solve to freely search their topic while others are given guidance toward specific resources that fit the topic at hand. Technology, such as the Internet, can provide yet other students the ability to communicate with others in a bias-free environment.

The purpose of this article, therefore, is to identify the impact that computers and technology have had on the field of special education and specifically to show the broadening use of technology over time in the lives of individuals with exceptionalities. Throughout this article, unless otherwise noted, the term *technology* will be used to include all aspects of instructional technology and assistive technology, including but not limited to computers.

For this retrospective look at technology in special education, we determined to look back to the year 1981, which approximately estimates when computers were first introduced in schools. A literature search was conducted by each of the authors in her/his area of expertise using both online and hand-search methods. Each author examined the flagship journal(s) in her/his area using the key terms *technology, assistive technology,* and *computers.* The data were analyzed using a naturalistic approach that allows for the emergence of themes (Lincoln & Guba, 1985). The emerging themes were then cross-checked by the authors to identify overall trends in the field. The results are presented by subfield, and a review of the overall trends can be found in the conclusion. The general headings, which match the subfields investigated, include: Learning Disabilities, Mental Retardation, Deaf/Hard of Hearing, Gifted and Talented.

LEARNING DISABILITIES

The research on using technology for students with learning disabilities reflects the complex instructional and assessment nature of the field of learning disabilities. A thorough investigation of three flagship journals–*Journal of Learning Disabilities, Journal of Special Education Technology,* and *Exceptional Children*–revealed several recurring themes: (a) computer-assisted instruction (CAI), (b) multimedia, and (c) tools for learning.

Historical Trends

Computer technology in the early 1980s for students with learning disabilities was comprised primarily of instruction commonly referred to as *computer-assisted instruction* (CAI). Such instruction generally consisted of drill-and-practice lessons to build specific skills. Researchers and educators implemented CAI to provide individualized instruction to students with learning disabilities (Bahr & Reith, 1989; McDermott & Watkins, 1983; Woodward, Carnine, Gerten, Gleason, Johnson, & Collins, 1986). Computers used in this capacity were viewed as playing the role of the tutor (Woodward, Gallagher, & Reith, 2001). This role came about as the computer was identified as an extremely efficient medium for delivering various levels of academic instruction, allowing students to work at their own pace and skill level and providing them with immediate feedback. In addition to tutorial software, drill-and-practice software provided learners with a multitude of opportunities to practice a single skill already taught. Computer-assisted technology seemed a natural fit into the traditional direct instruction curriculum that was typically found in special education classrooms.

As classroom instruction began to change, a new dimension to CAI was investigated. Researchers began to look at instructional design variables for effective instruction for students with learning disabilities (Woodward & Cuban, 2001). In the early 1990s researchers (e.g., Anderson-Inman, 1990-91; Boone & Higgins, 1993) developed computer-assisted instruction that engaged the learner through hypermedia. Higgins, Boone, and Lovitt (1996) investigated the use of hypermedia study guides and information retention with students identified as having learning disabilities and students receiving remedial services. Findings revealed that hypermedia study guides were viable educational tools. A three-year, school-based research study conducted by Boone and Higgins (1993) investigated the use of hypermedia support and basal readers. This study confirmed the effectiveness and use of hypermedia software for students in special education who participate in the general education curriculum.

Although the body of research in the area of hypermedia-based instruction is relatively small and could benefit from further investigation, instructional benefits of hypermedia and its use by students with learning disabilities have been reported at the elementary, middle, and high school grade levels (Anderson-Inman, 1990-91; Boone & Higgins, 1993; Higgins & Boone, 1990, 1991, 1993; Lewis, 2000; MacArthur & Haynes, 1995).

Multimedia

As technology began to advance in the late 1980s and early 1990s, researchers working in the field of learning disabilities began to investigate the power of graphics, and multimedia for learning. Multimedia–a combination of graphics, video, animations, pictures, and sound–provides diverse learning instruction and has been used for years in the classroom. Multimedia instruction provides the learner with ample opportunities to become interactive in the learning process.

The Cognition and Technology Group at Vanderbilt (CTGV) completed extensive research on the application of multimedia instruction. The major focus of their work involved the use of videodisc environments. Such situated environments provide rich opportunities and realistic contexts that encourage the active construction of knowledge by learners (Cognition and Technology Group at Vanderbilt, 1993).

As a result of advancing technology, more and more multimedia applications have become computer-based, making a shift from a receptive mode to a more interactive mode. Research conducted by Daiute and Morse (1994) involved the use of multimedia writing tools for students with disabilities. Findings concluded that students could experience writing success through the power of multimedia. Multimedia was found to be one way teachers can help children connect their specific perspectives and ways of expressing themselves to a common curriculum.

Multimedia makes important information more obvious (Najjar, 1996). Research supports the positive benefits of multimedia instruction for students with learning disabilities or those who may have limited prior knowledge in a particular academic area. Multimedia learning materials engage the learner in multiple representations of content to be learned.

Tutor versus Tool Metaphor

As technology became more common in our classrooms, educators and researchers were discovering the role of technology in the instructional process. The role of computers began to shift from "tutor to tool" (Woodward & Cuban, 2001). Technology had shifted from providing instruction to providing support for completing learning tasks and processes. Word processors, word prediction, speech recognition, spell checkers, text-to-speech programs, graphic organizers, and online resources provided students with learning disabilities opportunities to strengthen their academic weaknesses and complete a desired learning task with hope that academic growth would be achieved.

Word processing. As early as 1989, educators were discussing the liberating effects experienced by students with reading difficulties when basic word-processing applications were integrated into their language experience lessons (Sharp, 1989). Word processing and spell checkers have long been recognized as valuable tools in improving student writing, and those with learning disabilities especially benefit by being afforded the opportunity to edit easily and produce a highly legible finished product (Graham & MacArthur, 1998; Lewis, Graves, Ashton, & Kieley, 1998; MacArthur, 1996, 1998, 1999; MacArthur & Graham, 1987; MacArthur, Graham, & Schwartz, 1991; Outhred, 1989). Such a product would have been difficult to produce by these students without accessibility to word-processing applications (Woodward & Rieth, 1997).

Word prediction. Word prediction software provides the student with learning disabilities a tool to make the writing process more approachable. Such programs were found to enhance the text-entry speed of students with learning disabilities by allowing the student to simply recognize a word instead of spelling it out by individual letters (Lewis et al., 1998; MacArthur, 1999). Additional research conducted by MacArthur (1999) revealed that word prediction can make a substantial difference for those individuals with severe writing problems that interfere with the readability of their writing.

Speech recognition. The advancement/improvement of speech recognition technology is changing rapidly. De La Paz (1999) states that "in anticipation to such technological advancements, a small but growing group of researchers has conducted research during the past 10 years to determine how this technology might best be used with persons with learning and writing problems" (p. 174).

Speech recognition has been researched both as assistive technology to overcome difficulties in writing and as a tool to build remedial skills in reading and spelling (Elkind, Black, & Murray, 1996; Higgins & Raskind, 1995; Higgins & Zvi, 1995). Results were encouraging; students exhibited significant improvement in writing composition using speech recognition as compared to writing with word processing, or pencil and paper, or dictation to another person (Higgins & Raskind, 2000). In addition, the use of speech recognition to build remedial skills demonstrated an increase in word recognition, speed, accuracy, and reading comprehension.

As we investigate the effectiveness of speech recognition and other computer technologies for students with learning disabilities, it is essential to not only investigate the role that technology plays but also the strategies and metacognitive skills that are necessary to engage the individual in the specific learning tasks. With a better understanding of these components we can assist students in learning for understanding and provide them with the tools to create knowledge that is useful (Hasselbring, 2001).

MENTAL RETARDATION

A review of the flagship journals in mental retardation resulted in the identification of three general themes: historical trends, technology as a tool, and barriers. Each of these categories will be discussed according to specific themes revealed as a result of the review.

Historical Trends

Equal access to all aspects of life has always been an issue for individuals with mental retardation. Access for these individuals has relied heavily on the use of adaptive devices and technologies. Prior to the passage of P.L. 94-142 and the deinstitutionalization of individuals with mental retardation in the 1980s, most devices used by individuals with metal retardation would be considered "low tech." Low tech devices–described as simple, passive, and having few moving parts–include adaptive switches, cell systems, communication boards, adaptive books, adaptive eating utensils, tactile enhancement tools, etc. (Angelo, 1995; Mann & Lane, 1995; Parette, 1997). P.L. 94-142 and deinstitutionalization brought individuals with mental retardation into the community and public schools by mandating a free and appropriate education. To meet the learning needs of these students, the focus of technology moved from "low tech" to "high tech" devices. High tech devices, described as being more complex, usually incorporating sophisticated electronic components, include augmentative and alternative communication devices, modified or alternative keyboards, Braille printers and text-to-speech devices, and computers for educational tasks (Huntinger, 1996; Inge & Shepherd, 1995; Parette, 1997). It was ultimately shown that technology, as a teaching tool, would help give individuals with mental retardation equal access to the appropriate education they deserved.

Technology as a Tool

Technology as a teaching tool immediately, profoundly, and positively impacted the education of individuals with mental retardation. The use of assistive technology devices for individuals with mental retardation was shown by Wehmeyer (1998) to increase self-determination, independence, and integration skill. In addition, assistive devices allowed for "positive changes in inter- and intrapersonal relationships, sensory abilities and cognitive capabilities, communication skills, motor performance, self-maintenance, leisure, and productivity" (Parette, 1997, p. 268).

While many of the "low tech" and "high tech" assistive technology devices have greatly increased access to the learning environment for individuals with mental retardation, the introduction of the computer as a teaching tool, and subsequent supporting software, can be viewed as the greatest agent of change in relation to both the curricula taught and the teaching methods employed for individuals with mental retardation. Technology, in the form of interactive computers and software, is now being used to enhance the learning of these individuals by providing alternative pathways to acquiring knowledge and skills.

Initial studies in the 1980s and early 1990s identified computers, specifically computer-assisted instruction, as an effective teaching tool to support the acquisition of basic learning skills (Chen & Bernard-Opitz, 1993; Iacona & Miller, 1989; Thomas, 1981). More currently, the trend in research and in the special education literature has become the use of technology to enhance and/or open new avenues of learning and communication for individuals with mental retardation. Technology is now being used to develop functional curricula to better teach academic courses in schools and to help better prepare individuals with mental retardation for the transition to life after school.

Preparing individuals with mental retardation for the workplace through the use of technology has been an emerging theme in special education literature. Morgan, Gerity, and Ellerd (2000) used video and CD-ROM technology to help individuals with severe disabilities establish job preferences. Kyhl, Alper, and Sinclair (1999) used videotaped instruction to aid in job acquisition, and Furniss et al. (1999) looked at the use of palmtop-based devices to aid individuals with severe intellectual disabilities in the workplace setting.

A second theme evident in the literature is the use of assistive technology devices as a means of opening avenues of communication for individuals with mental retardation. Voice output communication aids, used to produce synthetic or digitized speech, have been used successfully with individuals with autism and related disabilities (Beukelman & Mirenda, 1992; Mirenda, Wild, & Carson, 2000; Schepis, Reid, Behrmann, & Sutton, 1998). Although viewed as controversial in the field of education, facilitated communication, the use of keyboards or alphabet boards, has been used as a means of communication for individuals with severe mental retardation, autism, or other related disorders (Sheehan & Matuozzi, 1996; Salomon-Weiss, Wagner, & Bauman, 1996).

A third emerging theme in special education literature is the use of a variety of technology to aid individuals with mental retardation in the acquisition of lifeskills. Developing and maintaining meaningful relationships have historically been problematic for these individuals. Renbald (1999) used technology to aid in the development of social networks of individuals with mental retardation. Browning and White (1986) used an interactive video-based curriculum to teach life-enhancement skills to these individuals.

Lastly, technology is now being used to help individuals with mental retardation produce work in the classroom for ongoing assessment. Denham and Lahm (2001) outlined how, through the use of assistive technologies, students with moderate to severe disabilities construct alternative portfolios of their work. Through the use of adaptive tools such as IntelliKeys keyboards and Overlay Maker, students were able to construct portfolios of their year-long work. These tools have allowed students with mental retardation to produce products similar to their nondisabled peers.

The Future of Assistive Technology–Overcoming Barriers

The future use of assistive technology for students with mental retardation does not necessarily lie in the development and implementation of new technologies but in the proper and full implementation of current technologies. The Association for Retarded Citizens (The Arc), a national advocacy organization that represents individuals with mental retardation and their families, has repeatedly voiced concerns related to access to technology for people with mental retardation. Wehmeyer (1999), summarizing the position of The Arc stated, "It appears that, for a variety of reasons, assistive technology devices remain largely underutilized by people with mental retardation" (p. 49). Studies by Wehmeyer (1999) and Derer, Polsgrove, and Rieth (1996) support The Arc's view that many appropriate and helpful assistive technology devices are being underutilized by these individuals.

Researchers have identified a number of issues that help to explain the current underutilization of assistive technology devices by individuals with mental retardation. Issues include the abandonment of technology (Parette, 1997), the cost of purchasing devices (Parette, 1997; Walker, 1991; Wehmeyer, 1999), the lack of information about what technologies are available and their use (Wehmeyer, 1999, 1998), the identification of appropriate technology features (Batavia & Hammer, 1990; Parette, 1997; Schere, 1993), the lack of assistive technology devices that can be used by individuals with mild to severe cognitive disabilities (Wehmeyer, 1998), and, lastly, the development of devices that are too complex (Perlman, 1993; Wehmeyer, 1998).

Access to all aspects of what society has to offer has always been at the forefront of issues for individuals with mental retardation. Technology as a tool, whether "low tech" or "high tech," has greatly increased access to public education for individuals with mental retardation. The future development of technologies is sure to offer an even greater level of access to the community and education as long as current and future barriers to the use of technologies for individuals with mental retardation are addressed.

DEAF/HARD OF HEARING

Traditional uses of technology have provided tremendous support to individuals with a hearing loss. Advances in computer use, however, have also provided challenges to persons with a hearing loss because computers are inherently an auditory-visual medium (Strepp, 1994). Although this visual component has allowed for presenting visual communication, the literature available from technology and special education journals has focused on instruction with technology and has dealt with the focus of the development and use of technology to work with or around the hearing loss. The two main journals in the area of deafness (*American Annals of the Deaf* and *Volta Review*) have even had special theme issues on technology, in some cases more than once, over the past 20 years. *American Annals of the Deaf* has included a technology issue section in each journal published, further highlighting the importance of technology to the field.

For individuals who are deaf/hard of hearing the overarching focus of the literature has been around classroom instruction, as well as specific technology to assist with the hearing loss or to facilitate the auditory educational environment. The past 20 years of professional journals have demonstrated a parallel development and distribution of each of these notions over time. These specific research issues have included closed captioning, real-time captioning, text telephones (TTY/TDD), FM systems, and mechanisms related to speech and speechreading.

Historical Trends

Even with the auditory quandary that classroom computers pose, they have also presented a new visual access for learning that was capitalized early on to assist with instruction and with individuals who are deaf/hard of hearing. As early as 1981 the *Volta Review* published an entire issue on learning technology for individuals who are hearing impaired that presented specific "tools" to support learning for individuals with a hearing loss (i.e., closed captioning, real-time captioning, and speech programs) as well as instructional technology for language acquisition and language learning (Withrow, 1981). Twenty years later the issues remain the same.

A number of surveys have attempted to identify the technology schools possess and the needs for such technology (Corbett & Micheaux, 1996; Deninger, 1985; Harding & Tidball, 1982; Harkins, Loeterman, Lam, & Korres, 1996; Pillai, 1999; Rose & Waldron, 1984). Corbett and Micheaux (1996) identified a few residential schools for individuals who are deaf that have clearly put a considerable amount of money into hardware, software, and connections for instructional technology, to improve educational and social programs. In other classrooms across the country representing more public school programs, not only was the need for more equipment identified but also teacher training and time devoted to instructional technology (Harkins et al., 1996; Pillai, 1999). A current survey of teacher education programs for the individuals who are deaf/hard of hearing identified the continuous need for the integration of technology in the classroom and teacher education (Roberson, 2001).

Instruction and Learning

Early in the history of technology use, special computer programs for the individuals who are deaf/hard of hearing were designed and used in residential settings, offering drill and practice primarily to work on language development, later moving into speech development and other curricular areas (Richardson, 1981). There was a call for instructional applications of computers to broaden the diversity of instructional programs for students who are deaf/hard of hearing (Stuckless & Carroll, 1994).

The literature has described ways in which integrating a variety of media will assist in instruction (Hasselbring, 1994) and language learning of individuals who are deaf/hard of hearing (Volterra, Pace, Pennacchi, & Corazza, 1995). In one study word prediction technology with individuals who are deaf/hard of hearing was shown to improve word fluency (Laine & Follansbee, 1994).

Specific technologies for instruction and learning include a focus on e-mail, videodisc, World Wide Web (WWW), virtual reality, and hypermedia. E-mail used with individuals who are deaf/hard of hearing and hearing students to communicate curriculum through written communication has been very successful. Since oral communication can be difficult for some individuals who are deaf/hard of hearing, this collaborative writing tool assists students with a hearing loss in this communication process (Weiserbs, 2000).

Videodisc technology has been used to create interactive instructional programs to successfully teach speechreading (Slike, Thornton, Hobbis, Kokoska, & Job, 1995). A unique program was designed and tested targeting three-dimensional virtual reality programs with students who are deaf/hard of hearing. The study found that these programs could improve flexible thinking. Additional learning opportunities were provided through the use of virtual reality (Passig & Eden, 2000). Clymer and McKee (1997) described a survey expressing the high rate of use of the WWW with students who are deaf/hard of hearing. In dealing with the auditory component of computer technology, hypermedia was used to create an instructional tool utilizing sign language and allowing for the use of connecting the sign to written language for the development of literacy and language (Aedo, Miranda, Panetsos, Torra, & Martin, 1994).

Technologies Applied to the Field

Technology had provided for the creation of text telephones (TTY) and other telecommunication technologies, which have seen an increase in access as continuing technology has allowed for convenience in size and mobility (Beck, 1995). Over time the TTY has been often exchanged for computers, allowing individuals to communicate "disability free" via e-mail, instant messages, and chat rooms (for example, Beck, 1995; Weiserbs, 2000).

Decoders were built into televisions and films were closed-captioned for educational purposes (Hairston, 1994), which opened educational avenues in school to a large amount of material previously inaccessible to individuals with a hearing loss (Caldwell, 1981). Real-time captioning was initially used to provide a visual process for print to assist with language acquisition (Stuckless, 1981) and has since moved to lectures and live news to provide access to current information.

Assistive listening devices have been created to provide access to auditory components of the educational setting. Audio loop systems provide mobility in the classroom for students with very mild or temporary hearing loss (Beck, 1995; Nelson & Nelson, 1997). FM systems are set up as radio signals to provide clarity of auditory information in one-on-one and group settings (Lewis, 1995). The research has demonstrated how FM systems have impacted (Boothroyd, 1990) and improved the educational setting for all degrees of hearing loss (Crandell & Smaldino, 1999; Flexer, 1997; Flexer, Wray, Black, & Millin, 1987).

There have been tremendous advancements in technological tools and the infusion of computers for instruction with students who are deaf/hard of hearing. The technology and the professionals in the field are at a critical juncture to move forward with future advancements for instruction and learning for students who are deaf/hard of hearing.

GIFTED AND TALENTED

A review of the extant literature on technology as it relates to the field of gifted education revealed three general categories: historical trends, technology as an agent for change, and distance learning. It should be noted that, generally, the literature follows the trends in innovation found in the general technology literature. That is to say, as technology became available in the market, it was quickly infused into the curriculum and programming for gifted and talented students.

Historical Trends

Preparing students for a technologically demanding society is a common theme throughout much of the literature on gifted programming. In an update on a 1978 article on the needs for preparing gifted students for the future, Torrance, Goff, and Kaufmann (1989) identified technology proficiency as a primary goal. Instruction of technology mirrors many of the goals and objectives of gifted education like critical and creative thinking (Corrigan, 1994; Little, 2001; Mann, 1994; Shaughnessy, Jausovec, & Lehtonnen, 1997; Weaver & Wallace, 1980). The infusion of computers and technology has not only changed what we teach but also how we teach (Olszewski-Kubilius, 2001). As will be seen later in this article, the promise of technology also addresses the needs of providing programming in rural areas (Spicker, Southern, & Davis, 1988).

There is a positive correlation between technological advancement in society and historical trends identified in gifted education (Corn, 1999; Imbeau, 1999; Stewart, 1999). Advances in technology have provided critical impetus for change in the field and will continue to do so both in the implementation and curricular aspects of programming for the gifted.

Agent for Change

There are numerous articles in the literature on gifted education that describe attempts to infuse technology into the classroom. In these cases, technology is seen as a tool that affects various levels within the curriculum. As an agent for change, technology can be infused to enhance a single lesson or to alter the entire philosophical nature of the curriculum.

Technology can be viewed as either a means to an end or the end itself. The literature is replete with articles that describe technology as a vehicle for conveying content. In these cases, the content or skills are the primary goal of the instruction, and the technology is infused to accentuate or facilitate the instruction. Traditionally, the use of technology was more commonly found in areas like math and science enrichment. Robotics, Logo, and other computer-aided design programs were popular additions to the activities in math classes (Grandgenett, 1991). Early on, Doorly (1980) promoted the use of computers in implementing mathematics instruction. She found developmental gains in the primary grades in basic number operations. Learning to develop computer programs was also a popular use of computers in math programs (Hershberger & Wheatley, 1989). By the nineties, the use of technology began to permeate other areas such as art, language arts, and thinking skills training (Banbury, Walker, & Punzo, 1990; Bowen, Shore, & Cartwright, 1992; Heaney, 1992; Riley & Brown, 1997; Smith, 1994; Troxclair, Stephens, Bennett, & Karnes, 1996).

Similarly, the literature also follows the trends in computer and technology advancement. Early articles discussed the use of computer-assisted technology and software packages like Logo, Hyperstudio, and various word-processing, spreadsheet, and basic drawing programs (Beasley, 1985; Flickinger, 1987; Jensen & Wedman, 1983; Kanevsky, 1985; Sisk, 1978). Later, the interest in more complex tools like interactive video, multimedia, artificial intelligence, virtual reality, and simulation software became more prevalent in the literature (Barr, 1990; Benno, 1998; Boyce, 1992; Bulls & Riley, 1997; Lewis, 1996; Riley & Brown, 1998a, 1998b; Strot, 1997a, 1997b; Wellington, 1993).

Additionally, using computers as tools to enhance the established curriculum was also noted in the literature. Howard (1994) suggested that using computers could enhance the learning opportunities for students who are gifted/learning disabled. Ross and Smyth (1995) described the importance of promoting thinking skills and how computer formats may enhance students' experiences with more difficult skills. Strot (1998) suggested that individualized instruction could be enhanced by the infusion of computers into research design and implementation projects. Simulation programs, database design, and research can all be added to existing research projects to further augment established activities. Similar studies described the infusion of technology into established units of study to improve the learners' experience and interest with the material and skills (Berger, 2001; Christopher, 1999; Duwell & Bennett, 2000; Strot, 1999).

Finally, there were few articles describing empirical studies that employed technology as a variable. Steele, Battista, and Krockover (1982) found in a study of fifth-grade math that infusing technology positively influenced the students' affective and cognitive outcomes. In a study of elementary and middle school students, Middleton, Littlefield, and Lehrer (1992) found gender and age differences on student attitudes for activities that included computers. Following a review of the literature on mathematics, Sowell (1993) suggested that further research is needed in the area of the effectiveness of computers in math programs. Shermis, Fulkerson, and Banta (1996) studied the use of computerized adaptive math tests and made suggestions for the potential this technology could have on talent identification. Kaniel, Licht, and Peled (2000) found similar positive results in a study using computer software to enhance metacognitive skills.

In addition to following trends in availability, as technology has become more prevalent in schools and society in general, there has been a subsequent increase in the literature on the philosophical nature of infusion. Morgan (1993) discussed infusion in terms of general school reform. Infusion was seen as a vehicle for impacting productivity and enhancing the instructional environment. Most recently, distance learning has become a popular avenue for instruction employing technology, which greatly alters the instructional environment and has had a direct impact on pedagogical change.

Distance Learning

The final category, comprised of various issues related to distance learning, has become a popular topic in the literature on gifted education. Articles in this category describe both the how-to issues and those related to pedagogical change.

Although Spicker, Southern, and Davis (1988) referred to the importance of distance learning for rural programs, there are few references to this important aspect of technology until later in the next decade. Like Spicker et al. (1988), McBride and Lewis (1993) asserted that telecommunication courses provide valuable resources to learners in rural areas because they provide resources to students that would otherwise be unavailable. This philosophy is one that is behind the distance learning opportunities like the Education Program for Gifted Youth (EPGY) at Stanford University that provides computer-based accelerated math and science courses for students across the country. Several authors have reported on the effectiveness of this instructional delivery system for students who require accelerated programs (Gilbert-Macmillan, 2000; Ravaglia, Suppes, Stillinger, & Alper, 1995; Washington, 1997).

Caution should be taken by those who wish to incorporate distance learning into the curriculum for gifted learners, as the very same objectives and standards should be applied to distance education as to other forms of instruction for gifted learners (Adams & Cross, 2000). Distance learning provides many positive outcomes for gifted learners but care must be taken that the technology does not overpower the users. Interaction and rigor can be maintained but must be carefully planned. Berger (2000) discussed how the rapid growth of the Internet could be used to make learning more accessible because of the plethora of resources now available via the World Wide Web. Teachers, however, need to be well versed in these resources in order to maximize the experience for learners. McKinnon and Nolan (1999) made excellent recommendations for programs using distance learning. Their emphasis was on the interactive nature of the technology, but advise that organization is the real key to success.

Many articles described specific programs, either intra- or extracurricular, that used computers within the expected coursework. These publications described the program specifically, and the technology was mentioned as part of the overall plan of the program. In other words, the technology used was not integral to the overall program but simply a small component of the coursework. It is worth noting that computers and technology are common features to gifted programs, whether within the scope of the curriculum or used as part of an enrichment program.

OVERALL TRENDS

The use of technology as reported in the literature on special education follows the historical timeline of available technology. Computers have been used in the various special and gifted education programs for as long as they have been available. Likewise the complexity of the infusion within programs mirrors the profundity of use by the wider society. As technology becomes more commonplace in schools and the sophistication of student use increases, the issues become more philosophical in nature. Educators need to be aware of their own pedagogical beliefs and beliefs about technology since these beliefs direct the modification and implementation of innovative technologies for the classroom (MacArthur, 2001).

It is evident that the infusion of technology is specifically tied to the mission and goals of the special education program. For example, the literature reveals that technology for students with learning disabilities is characterized by remedial, instructional enhancement, and productivity tools. Technology involving students with mental retardation is slowly shifting from remedial to functional skills acquisition, addressing the demand for lifelong skills and community integration. In the literature regarding individuals who are deaf/hard of hearing, technology is infused for auditory enhancements and overall access to the curriculum. Within the gifted and talented literature, technology is used to enhance or enrich the curriculum.

CONCLUSION

Educators need to provide each student with an appropriate education that meets his/her need for challenge, interest, and learning style. Educators now have to ask themselves whether the use of technology provides support and access for the learning activity, enhances the activity, or detracts from the effectiveness of the instruction. Technology is a tool; it is a means to an end, and that end is learning itself. The impact of technology is moving beyond integration at the classroom level to infusion at the curricular level.

While some continue to search for the perfect "teaching machine," many have abandoned this quest in exchange for a different vision. Gradually, a shift has occurred from using technology to provide remediation through drill-and-practice applications to encouraging students to use the computer in more self-directed ways to encourage critical thinking.

Students with exceptionalities generally look forward to using computers in the classroom and teachers capitalize on this desire. Unfortunately, research has indicated that teachers rationalize using computers in classrooms largely on the basis of its potential benefits for motivation and self-esteem and not on academic value or gains to achievement (Woodward & Rieth, 1997). More needs to be done to illustrate the curricular value of technology that reinforces what we value most in education, learning. Providing an appropriately challenging environment does not have to be at the expense of the curriculum. Technology can provide a vehicle for instruction that respects the needs of all learners without compromising the act of learning.

Review of the literature revealed that classroom technologies have the potential to positively impact the academic growth and development of students with exceptionalities. These students have benefited from the purposeful use of technology. However, for technology to truly make an impact in special education, a push toward deeper infusion into the curriculum is needed. Those with exceptionalities must find technology accessible and available, and teachers must be comfortable incorporating it into their daily instructional routines. Technology can and should move to a more "transparent" position, as teachers and students are able to use it more easily and creatively. In this type of classroom, teachers and students "see through" the technology and are able to better focus on more advanced learning goals of the curriculum.

The infusion of technology into the classroom and curricula during the late 20th century was largely reactive in nature. With limited coursework in teacher preparation programs, limited in-service exposure to technology, and the sheer speed of technological advances, educators were limited in their ability to thoroughly understand and fully infuse technologies that were currently available. The good news, however, is that, as technology advances there will be more user-friendly hardware and software from which to choose. In addition, as technology becomes more integrated into daily life, there will be a natural evolution into the classroom.

As we progress into the 21st century, a more proactive approach to the infusion of technology into the classroom and curricula is occurring. No longer are we as educators content with simple activities that allow students to use already-mastered skills. The primary thrust for infusion has infiltrated curriculum planning with an emphasis on scope and sequence. A major emphasis in teacher preparation programs to address the priority of infusing technology in all education is reflected in federal grant initiatives like Preparing Tomorrow's Teachers to use Technology (PT3). The emphasis for these grants is appropriately on training at all levels, including training the trainers in education programs.

In conclusion, this review has revealed that within the field of special education, there is considerable consensus with regard to the use of technology in the classroom. While there are variations in the specific hardware or software employed, there is much overlap in basic pedagological issues. Infusion of technology is non-negotiable in all educational settings and for students of all abilities.

REFERENCES

Adams, C. M., & Cross, T. L. (2000). Distance learning opportunities for academically gifted students. *Journal of Secondary Gifted Education, 11*, 88-96.

Aedo, I., Miranda, P., Panetsos, F., Torra, N., & Martin, M. (1994). A teaching methodology for the hearing impaired using hypermedia and computer animation. *Journal of Computing in Childhood Education, 5*, 353-369.

Anderson-Inman, L. (1990-91). Enabling students with learning disabilities: Insights from research. *Computing Teacher, 18*, 26-29.

Angelo, D. H. (1995). *ACC in the family home.* In S. L. Glenn & D. C. DeCoste (Eds.), *Handbook of augmentative and alternative communication* (pp. 523-541). San Diego, CA: Singular.

Bahr, C., & Reith, H. (1989). The effects of instructional computer games and drill and practice software on learning disabled students' mathematics achievement. *Computers in the Schools, 6*, 87-101.

Banbury, M. M., Walker, H., & Punzo, R. (1990). Thinking cap: A computer art program for gifted and talented students. *Gifted Child Today, 13*, 32-35.

Barr, D. (1990). A solution in search of a problem: The role of technology in educational reform. *Journal for the Education of the Gifted, 14*, 79-95.

Batavia, A. I., & Hammer, G. S. (1990). Toward the development of consumer-based criteria for the evaluation of assistive devices. *Journal of Rehabilitation Research and Development, 27*, 425-436.

Beasley, W. A. (1985). The role of microcomputers in the education of the gifted. *Roeper Review, 7*, 156-159.

Beck, S. G. (1995). Technology for the deaf: Remembering to accommodate an invisible disability. *Technology for the Deaf, 13*, 109-122.

Benno, M. (1998). Virtual reality. *Gifted Child Today, 21*, 12-14.

Berger, S. (2000). Technology in the 21st century. *Understanding Our Gifted, 12*, 3-8.

Berger, S. (2001). Surfing the net: We the people. Using interest as a motivator. *Understanding Our Gifted, 13*, 23-25.

Beukelman, D., & Mirenda, P. (1992). *Augmentative and alternative communication: Management of severe communication disorders in children and adults.* Baltimore: Brookes.

Blackhurst, A. E., & Edyburn, D. L. (2000). A brief history of special education technology. *Special Education Technology Practice, 2,* 21-36.

Boone, R., & Higgins, K. (1993). Hypermedia basal readers: Three years of school-based research. *Journal of Special Education Technology, 12,* 86-106.

Boone, R., Higgins, K., & Notari, A. (1996). Hypermedia pre-reading lessons: Learner centered software for kindergarten. *Journal of Computing in Childhood Education, 7,* 39-69.

Boothroyd, A. (1990). Impact of technology on the management of deafness. *Volta Review, 92,* 74-90.

Bowen, S., Shore, B. M., & Cartwright, G. F. (1992). Do gifted children use computers differently? A view from "The Factory." *Gifted Education International, 8,* 151-54.

Boyce, C. (1992). Interactive video. *Gifted Child Today, 15,* 22-23.

Browning, P., & White, W. A. T. (1986). Teaching life enhancement skills with interactive video-based curricula. *Education and Training of the Mentally Retarded, 21,* 236-244.

Bulls, M. R., & Riley, T. L. (1997). Weaving qualitatively differentiated units with the World Wide Web. *Gifted Child Today, 20,* 20-27, 50.

Caldwell, D. C. (1981). Closed-captioned television and the hearing impaired. *Volta Review, 83,* 285-290.

Chen, S. H. A., & Bernard-Opitz, V. (1993). Comparison of personal and computer-assisted instruction for children with autism. *Mental Retardation, 31,* 368-376.

Christopher, M. (1999). Math in architecture: Using technology to connect math to the real world. *Gifted Child Today, 22,* 24-31.

Clymer, E. W., & McKee, B. G. (1997). The promise of the World Wide Web and other telecommunication technologies within deaf education. *American Annals of the Deaf, 142,* 104-105.

Cognition and Technology Group at Vanderbilt. (1993). Examining the cognitive challenges and pedagological opportunities of integrated media systems: Toward a research agenda. *Journal of Special Education Technology, 12,* 118-124.

Corbett, E. E., & Micheaux, P. A. (1996). How some schools for deaf and hard of hearing children are meeting the challenges of instructional technology. *America Annals of the Deaf, 141,* 52-58.

Corn, A. L. (1999). Missed opportunities: But a new century is starting. *Gifted Child Today, 22,* 19-21.

Corrigan, S. Z. (1994). For the sake of the children. *Gifted Child Today, 17,* 22-23, 30, 41.

Crandell, C. C., & Smaldino, J. J. (1999). Improving classroom acoustics: Utilizing hearing-assistive technology and communication strategies in the educational setting. *Volta Review, 101,* 47-50.

Daiute, C., & Morse, F. (1994). Access to knowledge and expression: Multimedia writing tools for students with diverse needs and strengths. *Journal of Special Education, 12,* 221-253.

De La Paz, S. (1999). Composing via dictation and speech recognition systems: Compensatory technology for students with learning disabilities. *Learning Disabilities Quarterly, 22,* 173-182.

Denham, A., & Lahm, E. A. (2001). Using technology to construct alternative portfolios of students with moderate and severe disabilities. *Teaching Exceptional Children, 33*(5), 10-17.

Deninger, M. L. (1985). Is it still an apple for the teacher? *American Annals of the Deaf, 130,* 332-339.

Derer, K., Polsgrove, L., & Rieth, H. (1996). A survey of assistive technology applications in schools and recommendations for practice. *Journal of Special Education Technology, 13,* 62-80.

Doorly, A. (1980). Microcomputers for gifted microtots. *Gifted Child Today, 14,* 62-64.

Duwell, M. J., & Bennett, E. (2000). Weaving technology into gifted curriculum. *Understanding Our Gifted, 12,* 9-13.

Flexer, C. (1997). Individual and sound-field FM systems: Rationale, description, and use. *Volta Review, 99,* 133-162.

Flexer, C., Wray, D., Black, T., & Millin, J. (1987). Amplification devices: Evaluating classroom effectiveness for moderately hearing-impaired college students. *Volta Review, 89,* 347-356.

Flickinger, G. G. (1987). Gifted students and Logo: Teacher's role. *Roeper Review, 9,* 177-178.

Furniss, F., Ward, A., Lancioni, G., Rocha, N., Cunha, B., Seedhouse, P. et al. (1999). A palmtop-based job aid for workers with severe intellectual disabilities. *Technology and Disability, 10,* 53-67.

Gilbert-Macmillan, K. (2000). Computer based distance learning for gifted students: The EPGY experience. *Understanding Our Gifted, 12,* 17-20.

Graham, S., & MacArthur, C. (1998). Improving learning disabled students' skills at revising essays produced on a word processor: Self-instructional strategy training. *Journal of Special Education, 22,* 133-152.

Grandgenett, N. (1991). Roles of computer technology in the mathematics education of the gifted. *Gifted Child Today, 14,* 18-23.

Hairston, E. E. (1994). Education media technology for hearing-impaired persons: A federal perspective. *American Annals of the Deaf, 139,* 10-13.

Harding, R. E., & Tidball, L. K. (1982). A national microcomputer-software survey of current microcomputer usage in schools for the hearing impaired. *American Annals of the Deaf, 127,* 673-683.

Harkins, J. E., Loeterman, M., Lam, K., & Korres, E. (1996). Instructional technology in schools educating deaf and hard of hearing children: A national survey. *American Annals of the Deaf, 141,* 59-65.

Hasselbring T. S. (1994). Using media for developing mental models and anchoring instruction. *American Annals of the Deaf, 139,* 36-44.

Hasselbring, T. S. (2001). A possible future of special education technology. *Journal of Special Education Technology, 16,* 15-21.

Heaney, L. F. (1992). Children using language: Can computers help? *Gifted Education International*, 8, 146-50.

Hershberger, J., & Wheatley, G. (1989). Computers and gifted students: An effective mathematics programs. *Gifted Child Quarterly*, 33, 106-109.

Higgins, E. L., & Raskind, M. H. (1995). An investigation of the compensatory effectiveness of speech recognition on the written composition performance of postsecondary students with learning disabilities. *Learning Disabilities Quarterly*, 18, 159-174.

Higgins, E. L., & Raskind, M. H. (2000). Speaking to read: The effects of continuous vs. discrete speech recognition systems of the reading and spelling of children with learning disabilities. *Journal of Special Education Technology*, 15, 19-30.

Higgins, E. L., & Zvi, J. (1995). Assistive technology with postsecondary students with learning disabilities: From research to practice. *Annals of Dyslexia*, 45, 123-142.

Higgins, K., & Boone, R. (1990). Hypertext computer study guides and the social studies achievement of students with learning disabilities, remedial students, and regular education students. *Journal of Learning Disabilities*, 23, 529-540.

Higgins, K., & Boone, R. (1991). Hypermedia CAI: A supplement to an elementary school based reader program. *Journal of Special Education Technology*, 11, 1-15.

Higgins, K., & Boone, R. (1993). Technology as a tutor, tool, and agent for reading. *Journal of Special Education Technology*, 12, 29-37.

Higgins, K., Boone, R., & Lovitt, T. C. (1996). Hypertext support for remedial students and students with learning disabilities. *Journal of Learning Disabilities*, 29, 402-412.

Howard, J. B. (1994). Addressing needs through strengths: Five instructional practices for use with gifted/learning disabled students. *Journal of Secondary Gifted Education*, 5, 23-34.

Huntinger, P. L. (1996). Computer applications in programs for young children with disabilities: Recurring themes. *Focus on Autism and Other Developmental Disabilities*, 11, 105-114.

Iacono, T. A., & Miller, J. F. (1989). Can microcomputers be used to teach communication skills to students with mental retardation? *Education and Training in Mental Retardation*, 24, 32-44.

Imbeau, M. B. (1999). A century of gifted education: A reflection of who and what made a difference. *Gifted Child Today*, 22, 40-43.

Individuals with Disabilities Education Act Amendments of 1997, Pub. L. No.105-17. (1998).

Inge, K. J., & Shepherd, J. (1995). Assistive technology applications and strategies for school system personnel. In K. F. Flippo, K. J. Inge, & J. M. Barcus (Eds.), *Assistive technology: A resource for school, work, and community* (pp. 133-166). Baltimore: Brookes.

Jensen, R., & Wedman, J. (1983). The computer's role in gifted education. *Gifted Child Today*, 6, 10-11.

Kanevsky, L. (1985). Computer based math for gifted students: Comparison of cooperative and competitive strategies. *Journal for the Education of the Gifted*, 8, 239-255.

Kaniel, S., Licht, P., & Peled, B. (2000). The influence of metacognitive instruction of reading and writing strategies on positive transfer. *Gifted Education International, 15*, 45-63.

Kyhl, R., Alper, S., & Sinclair, T. J. (1999). Acquisition and generalization of functional words in community grocery stores using videotaped instruction. *Career Development for Exceptional Individuals, 22*, 55-67.

Laine, C. J., & Follansbee, R. (1994). Using word-prediction technology to improve the writing of low-functioning hearing-impaired students. *Child Language Teaching and Therapy, 10*, 283-297.

Lewis, D. E. (1995). FM systems: A good idea that keeps getting better. *Volta Review, 97*, 183-196.

Lewis, J. D. (1996). Confessions of an Internet junkie: View from the "information highway." *Gifted Child Today, 19*, 40-45, 48.

Lewis, R. B. (2000). Musing on technology and learning disabilities on the occasion of the new millennium. *Journal of Special Education Technology, 15*, 5-12.

Lewis, R. B., Graves, A. W., Ashton, T. M., & Kieley, C. L. (1998). Word processing tools for students with learning disabilities: A comparison of strategies to increase text entry speed. *Learning Disabilities Research & Practice, 13*, 95-108.

Lincoln, Y. S., & Guba, E. G. (1985). *Naturalistic inquiry.* Newbury Park, CA: Sage.

Little, C. A. (2001). Probabilities and possibilities: The future of gifted education. *Journal of Secondary Gifted Education, 12*, 166-169.

MacArthur, C. A. (1996). Using technology to enhance the writing processes of students with learning disabilities. *Journal of Learning Disabilities, 29*, 344-354.

MacArthur, C. A. (1998). Word processing with speech synthesis and word prediction: Effects on the dialogue journal writing of students with learning disabilities. *Learning Disabilities Quarterly, 21*, 151-66.

MacArthur, C. A. (1999). Overcoming barriers to writing: Computer support for basic writing skills. *Reading and Writing Quarterly, 15*, 169-192.

MacArthur, C. A. (2001). Technology implementation in special education. In J. Woodward & J. Cuban (Eds.), *Technology, curriculum and professional development: Adapting schools to meet the needs of students with disabilities* (pp. 115-120). Thousand Oaks: Corwin.

MacArthur, C. A., & Graham, S. (1987). Learning disabled students composing under three methods of text production: Handwriting, word processing, and dictation. *Journal of Special Education, 21*, 22-42.

MacArthur, C., Graham, S., & Schwartz, S. (1991). Knowledge of revision and revising behavior among learning disabled students. *Learning Disabilities Quarterly, 14*, 61-74.

MacArthur, C. A., & Haynes, J. B. (1995). Student assistant learning from text (SALT): A hypermedia reading aid. *Journal of Learning Disabilities, 28*, 150-159.

Mann, C. (1994). New technologies and gifted education. *Roeper Review, 16*, 172-176.

Mann, W. C., & Lane, J. P. (1995). *Assistive technology for persons with disabilities. The role of occupational therapy* (2nd ed.). Rockville, MD: American Occupational Therapy Association.

McBride, R. O., & Lewis, G. (1993). Sharing the resources: Electronic outreach programs. *Journal for the Education of the Gifted, 16*, 372-386.

McDermott, P., & Watkins, M. (1983). Computerized vs. conventional remedial instruction for learning disabled pupils. *Journal of Special Education, 17*, 81-88.

McKinnon, D. H., & Nolan, C. J. P. (1999). Distance education for the gifted and talented: An interactive design model. *Roeper Review, 21*, 320-325.

Middleton, J. A., Littlefield, J., & Lehrer, R. (1992). Gifted students' conceptions of academic fun: An examination of a critical construct for gifted education. *Gifted Child Quarterly, 36*, 38-44.

Mirenda, P., Wild, D., & Carson, P. (2000). A retrospective analysis of technology use patterns of students with autism over a five-year period. *Journal of Special Education Technology, 15*(3), 5-15.

Morgan, R. L., Gerity, B. P., & Ellerd, D. A. (2000). Using video and CD-ROM technology in a job preference inventory for youth with severe disabilities. *Journal of Special Education Technology, 15*(3), 25-33.

Morgan, T. D. (1993). Technology: An essential tool for gifted and talented education. *Journal for the Education of the Gifted, 16*, 358-371.

Najjar, L. J. (1996). Multimedia information and learning. *Journal of Educational Multimedia and Hypermedia, 5*, 129-150.

Nelson, D. G., & Nelson, D. K. (1997). Teacher and student satisfaction with freefield FM amplification systems. *Volta Review, 99*, 163-170.

Olszewski-Kubilius, P. (2001). Interview with Joyce VanTassel Baska. *Journal of Secondary Gifted Education, 12*, 57-61.

Outhred, L. (1989). Word processing: Its impact on children's writing. *Journal of Learning Quarterly, 22*, 262-264.

Parette, Jr., H. P. (1997). Assistive technology devices and services. *Education and Training in Mental Retardation and Developmental Disabilities, 32*, 267-280.

Passig, D., & Eden, S. (2000). Improving flexible thinking in deaf and hard of hearing children with virtual reality technology. *American Annals of the Deaf, 145*, 286-291.

Perlman, L. G. (1993). *The views of consumers with learning disabilities, mental retardation and their caregivers.* Washington, DC: Electronic Industries Foundation.

Pillai, P. (1999). Using technology to educate deaf and hard of hearing children in rural Alaskan general education settings. *American Annals of the Deaf, 144*, 373-378.

Ravaglia, R., Suppes, P., Stillinger, C., & Alper, T. (1995). Computer based mathematics and physics for gifted students. *Gifted Child Quarterly, 39*, 7-13.

Renbald, K. (1999). The potential for advanced technologies to broaden the outreach and social network of persons with mental retardation: A literature study. *Technology and Disability, 10*, 175-180.

Richardson, J. E. (1981). Computer assisted instruction for the hearing impaired. *Volta Review, 85*, 328-335.

Riley, T. L., & Brown, M. E. (1997). Computing for clever kids: Creating the future. *Gifted Child Today, 20*, 22-29.

Riley, T. L., & Brown, M. E. (1998a). Internet investigations: Solving mysteries on the information superhighway. *Gifted Child Today, 21*, 28-33.

Riley, T. L., & Brown, M. E. (1998b). The magic of multimedia: Creating leaders of yesterday, today, and tomorrow. *Gifted Child Today, 21,* 20-22, 24-26.

Roberson, L. (2001). Integration of computers and related technologies into deaf education teacher preparation programs. *American Annals of the Deaf, 146,* 60-66.

Rose, S., & Waldron, M. (1984). Microcomputer use in programs for hearing-impaired children: A national survey. *American Annals of the Deaf, 129,* 338-342.

Ross, J. A., & Smyth, E. (1995). Thinking skills for gifted students: The case for correlational reasoning. *Roeper Review, 17,* 239-243.

Salomon-Weiss, M. J., Wagner, S. H., & Bauman, M. L. (1996). A validated case study of facilitated communication. *Mental Retardation, 34,* 220-230.

Schepis, M., Reid, D., Behrmann, M., & Sutton, K. (1998). Increasing communicative interactions of young children with autism using voice output communication aid and naturalistic teaching. *Journal of Applied Behavior Analysis, 31,* 561-758.

Scherer, M. J. (1993). Living in the state of stuck. *How technology impacts the lives of people with disabilities.* Cambridge: Brookline.

Sharp, S. J. (1989). Using content subject matter with LEA in middle school. *Journal of Adolescent & Adult Literacy, 33,* 108-112.

Shaughnessy, M. F., Jausovec, N., & Lehtonen, K. (1997). Gifted education: Some considerations as we approach the year 2000. *Gifted Education International, 12,* 40-42.

Sheehan, C. M., & Matuozzi, R. T. (1996). Investigation of the validity of facilitated communication through disclosure of unknown information. *Mental Retardation, 34,* 94-107.

Shermis, M. D., Fulkerson, J., & Banta, T. W. (1996). Computerized adaptive math tests for elementary talent development selection. *Roeper Review, 19,* 91-95.

Sisk, D. (1978). Computers in the classroom. An invitation and a challenge for the gifted. *Gifted Child Today, 1,* 18-21.

Slike, S. B., Thornton, N. E., Hobbis, D. H., Kokoska, S. M., & Job, K. A. (1995). The development and analysis of interactive videodisc technology to teach speech-reading. *American Annals of the Deaf, 140,* 346-351.

Smith, R. B. (1994). Robotic challenges: Robots bring new life to gifted classes, teach students hands on problem solving, computer skills. *Gifted Child Today, 17,* 36-38.

Sowell, E. J. (1993). Programs for mathematically gifted students: A review of empirical research. *Gifted Child Quarterly, 37,* 124-132.

Spicker, H. H., Southern, W. T., & Davis, B. I. (1988). The rural gifted child. *Gifted Child Quarterly, 31,* 155-157.

Steele, K. J., Battista, M. T., & Krockover, G. H. (1982). The effect of microcomputer assisted instruction upon the computer literacy of high ability students. *Gifted Child Quarterly, 26,* 162-164.

Stewart, E. D. (1999). An American century of roots and signposts in gifted and talented education. *Gifted Child Today, 22,* 56-57.

Strepp, R. E. (1994). A technological metamorphosis in the education of deaf students. *American Annals of the Deaf, 139,* 14-17.

Strot, M. (1997a). Electronic explorations: Support for independent studies. *Gifted Child Today, 20,* 12-14, 16-17, 46-47.

Strot, M. (1997b). Publishing a Web page. *Gifted Child Today, 20,* 38-39.

Strot, M. (1998). Individualizing instruction with computer applications. *Gifted Child Today, 21,* 40-42.

Strot, M. (1999). A technology plan for math skills. *Gifted Child Today, 22*, 30-31.

Stuckless, E. R. (1981). Real-time graphic display and language development for the hearing impaired. *Volta Review, 85*, 291-300.

Stuckless, E. R., & Carroll, J. K. (1994). National priorities on educational applications of technology for deaf and hard of hearing students. *American Annals of the Deaf, 139*, 62-63.

Technology Related Assistance for Individuals with Disabilities Act of 1988 and Amendments (Catalogue No. 850, Senate Rep. No. 100-438). Washington, DC: U.S. Government Printing Office.

The Americans with Disabilities Act of 1990, Pub. L. No. 101-336 (1991).

Thomas, M. A. (1981). Educating handicapped students via microcomputer/videodisc technology: A conversation with Ron Thorkildsen. *Education and Training of the Mentally Retarded, 16*, 264-269.

Torrance, E. P., Goff, K., & Kaufmann, F. (1989). Are we teaching our children to think about the future? *Gifted Child Today, 12*, 48-50.

Troxclair, D., Stephens, K., Bennett, T., & Karnes, F. (1996). Teaching technology: Multimedia presentations in the classroom. *Gifted Child Today, 19*, 34-36, 47.

Volterra, V., Pace, C., Pennacchi, B., & Corazza, S. (1995). Advanced learning technology for a bilingual education of deaf children. *American Annals of the Deaf, 140*, 402-409.

Walker, P. (1991). Where there is a way, there is not always a will: Technology, public policy, and the school integration of children who are technology-assisted. *Children's Health Care, 20*, 68-74.

Washington, M. A. F. (1997). Real hope for the gifted. *Gifted Child Today, 20*, 20-22.

Weaver, R. A., & Wallace, B. (1980). Technology and the future of gifted child education. *Roeper Review, 2*, 19-21.

Wehmeyer, M. L. (1998). National survey of the use of assistive technology by adults with mental retardation. *Mental Retardation, 36*, 44-51.

Wehmeyer, M. L. (1999). Assistive technology and students with mental retardation: Utilization and barriers. *Journal of Special Education Technology, 14*(1), 48-58.

Weiserbs, B. (2000). Social and academic integration using e-mail between children with and without hearing impairments. *Computers in the Schools, 16*, 29-44.

Wellington, B. (1993). Connecting computers. *Gifted Child Today, 16*, 33-36.

Withrow, F. B. (Ed.). (1981). Learning technology and the hearing impaired. *Volta Review, 83*.

Woodward, J., Carnine, D., Gerten, R., Gleason, M., Johnson, G., & Collins, M. (1986). Applying instructional design principles to CAI for mildly handicapped students: Four recently conducted studies. *Journal of Special Education Technology, 8*, 13-26.

Woodward, J., & Cuban, J. (2001). *Technology, curriculum and professional development: Adapting schools to meet the needs of students with disabilities.* Thousand Oaks: Corwin.

Woodward, J., Gallagher, D., & Reith, H. (2001). No easy answer: The instructional effectiveness of technology for students with disabilities. In J. Woodward & J. Cuban (Eds.), *Technology, curriculum and professional development: Adapting schools to meet the needs of students with disabilities* (pp. 3-27). Thousand Oaks: Corwin.

Woodward, J., & Rieth, H. (1997). A historical review of technology research in special education. *Review of Educational Research, 67*, 503-536.

Ward Mitchell Cates
Betsy Price
Alec M. Bodzin

Implementing Technology-Rich Curricular Materials: Findings from the *Exploring Life* Project

SUMMARY. Eighteen high school biology teachers from a stratified sample of 13 distinct geographical United States regions participated in evaluating first-year prototypes of *Biology: Exploring Life*, which incorporates a print textbook; accompanying Web activities to explain and reinforce the text and promote active, hands-on learning; and wet lab investigations. This article discusses how we chose our teacher participants, compares our participant sample with the characteristics of early adopters of innovation, and details what we learned from our year-long investigation about implementing

WARD MITCHELL CATES is Professor, Lehigh University, College of Education, Bethlehem, PA 18015 (E-mail: Ward.cates@Lehigh.edu).
BETSY PRICE is Director of Associate Instructor Program, Westminster College, Salt Lake City, UT 84105 (E-mail: bprice@westminstercollege.edu).
ALEC M. BODZIN is Assistant Professor, Lehigh University, Bethlehem, PA 18015 (E-mail: amb4@lehigh.edu).

This article is based on a paper presented at the National Educational Computing Conference in San Antonio, Texas, in June 2002.

The preparation of this article was funded by a grant from the National Science Foundation (NSF), Grant IMD-9986610. The opinions expressed are those of the authors and do not necessarily reflect the position of NSF.

[Haworth co-indexing entry note]: "Implementing Technology-Rich Curricular Materials: Findings from the *Exploring Life* Project." Cates, Ward Mitchell, Betsy Price, and Alec M. Bodzin. Co-published simultaneously in *Computers in the Schools* (The Haworth Press, Inc.) Vol. 20, No. 1/2, 2003, pp. 153-169; and: *Technology in Education: A Twenty-Year Retrospective* (ed: D. LaMont Johnson, and Cleborne D. Maddux) The Haworth Press, Inc., 2003, pp. 153-169. Single or multiple copies of this article are available for a fee from The Haworth Document Delivery Service [1-800-HAWORTH, 9:00 a.m. - 5:00 p.m. (EST). E-mail address: docdelivery@haworthpress.com].

a technology-rich science product in real classrooms. The article concludes with recommendations for adopting of technology-rich science learning products in schools. *[Article copies available for a fee from The Haworth Document Delivery Service: 1-800-HAWORTH. E-mail address: <docdelivery@haworthpress. com> Website: <http://www.HaworthPress.com> © 2003 by The Haworth Press, Inc. All rights reserved.]*

KEYWORDS. Technology integration, technology implementation, technology product development, general biology, educational technology, computer uses in education

Twenty-one years ago, Bunderson (1981) predicted that technology (at that time, the videodisc) would become a dominant source of instruction within the decade, largely replacing the teacher. Ten years later, Heinich (1991) was still arguing for "certified resources," technology-based products that would displace teachers, an argument strongly supported by Perelman in *School's Out* (1992). A survey of classrooms today would reveal, however, that teachers–while perhaps playing a slightly different role–still dominate the educational landscape.

A brief survey of the literature over the past 20 years shows early adopters–in typical technology champion style–have prophesied the best was yet to come for teaching and learning using technology (see, for example, Bork, 1985; Dennis & Kansky, 1984; Freeman, 1987; Jacobsen, 1998; Norman, 1997; Sharp, 1993). Unfortunately, the extent to which technology has effected radical change in teaching and learning falls a bit short of the prophecy (Cuban, 2001). The major concerns about integration of technology in school settings in the last two decades' literature seem to focus on (a) availability of suitable technology (hardware), (b) access to well-designed educational software, (c) adequate teacher training in technology use, and (d) support for teachers in using technology with students. In the words of Baker (1981), computer-based instructional products and applications will only succeed if they can be integrated "into the enduring fabric of the educational system" (p. 23). This article examines how implementing technology-rich materials today reflects the same concerns expressed 20 years ago and attempts to illuminate some of the strands of that fabric.

Data from the National Center for Educational Statistics (1999) and the State-of-the-States Survey (2001) suggest that many schools have advanced beyond the first level of adopting technology: purchasing hardware and software, preparing school facilities, and wiring schools for Internet access. Many schools have also completed the second level of adoption: preparing teachers to operate computers. As a general rule, successful completion of the first and second levels makes record-keeping easier, improves the quality of presentations, and increases professional communication among teachers.

Despite the apparent readiness of school systems to advance to the next level of technology integration and the presence of better computer facilities than a few years ago, technology-rich curricular materials do not appear to have yet been implemented on a large scale. According to the State-of-the-States Survey (2001), 90% of the responding state-level directors of technology reported they either require or recommend integration of computers into the curriculum. However, state directors of technology also reported they would rate only 80% of their state's teachers as "average" in proficiency in integrating technology (Solmon, 1999). Further, these state directors suggested only 62% of their teachers used technology to enhance teaching, while fewer than 45% pursued higher level thinking activities with their students. Similarly, the directors rated only 11% of their teachers as above average in using project-based learning or cooperative groups.

Lemke and Coughlin (1998) studied factors that determine whether schools will be successful in raising the level of student use of computers for learning. Their study produced a list of key factors that mirrors the factors identified in the past 20 years' literature. Missing from their list, however, was a well-developed, comprehensive curriculum that can be used for an entire course of study. Such year-long curricula that integrate technology may be crucial to helping teachers bring about the kind of systemic change that technology integration may demand (*CEO Forum*, 1997; Mann, 1998; Sherman, 1998). There appears to be much support for the desire for such curricula (Bailey, 1997; Dockstader, 1999; Ediger, 1997; Fine, 1999; Gunter & Wiens, 1998; Hall & Mantz, 2000). This support is further reinforced by the fact that 22% of the state-level directors of technology, when asked why computers are not used in schools, responded that schools needed to revise the curriculum.

To address just this need, the present project integrated technology into the full-year curriculum. The product uses a 4 E's learning cycle model, a modification of the 5 E's instructional model (Biological Sciences Curriculum Study, 1993) that integrates computer media throughout. The "E's" represent various phases of the constructivist learning cycle (*Engage, Explore, Explain, Evaluate*). The product, whose prototyping was funded by the National Science Foundation, integrates a shorter (800-page), concept-oriented textbook, a collection of inquiry-based lab and field activities, and an extensive World Wide Web site that provides an interactive learning environment for students. These components are designed to work together to help teachers provide a more interactive classroom in which computers support and enhance delivery of the curriculum. Unlike textbooks "published" (posted) on the Web largely as Acrobat PDF files or other forms of documents and worksheets, *Biology: Exploring Life* materials go beyond simple reading, teacher lesson plans, and activity worksheets. Web activities explain and reinforce the text and promote active, hands-on learning. They encourage students to explore, analyze, draw conclusions, and share their findings.

Hoover and Abhaya (1995) argued, however, that many "educational" sites are not well-suited to classroom use because (a) they lack strong instructional (pedagogical) design and (b) scientists (content specialists) have difficulty collaborating with educators and Web site designers to produce the most efficacious sites. In addition, a number of authors argue that teachers need professional development to help them learn how to integrate technology into teaching and learning and that we need newer models for such development activities (see, for example, Black, 1998; Smith-Gratto & Fisher, 1999).

In order to develop a useful and adoptable product, we needed to explore how melding a print textbook with online activities influenced what teachers in real school settings could do. The developers produced prototype materials and then asked a sample of teachers to implement them in real classrooms under a wide range of technological configurations. The major questions we, as evaluators, sought to answer through our study were as follows:

1. How ready are biology teachers who are early adopters of technology to employ a curriculum that requires students to use computers on a regular or even daily basis?
2. What motivation, additional education, hardware, or skills do teachers require in order to integrate almost-daily computer use into the curriculum?
3. Do high schools have the adequate technology facilities to implement a curricular program that incorporates students using computers on an almost-daily basis?
4. How might existing schools change to support a technology-based curricular program?

PARTICIPANTS

Three evaluation workshops were conducted at different developmental stages during the first year of our project. To attract participants, we posted calls for participation on national and state educational listservs and bulletin boards. Biology teachers who were interested in participating in the *Biology: Exploring Life* evaluation completed a 44-item computer experience questionnaire. This questionnaire allowed us to identify participants' varied demographics and background characteristics, including geographical area, socioeconomic level of the school, years using the Internet for teacher planning/preparation, perceived preparation to use the computer and Internet in classroom activities, training to integrate instructional technologies into curricula, number of computers in the classroom and school, student-to-computer ratio, and reported technology use in the classroom.

Forty-two high school biology teachers, one pre-service biology teacher, and one science supervisor were selected from a stratified sample of 13 distinct geographical regions that included Alaska and Hawaii. These 44 people participated in the evaluation of the first-year prototypes, reviewing the materials in various stages of development at one of the three evaluation workshops (August 2000, October 2000, and March 2001). Although the 42 teachers had volunteered to implement the materials in their classrooms, only 18 were able to do so during the 2000-2001 school year. They pilot-tested the *Biology: Exploring Life* materials with 783 students. The loss of 24 teachers was due primarily to scheduling problems and the timing of the workshops in relation to when the content in the prototypes was covered in their classrooms. For this reason, some of these teachers agreed to participate in the second year's field test instead. In addition, five classrooms were chosen for field observations based on arbitrary volunteer selection.

DATA COLLECTION

As noted earlier, we collected data on teachers' past practices, teaching experience, use of computers, and professional development. At the three workshops, teacher participants evaluated how well prototype materials met national and local teaching standards and assessed the cognitive and interest level of students. In addition, they appraised the quality of prototype use of the interactive qualities of computers and the Web. To determine the use of the materials in the classroom, the evaluation team conducted five classroom field observations during the school year. Students completed measures of biology content knowledge and concept understanding before and after using chapter materials, and each teacher submitted a questionnaire and a journal with open-ended responses after using each chapter. To collect a richer and more detailed set of teacher impressions, a member of the evaluation team conducted follow-up phone interviews with teacher participants who completed two or more units. To obtain a richer pool of student reactions to the prototypes, we selected two volunteer teachers and examined their students' submitted journals.

FINDINGS

Findings are discussed below in terms of the teachers' self-report data prior to implementing the materials in the school setting and then what we learned about their actual use of the materials in the pilot. Although student knowledge of biology, as measured by all four pre- to post-pilot measures, increased significantly [$t(477) = 18.64$; $t(212) = 15.11$; $t(85) = 9.94$; $t(77) = 4.79$; all findings $p = .001$] and students reported strong favorable reactions to the prototype materials, this paper focuses on the teachers' experience. Thus, we discuss student findings only in relation to how they might affect teacher actions and decisions in implementing such a technology-rich product.

PARTICIPANT SELF-REPORT DATA BEFORE THE PILOT

This section is divided into four main parts: *participants as early adopters, reduced planning time, computer facilities and support,* and *participant use of technology.*

Participants as Early Adopters

According to Rogers (1986), adopters of technology fall into fairly clearly defined categories. Innovators and early adopters lead the way, early majority folks hold the middle ground, while late majority adopters and laggards wait longest. Given that we used the Web and e-mail as principal means of soliciting a volunteer sample, we assumed our participants might well fall on the leading edge of Rogers' adoption-of-innovation curve (as applied to educational technology use). Teachers' reported use data offered some support for this assumption.

Our teachers reported that they used computers for preparation and planning once a week or more (97%) and rated themselves as well or very well prepared to use technology (83%). The vast majority of our participating teachers (88.1%) reported they had used computers for three or more years in teacher planning and preparation and had completed professional development in the past three years related to technology use or implementation. Similarly, all participants (100%) reported that they had assigned their students Web-based research tasks, while 92.9% reported they had assigned students data-analysis and problem-solving tasks using computers or the Web. Those same respondents reported that they felt ready to use computers for their own professional use, as well as with their students. Participants reported notable levels of participation in professional development activities; 76.2% said they had completed nine or more hours in the past 3 years, while one-third reported taking more than 32 hours in that same period. Despite such training, most in our sample identified their own independent learning (97.6%) and interactions among colleagues (83.3%) as main sources of their knowledge about technology and its use. This contrasts with 35.7% who reported that at least a moderate extent of their training came from college courses.

Reduced Planning Time

Participants noted on their questionnaires during the first workshop that additional planning time would be needed to infuse technology into their biology curriculum. This is consistent with the assertions of writers who have suggested technology implementations increase the demand on teacher planning time, and restrictions in available time may act as a limiting factor (Cummings, 1998; Heck & Wallace, 1999; Schnackenberg, Asuncion, & Rosler, 1999).

However, during focus groups prior to the field test, the teachers espoused the belief that the prototype materials would actually save planning time. Because these materials included interactive activities that enhanced the text, offered links that were kept up to date, and because the publishers were responsible for keeping information updated, participants opined that they would spend less time searching and more time teaching. Because the program offered activities at various cognitive levels, participants also thought the prototype materials might save time adjusting materials for different class levels and interests.

Computer Facilities and Support

Many teachers in our study (73.8%) reported that they expected adequate support for a technology-integrative curriculum from their administrators. Most (54.8%) rated the number of computers in their school as sufficient to use a Web-based curriculum. Similarly, most respondents (61%) reported that their districts had a computer training requirement.

Participating teachers reported differential access to computers in their instructional settings. Twenty-five percent of the participants responded that they had what we would call a "classroom set"; that is, 10 or more computers in the classroom. Forty-nine percent of the teachers reported having two to nine computers, and only 26% reported just one computer in the classroom. Almost all of the teachers (97.6%) reported, however, that they also had access to a computer lab.

Participant Use of Technology

At the same time that we saw evidence that our sample might be more active in using technology in schools, we were surprised at the ways teachers reported actually using computers in schools. The three most reported activities–searching for possible activities to use with students, communicating with colleagues, and word processing–were uses supporting *teaching*, not uses involving *students* in the classroom directly. When we looked at how students in their classrooms used computers, most of the reported activities were data collection and reporting.

A majority of the teachers (66.7%) responded that they did not use comput-ers for classroom multimedia presentations at all, or did so infrequently. This finding seems consonant with McDermott and Murray's (2000) contention that the use of computers still remains teacher-centered as opposed to learner-centered. The finding seems particularly important here, however, because our prototype materials were student-centered and required teachers to have stu-dents use computers in the classroom almost daily.

PILOT RESULTS

This section is organized around four headings. The first three parallel the previous discussion: *planning time not reduced, inconsistent computer facili-ties issues,* and *teacher use of technology.* The fourth heading, *findings related to specific learners,* relates to how specific populations of students interacted with the prototypes.

Planning Time Not Reduced

Despite teachers' prediction of reduced planning time requirements, once the field test was underway, the majority of teachers reported that they spent *additional* time planning and preparing to teach. Most of that extra time was spent dealing with the technical requirements: arranging computers, adjusting schedules around labs times, and installing software and Web browser plug-ins. Many teachers reported spending planning time developing supplemental worksheets to be used as accountability measures when students completed online tutorials. As anticipated, teachers did feel that the program reduced the amount of time they spent searching for support materials, and respondents suggested that they would be able to spend less time planning if their school computers were properly configured and if the publisher developed work-sheets to be used with materials.

Inconsistent Computer Facilities and Support

Once they were using the prototype materials on a regular basis, a number of our pilot teachers discovered their school buildings did not have an adequate support system for implementing such technology-intensive curricular materi-als. As we talked to teachers, we found that there was little consistency in schools' student computer facilities. Some distributed computers so that every room had a computer, while other schools centralized all computers for student use in computer labs. We observed that some teachers who valued technology were unwilling to wait for their school budgets to equip individual classrooms with computers. Instead, they had acquired computers for their classrooms through grants and private funds. This meant that, within the very same school, some teachers had technology-rich classrooms while others had almost no classroom technology. Ironically, this produced a "digital divide" *within* a school wider than the difference *between* that school and others.

Many of the teachers had planned to use their school's computer lab to do the activities. However, teachers often discovered they were not able to access their computer lab or that lab availability was restricted with little scheduling flexibility. Sometimes this meant our teachers were left having to adjust a week or even a month of lessons in order to get lab time. Such availability might determine whether the materials got used at all: One teacher was called out of town and her class missed the computer lab day. When she returned, she was unable to reserve another day right away. Unfortunately, she had used up the time that was allotted by her core curriculum to the concept covered by the prototype's Web-based activities and had to move on to other materials.

Most biology classrooms are not designed to accommodate a large number of computers. Often there are not enough electrical outlets and few (or no) Internet connections. Some schools lined computers up in neat rows that left little room for students to work in pairs or even work independently because of the crowded linear layout. Our observations indicated that wireless computers offered greater classroom arrangement flexibility than using a computer lab, permitting more collaboration and small group work. However, even with wireless computers, difficulties occurred. In one classroom, students had to walk around the room, holding their computers like divining rods to find the service area of their wireless computer hub. Their room was, by the pernicious nature of the technology gods, located in an area that received three separate signals from disparate ends of the school.

Facilities were only part of the problem, however. Most reported difficulties related to preparing computers to use the program. The computers required minimum system requirements of 64 MB of RAM, Internet Explorer 5 or higher as the Web browser, 350 MHz CPU speed, at least 56K connection speed, and installation of Flash 5 and QuickTime 4 plug-ins to the Web browser. Every school had a unique network system configuration, requiring knowledge of how addresses needed to be configured for network access. Most teachers required computer support persons to help them confirm that their computers met the minimum requirements and were properly configured. This included help with downloading and installing the Web browser and necessary plug-ins. When adequate technical support was not available, teachers needed to be technologically savvy in order to prepare available computers to implement the curriculum.

Communication between teacher and computer support persons varied greatly from school to school, as did responsiveness. Some teachers were able to call system administrators, who quickly came to configure computers, while others had system administrators who responded slowly or didn't show at all. One teacher had computers in her room for six months before they sent a technician in to set them up and to connect them to the Internet. The knowledge level of the system support people in different schools also varied greatly. In one case, a teacher checked with the system administrator and was assured that the school's computers would be able to run the program. When she began the pilot test, she found that the computers were woefully inadequate.

School system technology policies also created problems. Some systems had blocking software that inhibited learners from accessing externally linked Web sites that were linked to prototype activities. Some systems restricted teachers from downloading necessary plug-ins or upgrading their version of Internet Explorer. Two teachers had problems with their systems not connecting to the Web site. Because of computers with less memory, one teacher had to download plug-ins each morning and then take them off at night. Often, school Internet connections were slow, frustrating both students and teachers.

Regardless of how much technical support teachers had in their schools, all teachers became emergency technicians while pilot testing the prototype materials, troubleshooting problems as necessary during class. Many teachers had to learn to download software, reboot computers, and set up audio capabilities on their computers. The amount of time and type of problem were usually minor annoyances. However, for almost 43% of our pilot teachers (18 teachers out of the 42) it constituted enough of a hardship that pilot testing was aborted.

Teacher Use of Technology

As we observed teachers in the classroom, it was apparent that being an innovator was not always fun or easy. Few teachers had complete availability or the perfect arrangement of computers. Many teachers had difficulties thinking of ways in which they could adapt use of computers to facilitate their teaching. As previously mentioned, most of the teachers had not used computers with the students on a regular basis or as a critical component for teaching. In order to implement the prototype materials, many teachers had to adjust their normal styles of teaching.

There was no one pattern to how teachers used the prototype materials. Teachers spent from 2 to 20 days implementing the chapters. How teachers used materials and which materials teachers selected for use appeared to be influenced by their comfort level in working with technology, as well as their need to meet local standards and core curriculum requirements. Teachers also selected different components based on the ability levels of their students and the sorts of instructional activities best supported by the arrangement and location of available computers.

It appears that many biology teachers in our sample did not know how to make the most of available computers in their classrooms. Of those teachers who had multiple computers in their classrooms, few reported using them as learning stations. Likewise, few teachers said they used an LCD projector to project visualizations on a screen or a television monitor to call attention to biological concepts presented in the materials. One teacher, who did not know she had the ability to connect her computer to her classroom television monitor, decided to print out an animation screen to illustrate the biological concepts that were presented in the animation. Another teacher, despite having enough computers in her classroom for the students to work in groups, took her students to the library computer lab to do the activities, since she believed the only way to work with prototype materials was individually (one computer per student). Similarly, many teachers were unaware of new products just coming out, like wireless computers, hand-held computers, and SmartBoards that would offer more ways to present interactive segments of the prototype materials.

Many teachers customized the instructional design of materials to accommodate their pedagogical styles. The materials are designed so that teachers can selectively choose different components to meet the diverse needs of their students. For example, one teacher chose to use the Web components to enhance her lecture material. In contrast, after implementing the wet lab, another teacher had students use the computer activities to check their understanding of concepts presented in the lab and to reinforce that learning.

Most teachers did not implement all computer-based activities in a chapter. When teachers had limited time, wet labs were the first activities to be omitted, and teachers tended to use the WebQuests at the beginning of the chapters as an introduction to the chapter's content. Interactive tutorials were next most likely to be used by teachers to illustrate concepts or to reinforce vocabulary.

Teachers experienced management issues when using the prototype materials in a computer lab. In computer labs, eye contact was a problem with students seated behind computer monitors or with their backs to the teacher. Computer audio could also be a problem: As an extreme example, the students in one lab were completing an activity in which a bear burps after he has eaten an apple. They decided to devote time to trying to get all computers to play the bear's burp in unison and the teacher had trouble getting them back on task.

It is difficult for a teacher to be the center of activity in a computer lab. Teachers who were accustomed to using a teacher-centered approach expressed some uncertainty, therefore, about what role to play when using computer activities. One teacher commented that she felt a bit useless and didn't quite know what to do when the students became focused on the computers and busy with the activities. Student data suggested that teachers were not the only ones aware of the change: Several students noted in their journals that their learning became more intrinsic and relied less on the teacher's direct instruction. Many students said they enjoyed the shift in emphasis to a more student-centered atmosphere. However, not all students preferred learning autonomously with computers. In two schools, higher-level biology students reported that they preferred a more traditional textbook-centered curriculum over the prototype materials.

We deemed a successful implementation of the prototype materials to be one in which classroom students were able to use the prototype materials assigned by the teacher and learned biology. A variety of factors contributed to successful implementation. In the most successful classrooms, the teachers appeared to have a pedagogical style that permitted them to incorporate the materials without radically changing their approach to teaching. Such a style usually was one that permitted a combination of teacher-centered and student-centered learning, with easy transitions between the two. Structuring the classroom environment for students to work in small groups proved to be a most advantageous way to implement the materials. Teachers circulated among groups, guiding activities and assisting the students, while students often discussed concepts among themselves to derive responses to questions in the tutorials. Teachers who had multiple ways to use computers and multiple types of related technology also appeared to have more success. For instance, teachers who used a combination of projected computer animations for whole-group guided discussion and stand-alone computers for small group activities also reported success implementing the materials. Similarly, five to seven computers spread out to allow students to work in small groups and wireless connections where students could form their own work groups dynamically seemed good ways to configure student-centered activities.

Findings Related to Specific Learners

Some student findings had implications for teachers implementing such a technology-rich product. In particular, we saw some evidence that this approach might have had unanticipated effects on specific populations of learners. For instance, one teacher noted that the academic performance of her students with Individual Education Plans (IEPs) for learning disabilities improved while implementing the program. The most dramatic observation was a student whose average mark improved from a D to a B. In an unfortunate confirmation of the learner's preference for the prototype approach, the student's mark slipped back to a D when the textbook-centered curriculum was reinstated at the end of the pilot test. In the same class, grades for two English-as-a-second-language students also improved while using the prototype materials. During study hall, they were able to access the Web site and complete activities at their own pace. While novelty may play some role in these findings, it is worth noting that the implementation covered a period of one to three weeks per chapter for each of the three chapter prototypes.

In contrast, analysis of student journals indicated that low-proficiency readers had more difficulty reading text on a computer monitor than from a textbook. These learners also became disorientated with activities that launched more than one browser window. For instance, some of the WebQuests required learners to navigate across Web sites, opening several concurrent windows. As a result, such students appeared to have trouble staying focused and on task, jumping instead between and among Web sites.

RECOMMENDATIONS

As a result of the first year's pilot test, we are able to make a few recommendations that we have already implemented in the second year's field test. They may well also apply to implementing other kinds of technology-rich science materials.

1. *Technology-rich products still demand more technological sophistication than many teachers currently possess and more technical support than many schools currently provide.*

Cutting-edge really means that early implementers bleed so that later users may have fewer problems. As we saw in our pilot, present levels of technology call for a lot of troubleshooting. Until things become simpler, teachers need to be adept troubleshooters if they wish to use technology-rich materials in their classrooms. Given the troubles that some of our teachers had with technical support in their buildings, administrations who wish to see their teachers use such materials may well need to make certain that the necessary level of technical support—and responsiveness—is there for teachers. In addition, teachers need to be made aware of the sorts of teaching technologies that exist, from large monitor connections to data projectors, to SmartBoards and amplified speaker connections. Not only should schools help their teachers understand what these technologies are and how to use them in teaching, but technology-rich materials produced for use in school settings should include good instructions on how to use those materials in a wide range of delivery techniques.

2. *Teachers wishing to implement technology-rich materials may need to rely on a more diverse set of computer configurations than just using the computer lab.*

Our teachers certainly encountered a number of problems in working with computer labs. Availability and scheduling problems made it difficult to complete activities where they fell in the curriculum. If teachers want to stay on schedule, they may need to think in terms of a combination of approaches, only some of which might occur in a computer lab. And any activities in the computer lab need to be scheduled well in advance. Further, for technology-rich learning products to succeed, schools need to recognize the importance of instructional uses of computer labs, not simply use of such facilities for word processing and other activities calling for the use of tool/productivity programs. Similarly, schools need to plan for classroom Internet access.

Technology continues to advance. Wireless computers certainly appeared to help those teachers who had them to implement our prototypes in more flexible ways. Unfortunately, once a technology solution finds its way into a school, competition for that resource becomes greater. For instance, a teacher in our sample had received a grant to purchase wireless laptop computers for her school's biology department. At the beginning of the school year, she was the only teacher using the equipment. However, as more and more teachers began using her wireless laptop computers, she had more and more trouble scheduling them for her own use with our prototypes.

3. *Technology-rich materials may change the nature of teacher planning for instruction.*

While our teachers did not achieve the anticipated saving in planning time, the way in which they used their planning time did change a bit. It may be that having such rich materials means that teachers spend their advance time planning which parts of the product to implement when; how to prepare students for their interactions with the materials; which things to cover in whole-class settings, which in small groups, and which individually; how to match materials and activities to one's individual teaching style and philosophy; and how to assess student learning after using the materials. Of course, another use of planning time will continue for the present to be setting up the technology and preparing the setting for its use.

4. *Professional development may need to focus more on helping teachers and administrators understand how best to implement learner-centered approaches.*

Our findings suggest that many teachers (and perhaps administrators) may not have as broad an understanding of learner-centered approaches to teaching biology as they might. It is worth noting that high school science teachers may be more likely to have a science degree than a science education or education degree and may not have received training in incorporating technology into instructional contexts (National Center for Education Statistics, 1999). If such teachers are to employ more learner-centered approaches as recommended in the National Center for Education Statistics report, professional development focused on acquiring a diverse repertoire of pedagogical approaches may prove useful.

.5. *While it might seem logical to delay adoption of technology-based curricular materials until lots of high-powered computer equipment is widely distributed in schools, it may make more sense to start using products like this and let curricular demand dictate acquisition of more computer technology.*

There's an old saying in the computer industry: *Software sells hardware (not the reverse).* Technology-using teachers do not seem to wait for the perfect hardware before they find strong technology-based curriculum materials. Instead, they acquire and adopt strong curricular materials and then use the technological demands of those materials to justify acquiring more computer technology.

REFERENCES

Bailey, G. D. (1997). What technology leaders need to know: The essential top 10 concepts for technology integration in the 21st century. *Learning and Leading with Technology, 25*(1), 57-62.

Baker, F. (1981). Computer-managed instruction: A context for computer-based instruction. In H. E O'Neil, Jr. (Ed.), *Computer-based instruction: A state-of-the-art assessment* (pp. 23-64). New York: Academic.

Biological Sciences Curriculum Study. (1993). Developing biological literacy: A guide to developing secondary and post-secondary biology curricula. Colorado Springs, CO: Author.

Black, E. D. (1998). *Staff development baseline needs assessment. Analysis of a statewide survey of directors and full-time instructors.* (ERIC Document Reproduction Service No. ED428176).

Bork, A. (1985). *Personal computers for education.* New York: Harper & Row.

Bunderson, C. V. (1981). Courseware. In H. E O'Neil, Jr. (Ed.), *Computer-based instruction: A state-of-the-art assessment* (pp. 91-125). New York: Academic.

CEO Forum. (1997). *School technology and readiness report: From pillars to progress. The CEO forum on education and technology, Year one.* Washington, DC: CEO Forum. (ERIC Document Reproduction Service No. ED416819).

Cuban, L. (2001). *Oversold and underused: Computers in the classroom.* Cambridge, MA: Harvard University Press.

Cummings, C. A. (1998). *Teacher attitudes and effective computer integration.* Master's research paper. Charlottesville, VA: University of Virginia. (ERIC Document Reproduction Service No. ED419512).

Dennis, J. R., & Kansky, R. J. (1984). *Instructional computing: An action guide for educators.* Glenview, IL: Scott, Foresman.

Dockstader, J. (1999) Teachers of the 21st century know the what, why, and how of technology integration. *Technological Horizons in Education Journal, 26*(6), 73-74.

Ediger, M. (1997). *Computer literacy in the public schools.* (ERIC Document Reproduction Service No. ED412919).

Fine, L. (1999). *Improving the integration of technology into the sixth-grade curriculum in a middle school.* EdD Practicum I Report, Nova Southeastern University. (ERIC Document Reproduction Service No. ED437909).

Freeman, D. (1987). Information handling on computer in the humanities classroom: Process, practice, and perspectives. In W. A. Kent & R. Lewis (Eds.), *Computer-assisted learning in the humanities and social sciences* (pp. 3-9). Oxford: Blackwell Scientific.

Gunter, G. A., Gunter, R. E., & Wiens, G. A. (1998, March). *Teaching pre-service teachers technology: An innovative approach.* Paper presented at the Society for Information Technology & Teacher Education International Conference, Washington, DC. (ERIC Document Reproduction Service No. ED421112).

Hall, G., & Mantz, C. (2000, February). *Middle school technology integration study.* Paper presented at the Society for Information Technology & Teacher Education International Conference, San Diego, CA. (ERIC Document Reproduction Service No. ED444564).

Heck, G. J., & Wallace, B. (1999). *Preparing to implement learner outcomes in technology: Best practices for Alberta school jurisdictions.* School Technology Task Group. (ERIC Document Reproduction Service No. ED429571)

Heinich, R. (1991). Restructuring, technology, and instructional productivity. In G. J. Anglin (Ed.), *Instructional technology: Past, present, and future* (pp. 236-243). Englewood, CO: Libraries Unlimited.

Hoover, S. J., & Abhaya, P. S. (1995). *Instructional design theory and scientific content for higher education.* Paper presented at the 1995 Annual National Convention of the Association for Educational Communications and Technology, Anaheim, CA.

Jacobsen, D. M. (1998). *Adoption patterns of faculty who integrate computer technology for teaching and learning in higher education.* Ottawa, Ontario: Social Sciences and Humanities Research Council of Canada.

Johnson, M. (2000, February 4). *New roles for educators.* Milken Family Foundation. Retrieved October 2, 2001, from http://www.mff.org/edtech/article.taf?_function=detail&Content_uid1=290

Lemke, C., & Coughlin, E. (1998, July 10). *Technology in American schools: Seven dimensions for gauging progress–A policymaker's guide.* Milken Family Foundation. Retrieved October 2, 2001, from: http://www.mff.org/edtech/publication.taf

Mann, M. (1998). *Technology in education. PREL briefing paper.* Pacific Region Educational Laboratory, A publication of the School Technology Task Group. Edmonton: Alberta Department of Education. (ERIC Document Reproduction Service No. ED415853).

McDermott, L., & Murray, J. (2000). *Study on the effective use and integration of technology into the primary curriculum.* Chicago, IL: Saint Xavier University. (ERIC Document Reproduction Service No. ED445669).

National Center for Education Statistics. (1999). *Teacher quality: A report on the preparation and qualifications of public school teachers* (NCES 1999-080). Washington, DC: U.S. Government Printing Office.

Norman, K. L. (1997, November). *Pushing the electronic limits: No paper, no pencils, no books.* Paper presented at the Society for Computers in Psychology, 27th annual meeting, Philadelphia, PA.

Perelman, L. J. (1992). *School's out: A radical new formula for the revitalization of America's educational system.* New York: Avon.

Rogers, E. M. (1986). *Communication technology: New media and society.* New York: Free Press.

Schnackenberg, H. L., Asuncion, J., & Rosler, D. (1999, February). *The education forum: A web-based resource for teachers.* Paper presented at the Annual Convention of the Association for Educational Communications and Technology, Houston, TX.

Sharp, V. (1993). *Computer education for teachers.* Madison, WI: Brown & Benchmark.

Sherman, L. (1998). The promise of technology. *Northwest Education, 3*(3), 2-9.

Smith-Gratto, K., & Fisher, M. M. (1999). An aid to curriculum and computer integration: Prototypes for teachers. *Computers in the Schools, 15*(2), 61-71.

Solmon, L. (1999, October 19). *Results from a study of 27 states' district technology coordinators.* Milken Family Foundation. Retrieved October 2, 2001, from http://www.mff.org/publications/publications.taf?page=277

State-of-the-States survey. (2001). *Technological Horizons in Education Journal.* Retrieved October 2, 2001, from http://www.thejournal.com/magazine/stateofthestates/

Lee A. Montgomery

Digital Portfolios in Teacher Education: Blending Professional Standards, Assessment, Technology, and Reflective Practice

SUMMARY. Digital portfolios can be powerful tools for facilitating reflective practice when based on sound developmental principles and adequately supported by mentoring, peer review, and other effective practices. This article explores the use of the digital portfolio to promote reflection by practitioners and suggests strategies that can be employed by teacher educators to maximize the benefits of these constructivist tools for learning, reflection, and assessment. *[Article copies available for a fee from The Haworth Document Delivery Service: 1-800-HAWORTH. E-mail address: <docdelivery@haworthpress.com> Website: <http://www.HaworthPress.com> © 2003 by The Haworth Press, Inc. All rights reserved.]*

KEYWORDS. Digital portfolios, professional standards, assessment, technology, reflective practice, computers

"If change is to occur, reflective thinking must become a taken-for-granted lens through which pre-service teachers conceptualize their practice" (Ross & Hannay, 1986, p. 14).

LEE A. MONTGOMERY is Associate Dean, Southern Utah University, College of Education, Cedar City, UT 84720 (E-mail: Montgomery@suu.edu).

[Haworth co-indexing entry note]: "Digital Portfolios in Teacher Education: Blending Professional Standards, Assessment, Technology, and Reflective Practice." Montgomery, Lee A. Co-published simultaneously in *Computers in the Schools* (The Haworth Press, Inc.) Vol. 20, No. 1/2, 2003, pp. 171-186; and: *Technology in Education: A Twenty-Year Retrospective* (ed: D. LaMont Johnson, and Cleborne D. Maddux) The Haworth Press, Inc., 2003, pp. 171-186. Single or multiple copies of this article are available for a fee from The Haworth Document Delivery Service [1-800-HAWORTH, 9:00 a.m. - 5:00 p.m. (EST). E-mail address: docdelivery@haworthpress.com].

When Cleborne D. Maddux (1984), Associate Editor for Research for *Computers in the Schools*, spoke of "breaking the Everest syndrome" in the journal's second issue almost two decades ago, he gave voice to a common concern held by many educators who found themselves at the threshold of a revolution in educational computing. Insistence on the part of computer advocates that computers should be used simply because they were there and the notion that computers would "deliver us from educational nirvana merely by existing" fueled fears that the fledgling educational computing movement, unless redirected, might turn out to be just another good idea that never arrived. (p. 38).

Writing in the first issue of the same journal, Maddux distinguished between Type I (using computers to make it quicker and easier to continue teaching the same topics in the same ways we have always taught them) and Type II uses (computer applications which support new and better ways of helping children learn). Applications which focus on drill and practice typify the first category while databases, spreadsheets, simulations programming applications, and problem-solving software are typical of Type II.

Maddux, Johnson, and Willis (2001) compared the characteristics of the two categories of applications and noted that most Type II applications were designed to "stimulate relatively active intellectual involvement on the part of the user" (p. 101). Jonassen (2000) coined the phrase "mind tools" to refer to Type II applications that promote problem-solving and other constructivist approaches to learning.

While the proliferation of Type II applications has been relatively slow, the ability of such applications to actively engage the learner's intellect in ways that lead to increased understanding suggests that Type II applications may have great potential when applied as tools for promoting reflective practice among pre-service educators.

Three powerful trends anchored in the educational reform movement are rapidly converging in ways that directly impact the evolution of the digital teaching portfolio and the preparation of teachers for the 21st century. The first of these trends, the movement of teacher preparation programs toward the adoption of professional teaching standards, drives the other two: the need for performance-based teacher assessment and an accompanying need for new technological tools to record and organize evidence of successful teaching.

Research on teacher effectiveness suggests that outstanding teachers learn from their experiences and constantly seek to refine their own professional practice. They remain current in the literature of their disciplines and continue to grow professionally. Master teachers continually try out new strategies and techniques in their classrooms, reflect on their successes and failures, and then adjust their professional practices accordingly. They often keep reflective journals and carry out formal action research projects to assist them in this process. Yet, most teachers would find it difficult to demonstrate how these varied experiences fit into the total framework of their professional development. Because the acquisition of complex knowledge, skills, and dispositions is a critical indicator of growing professional competency, it is important that teacher candidates who are preparing to enter the profession be able to articulate these competencies to themselves and others.

When employed as a tool for reflective practice, a digital teaching portfolio can enable both novice and accomplished teachers to make sense out of a myriad of professional experiences and bring into focus a clear picture of themselves as growing, changing professionals. Properly used, the digital portfolio can also be a meaningful and highly effective way to demonstrate to others the knowledge, skills, and dispositions teachers and teacher candidates have gained in the complex process of teaching.

PORTFOLIOS AND REFLECTIVE PRACTICE

While the use of teaching portfolios has moved from individual classrooms and teacher education programs to state departments of education and are the primary assessment used by the NBPTS, the electronic teaching portfolio is still very much in its infancy (Lyons, 1998a). There is not yet a systematic body of data documenting its uses and long-term consequences. While much research concerning the educational benefits of electronic portfolios remains to be undertaken, a survey of the literature linking reflective practice to the use of traditional portfolios provides promising glimpses of the powerful role these portfolios can play in producing a new generation of reflective practitioners (Moss, 1997).

The 1998 winter issue of *Teacher Education Quarterly* featured a number of studies on the use of portfolios in teacher education programs. Jones (1998), in the editor's preface, asserted that "portfolios have assumed a significant role in teacher education." Writing in the same issue, guest editors Bartell, Kaye, and Morin (1998) noted that portfolios were valuable to students for promoting reflection and self-directed growth, building good teaching habits, encouraging collaborative dialogue and enriched discussions, documenting growth over time, and "integrating the diversity of their teacher preparation experiences" (p. 5).

Anderson and DeMeulle (1998) surveyed 127 teacher educators throughout the United States to examine the use of portfolios in teacher preparation programs. Teacher educators reported using portfolios for a variety of purposes, including promoting student development, encouraging student self-assessment and reflection, providing evidence for assessment and accountability, and documenting professional growth. Ninety-two percent of the teacher educators surveyed agreed that the use of portfolios had a positive impact on the professional development of pre-service teachers because the portfolios were student-centered, defined by professional standards, and reflective. Further, the portfolios were viewed as "self-empowering tools that encourage pre-service teachers to assume more responsibility for their learning" (pp. 23-31).

Wolf (1996) described a teaching portfolio as a "collection of information about a teacher's practice" (p. 35). He emphasized that the portfolio should be more than a scrapbook of miscellaneous artifacts and lists of professional activities. According to Wolf, the introduction should include a statement of the student's teaching philosophy and goals but the heart of the portfolio should be a combination of teaching artifacts and written reflections. He emphasized that artifacts should be framed with clear identifications, contextual explanations, and reflective commentaries that examine the teaching documented in the portfolio. He also proposed that students include an informal self-assessment and that formal assessment be tied to standards such as those put forth by the NBPTS.

Grant and Huebner (1998) discussed the "powerful learning" that takes place when pre-service teachers incorporate personal beliefs into their professional practice. The authors defined "powerful learning" as a self-regulated learning process in which the teacher's mind is "proactive, problem-oriented, attentionally focused, selective, constructive and directed toward ends" (p. 34). They viewed constructivist patterns of thinking as particularly appropriate for teaching pre-service teachers and maintained that powerful learning took place when a meaningful question concerning professional practice was posed, data collected, and reflection on relationships between the data and the question undertaken.

Stone (1998) explored the importance of providing guidance and support when implementing teaching portfolios and the efficacy of introducing them early in the professional education program. He examined two groups of student teachers to determine an effective method for introducing pre-service teachers to the portfolio process. Each of the two groups was introduced to portfolios at different stages of their professional program and received varying levels of guidance and support. The majority (75%) of the group that received support near the beginning of their first student teaching experience believed that portfolios accurately communicated and documented learning and accomplishments. Only 48% of the second group, which began portfolio construction with their final student teaching assignment, agreed that portfolios were worthwhile in communicating and documenting learning. Stone concluded that the introduction of portfolios must be carefully planned and take place early in the teacher preparation program and that students must be taught how to select artifacts and reflect on their learning.

Lyons (1998b) analyzed the development of reflective practice in a longitudinal study of 10 graduates of Southern Maine's Extended Teacher Education Program. She conducted open-ended interviews with teaching interns during training and again two years later to determine how ideas concerning reflective practice changed over time. She concluded that there was a pattern of reflective processes developing and transforming over time though initial student reflection may have been rudimentary. Lyons believed that the critical conversations concerning the significance of portfolio entries provided a "scaffold that fosters teacher awareness of their knowledge of practice." Additional findings indicated that a beginning teacher's philosophy of education becomes embedded in practice through the process of reflection and that this process occurs through collaborative inquiry related to personal values of teaching and learning.

Borko, Michalec, Timmons, and Siddle (1997) utilized an action research cycle to examine student teachers who completed teaching portfolios as part of a seminar program at the University of Colorado, Denver. Interviews of the 21 student teachers participating in the study explored the benefits of using the portfolio as a tool for reflection. Portfolios were viewed as beneficial in making connections between theory and practice by most participants. Fifteen of the student teachers surveyed reflected on the connection between their philosophy and their teaching practice. While many planned to use portfolios for employment interviews, the researchers concluded that the primary goal of providing a tool for reflecting on student teaching experiences had been met.

MERGING STANDARDS, TECHNOLOGY, ASSESSMENT, AND REFLECTIVITY THROUGH PORTFOLIO DEVELOPMENT

"An electronic portfolio uses electronic technologies, allowing the portfolio developer to collect and organize portfolio artifacts in many media types (text, video, audio, and graphics). A standards-based portfolio uses a database or hypertext links to clearly show the relationship between the standards or goals, artifacts, and reflections. The learner's reflections are the rationale that specific artifacts are evidence of achieving the stated standards or goals" (Barrett, 2000a, p. 14).

While the notion of using portfolios as tools for assessment and reflective practice is not new, teacher educators are just beginning to explore the advantages of storing those portfolios in a digital format. As schools and colleges of teacher education have expanded their access to technology, an increasing number of options have become available for developing electronic teaching portfolios. Technological innovations, including Hypermedia programs, Web-page editors, PDF distillers, and commercial proprietary software such as Chalk and Wire's e-Portfolio have made the process of creating and storing electronic portfolios relatively easy, enabling teacher educators to take advantage of a number of advantages the digital format provides over traditional, paper-based portfolios (Montgomery, 2002).

A development of the 1990s, digital portfolios combine the use of electronic technologies to create and publish a portfolio that can be displayed on a computer monitor. As early as 1992, Shiengold recognized that using electronically stored portfolios can make student work accessible, portable, and more easily distributed. Niguidula (1993), working with the Exhibitions Project at the Coalition of Essential Schools to develop a digital portfolio methodology, recognized the value of paper-based portfolios but posed the question, "What are we going to do with all this stuff?" He described the "logistical nightmare of thousands of papers turning brittle and collecting dust" and proposed that educators create a tool using computer technology that allows "for a richer picture of what a student can know and do" (p. 1).

The International Society for Technology in Education (ISTE), in a report prepared for the National Foundation for the Improvement of Education (1997), described technology as providing new assessment tools that would enable students to engage in "authentic projects" that are more "real world in nature." ISTE asserted that information technologies "added new dimensions to portfolio assessment" and suggested that computer editing could facilitate the arrangement of portfolio artifacts, allowing one presentation to be used for a variety of purposes. ISTE further recommended the use of interactive multimedia stacks and Web pages to develop and store portfolio products.

Sheingold and Frederiksen (1994) argued that technology could provide students and teachers with a medium for conversations about the values and standards for student performance. They suggested that technology could help link assessment with reform through providing: (a) support for student work in extended, authentic learning activities; (b) portable, accessible, and replayable copies of performances in multiple media; (c) libraries of examples and interpretative tools; (d) greater participation in the assessment process; and (e) publication of works demonstrating student accomplishments. Further, technology could provide assessment evidence beyond the capability of text-based products that require the physical presence of an evaluator. Using electronic technologies, student work could be captured and preserved for review anywhere or at any time, eliminating the need for transporting and storing bulky paper portfolios.

Jackson (1998) studied the effects of the use of electronic portfolios at St. Mary's University of Minnesota. Teacher education students determined the characteristics they thought would make them effective teachers and reflected on their progress toward the acquisition of these characteristics using multimedia-based electronic portfolios. In addition to benefits derived from reflecting on their accomplishments, students reported the value of publicly sharing the contents of their portfolios with potential employers and expressed confidence in the possibility of infusing technology in their own classrooms.

Barrett (2000) supported the use of portfolios for authentic assessment of prospective teachers and proposed that professional standards provide the basis for portfolio organization. She maintained, "An electronic portfolio without clear links to standards is just a multimedia presentation or a fancy electronic resume or digital scrapbook. Without standards as the organizing basis for a portfolio, the collection becomes just that . . . a collection, haphazard and without structure; the purpose is lost in the noise, glitz and hype. High technology disconnected from a focus on curriculum standards will only exacerbate the lack of meaningful integration of technology to improve teaching and learning."

Barrett (2000) suggested that a portfolio should include student self-reflections on professional standards and argued that an electronic format was appropriate because:

1. Documents included in portfolios are generally created with a computer to begin with.
2. Hypertext links allow clear connections between standards and portfolio artifacts.
3. Creating an electronic portfolio can help students develop skills in using multimedia technologies.
4. If teachers develop electronic portfolios, their students may be more likely to do so.
5. Electronic portfolios are fun and technology makes it easier to manage the process, especially where storage, presentation, and duplication are are concerned.
6. Electronic portfolios make student work replayable, portable, examinable, reviewable, and widely distributable.

In the year 2000, the National Council for the Accreditation of Teacher Education (NCATE) introduced new standards that make effective use of technology a central requirement for teacher preparation programs. NCATE has called for a reappraisal of teaching practices and recommended a paradigm shift for teacher educators, with an emphasis upon the use of technology to support constructivist teaching and active learning. NCATE suggested that teachers incorporate a wide range of technological tools into their "instructional repertoire" and explore new roles that will help their students explore, discover, and interpret information that "inspires them to become lifelong learners." Powers (1998) recommended that NCATE technology standards developed by the International Society for Technology in Education (ISTE) be adopted as the foundation standards for all teacher candidates. In addition to mastering basic computer applications and operations, ISTE standards require candidates to demonstrate competence in using technology for professional growth and planning and delivering instruction. Powers also recommended that candidates demonstrate proficiency through the use of performance assessments and artifacts included in their professional teaching portfolios.

RESEARCH ON TEACHER REFLECTION

The notion of reflective practice as a goal of teacher education is not new. The seminal work of Donald Schon (1983) built on a foundation laid by Progressive educator John Dewey (1933), and teacher educators across the nation rallied to Schon's (1987) challenge to make reflective practice a central goal of teacher education programs. By the 1990s, the ability to engage in reflective practice was recognized as an important skill for both beginning and experienced teachers. With this renewed emphasis on reflective practice came new modes of teacher assessment, including the use of professional portfolios and other performance assessments suggested by the work of Lee Shulman (1992) and the NBPTS.

A review of the literature on reflection reveals that reflective practice is defined and implemented in teacher education programs in a myriad of ways (Clarke, 1995; Grimmett, Erickson, MacKinnon, & Riecken, 1990), but most of the definitions of "reflective practice" reveal a strong influence by Dewey and Schon. Dewey (1933) believed that reflective thinking involved: (1) a state of doubt or mental difficulty, in which thinking originates, and (2) an act of searching or inquiring, to find material that will resolve the doubt. For Dewey, reflective thinking was "deliberation," a type of thinking that closely resembled scientific thinking. Schon (1983, 1987) viewed reflective thought as being embodied in action. Reflective practice involved calling up previous knowledge and translating it into action to address a particular aspect of practice. Dewey defined reflective thinking from a perspective of problem solving, and both he and Schon viewed the world of professional practice as complex, unstable, and often conflicting.

Dewey's idea of "deliberation" and Schon's concept of "reflection embodied in action" have become a point of departure for many teacher educators who think about the nature of reflective practice and attempt to employ it in teacher education programs. Yinger (1981) viewed reflection as "contemplation" while Fenstermacher (1988) saw it as "practical arguments." Zeichner and Liston (1987) added a moral or ethical dimension to the definition, while Clarke (1995) disputed Schon's assertion that reflection occurs within the context of a single incident or conversation. Clarke viewed reflection as evolving from a series of thematic incidents occurring over relatively long periods of time.

One way of describing the characteristics of reflective thinking is through analyzing modes of delivery. While researchers differ on the hierarchical nature of reflection, they generally agree on three modes or levels of reflective thinking: (a) technical, (b) contextual, and (c) dialectical (Taggart & Wilson, 1998, p. 2).

Van Manen (1977) referred to the initial level of reflective thinking as "technical rationality" and served as a model for Lasley (1992), and Grimmett, Erickson, McKinnon, and Riecken (1990). He suggested that the first level of reflection dealt with methodological problems and theory development to achieve objectives. Valli (1990) also referred to the first level as technical rationality but insisted that it was actually a nonreflective level. His second level, "practical decision making," added reflection to the technical aspects of teaching.

According to Taggert and Wilson (1998), "practitioners reflecting at the technical level function with minimal schema upon which to draw when dealing with instructional problems" (p. 2). At this level, practitioners reflect on short-term measures such as getting through lessons and using instructional management approaches only in terms of meeting outcomes. Individual, often isolated, episodes are building blocks for developing the professional repertoire needed to reflectively handle non-routine problems. A lack of schema in dealing with educational problems forces many novice teachers to function at a technical level.

The contextual level, a second level of reflective practice (Grimmett et al., 1990; Lasley, 1992; Van Manen, 1977), involves classifying and reflecting upon the assumptions underlying classroom practice as well as upon the consequences of various strategies employed by the teacher. Contextual practitioners critically examine pedagogical matters relative to the relationship between theory and practice. The non-problematic nature of technical rationality gives way to problems which often stem from the practitioner's personal dispositions, biases, and beliefs. At this level, practitioners examine situations in context and question practice from a perspective of increased pedagogical knowledge and skills.

Critical reflectivity, Van Manen's (1977) third and highest level of reflectivity, involves questioning moral and ethical issues related to a teacher's professional practice. At this level, such principles as equality, caring, and justice are taken into consideration, and practitioners contemplate ethical and political contexts when planning and implementing instruction. Critically reflective practitioners recognize and attempt to compensate for personal biases and are concerned with the value of knowledge and social circumstances useful to students. The ability to make defensible choices and open-mindedly review a teaching event are characteristics of practitioners functioning at a level of critical reflectivity.

USING DIGITAL PORTFOLIOS TO PROMOTE AND DOCUMENT REFLECTIVE PRACTICE

The reflective thinking level at which a practitioner functions impacts both the meaning of experiences documented in the digital portfolio and what is learned from reflecting on those experiences. The work of Taggert and Wilson (1998) suggests a number of strategies useful in promoting reflection appropriate for the various levels.

Appropriate portfolio goals for teachers reflecting at a technical level might focus upon selecting and implementing a preset lesson to achieve an established, non-problematic objective. Since the practitioner at this level does not deliberate on the context of the situation, the acquisition of skills, methodological awareness, and technical knowledge are important. Identification of the relevancy of activities and objectives becomes increasingly important as technical practitioners transition into linking theory development to practice. Practitioners at this level benefit from making observations and processing information to validate pedagogical decisions.

Practitioners functioning at a technical level need genuine, continuous experiences and thoughtful discussion of problems and possible solutions that emerge from those experiences. Experimentation and application of solutions with clear explanations and meaningful activities are also important. Reflections should focus on pedagogy, content, and theory, and provide for use, examination, and analysis of varying instructional and management approaches. Knowledge of student characteristics will also assist the technical practitioner in reflecting on problems experienced in actual classroom settings.

Understanding concepts, contexts, and theoretical bases for classroom practices and defending those practices in light of their relevance to student growth are appropriate goals for practitioners functioning at the contextual level. Reflecting on assumptions and biases that impact practice helps contextual practitioners recognize the implications and consequences of their professional actions and beliefs. Understanding how their own personal characteristics interact with environmental and contextual factors of teaching and learning is especially important at this level. Through increased practice and the acquisition of theoretical knowledge, practitioners at this level begin to examine conflicting views of actions and consequences and develop defensible routines and "rules of thumb."

Teacher educators working with practitioners at this level should attempt to facilitate reflection upon situational constraints and external factors that impact effective teaching practices. Time for collegial support, input, and discussion to provide bridges between concepts, theories, and practices is especially appropriate. Timely feedback and guiding questions directed at promoting reflection on portfolio entries should be provided.

Portfolio goals for practitioners functioning at the dialectical or critical reflectivity level should focus upon identifying and analyzing knowledge systems and theories in context, discovering relationships between them and relating them to their own daily professional practice. Critical examination of underlying assumptions, norms and rules and practicing introspection, open-mindedness, and intellectual responsibility (Dewey, 1933), are appropriate topics for reflection at this level. Equally important is reflecting on the moral and ethical issues involved in day-to-day planning, teaching, and assessing.

Teacher educators can assist practitioners functioning at this level by assisting them to examine the appropriateness of their actions. The analysis of case studies, curricular approaches, conventional wisdom, and best practices enables dialectical practitioners to examine professional practice through the lens of optimum benefit for students. Portfolio activities grounded in action research should also be a natural product of reflective thinking at the dialectical level. Other activities might include analyzing stereotypes and biases through journaling, self-talk, and storytelling; practicing affective elements of caring and concern; and reflecting on the educational roles of school climate and social values.

THE PORTFOLIO AS A TOOL FOR SCAFFOLDING PROFESSIONAL AND ETHICAL DEVELOPMENT

A feature of the professional teaching portfolio that begins to come into focus when various reflective levels are considered is the opportunity the portfolio can provide for practitioners to author their own learning and professional development. Regardless of their level of functionality, the insights of self-reflection enable practitioners to examine ways that their own beliefs and actions impact students. Through a process of reflecting upon professional teaching standards and experiences encapsulated in portfolio artifacts, practitioners can scaffold their own ethical and professional development.

The work of Richard Stiggins (1987) provides a strong theoretical base for the value of this process. Stiggins advocates a three-prong process that involves engaging prospective teachers in assessment, recording their own progress, and communicating their own success. He maintains that involving candidates in these activities opens the assessment/development process and brings candidates in as full partners. In addition, a high level of involvement provides candidates a clear vision of the meaning of academic success and reveals to them where they stand relative to that vision. The result, according to Stiggins, is a clear sense on the part of the candidate of the path he or she must follow to improve his or her own practice. Another result is a classroom environment in which there are "no surprises" for candidates or professors.

Also consistent with the model advocated by Stiggins is the process of practitioner-involved record keeping, which is facilitated through portfolio development. Teachers can learn to be reflective practitioners by monitoring their own performance through repeated self-assessment utilizing professional standards and a uniform and constant set of performance criteria. Professional portfolios provide opportunities for practitioners to chart evidence of their success over time. Self-reflections about best practice and the changes they see in their own performance permit emerging educators to literally watch themselves grow. As candidates chart their progress, they assume control of and responsibility for their own professional growth and success. According to Stiggins, when candidates know from the onset of the learning process that they will be expected to tell the story of their own success, "they experience a fundamental deep-seated internal shift in their sense of responsibility for their own learning" (Stiggins, 1987).

Barton and Collins (1993) also emphasized the importance of the portfolio in establishing a context for candidate learning and setting goals for personal growth:

> The development of a portfolio begins with the act of establishing purposes. Students, with the help of an advisor, develop purposes for their studies by establishing what they need and want to learn in order to become master teachers. Once they establish these purposes, students seek to find and create practices that meet the need. Because the portfolio emphasizes purpose, students share real and authentic reasons to look for connections between theory and practice. (pp. 210-211)

DIGITAL PORTFOLIOS AND CONVERSATIONS WITH COLLEAGUES

The use of focused interviews and practitioner-directed portfolio conferences at strategic points throughout the portfolio development process constitutes another crucial component anchored in the work of Stiggins. Portfolio conversations refer to structured discussions about professional teaching practice between the portfolio author and other group members, including peers and teacher educators. These conferences focus on standards and the documented evidence of teaching collected and included in the portfolio as artifacts. A strength of the digital portfolio is the ease with which evidence can be presented to others in the group. Since the documents included in the portfolio are digital, they can easily be distributed and displayed for discussion.

Public discussion and debate about what constitutes good teaching brings candidates into the process of presenting the evidence of their own success relative to mastery of professional standards. As productive as teaching portfolios are for facilitating individual reflection and improving professional practice, their value increases dramatically when they serve as a focal point for conversations with colleagues about teaching (Wolf, Whinery, & Hagerty, 1995).

Shulman (1992) pointed out that teaching portfolios do not achieve their full value if they sit in a box (or an unopened computer file). They become valuable only when they become a point of departure for "substantive conversations" about the quality of a teacher's work.

Wolf, Whinery, and Hagerty (1995) suggested that the goal of a portfolio conversation should be to help the portfolio author and other members of the group improve their professional practice. To accomplish this goal, several conditions must be met: (a) the conversation must focus on standards and their relation to the teaching artifacts being presented, (b) clear guidelines for the session must be established to ensure effective interpersonal communication, (c) the discussion group must be carefully organized to maximize both the quality and quantity of input and feedback, and (d) the presentation of portfolio artifacts must relate to a specific set of standards and reflect an authentic teaching enterprise.

It is critical to focus on specific artifacts of teaching rather than upon teaching or education in general. Richert (1990) found that when discussions focused on artifacts, practitioners talked with colleagues about their teaching, and their conversations were more focused and reflective.

A common problem in portfolio conversations occurs when the discussion group loses sight of the primary purpose of the conversation: to guide the portfolio author in improving his or her teaching practice. This situation can often be averted by asking the portfolio author to present a particular artifact and request specific types of feedback from other group members. In this way, the author assumes the responsibility for directing the conversation about his or her work. Once the author's initial set of questions has been addressed, the group should raise additional questions about the artifact that the author may not have considered. The session should close with the portfolio author summarizing what was learned and what action he or she will take as a result (Richert, 1990).

SUPPORTING THE PORTFOLIO DEVELOPMENT PROCESS

Campbell, Melenyzer, Nettles, and Wyman (2000) emphasized the importance of a support system for electronic portfolio development that involves all the stakeholders, including teacher educators, public school mentors, and peers. Two essential types of collaboration and support are mentoring and peer support. The first method, collaboration, is a program-wide effort while the second, peer support, can be done in individual teacher education classrooms.

Mentoring is an effective way to initiate and facilitate academic growth for students just entering professional education programs. Mentors can provide valuable assistance through sharing their own professional portfolios with newcomers and discussing the standards that provide a framework for the collection of artifacts the portfolios contain. Mentors, who include teacher educators, public school practitioners, and advanced teacher education candidates, can serve as "critical friends" to students entering the professional education program. The role of the mentor includes emphasizing the importance of professional standards and encouraging initiates to collect important documentation that can be used as evidence of growth toward meeting those standards. Campbell suggested that participation in a mentoring program can be a highly motivating experience for both mentor and the initiate.

Peer support may take place in the context of the individual classroom. Students who need support can be referred to advanced students who have their portfolios well underway and who have demonstrated their proficiency through portfolio conferences or other assessment activities. According to Campbell, this type of support is especially useful for students who are struggling with articulating their self-reflections.

Peer editing is yet another way that peer support can be provided in the college classroom. This strategy is particularly helpful because it requires students to articulate their work for an audience other than the course instructor, adding a level of authenticity. Peer editing not only helps students improve their work but also models the collaborative nature of the work of real-life professionals.

CONCLUSION

As the demand for authentic, standards-based assessment of teacher performance continues to grow, teacher educators will need to develop new strategies for recording and presenting evidence of successful teaching. While the notion of using portfolios as an assessment tool in professional education programs is not new, teacher educators are just beginning to explore the advantages of digital formats for these assessment tools.

Appropriately used, a digital portfolio is far more than an electronic collection of course projects, assignments, and teaching memorabilia. A thoughtfully developed portfolio provides organized, standards-driven documentation of professional development and competency in teaching. When anchored in professional teaching standards, the digital teaching portfolio becomes a highly meaningful and effective way to demonstrate to others the knowledge, skills, and dispositions gained in mastering the complex art and science of teaching.

A critical goal of the professional teaching portfolio, whether presented in digital or traditional form, should be to facilitate the development of reflective practice. When this goal is addressed, a digital teaching portfolio can enable professional education candidates to assume responsibility for their own learning, make sense out of a myriad of teacher preparation experiences, and bring into focus a clear picture of themselves as growing, changing professionals.

REFERENCES

Anderson, R.S. & DeMeulle, L. (1998). Portfolio use in twenty-four teacher education programs. *Teacher Education Quarterly, 21*(1), 23-31.

Barrett, H.C. (2000). Strategic questions: What to consider when planning for electronic portfolios. *Learning and Leading with Technology, 26*(2), 6-13.

Barrett, H.C. (2000a). Create your own electronic portfolio. *Learning and Leading with Technology, 27*(7), 14-21.

Bartell, C.A., Kaye, C., & Morin, J.A. (1998). Guest editor's introduction. Teaching portfolios in teacher education. *Teacher Education Quarterly, 25*(1), 5-8.

Barton, J. & Collins, A. (1993). Portfolios in teacher education. *Journal of Teacher Education, 44*(3), 200-211.

Borko, H., Michalac, P., Timmons, M., & Siddle, J. (1997). Student teaching portfolios: A tool for promoting reflective practice. *Journal of Teacher Education, 48*(5), 345-358.

Campbell, D.M., Melenyzer, B.J., Nettles, D.H., & Wyman, R.M. (2000). *Portfolio and Performance Assessment in Teacher Education*. Boston: Allyn & Bacon.

Clarke, A. (1995). Professional development in practicum settings: Reflective practice under scrutiny. *Teaching and Teacher Education, 11*(3), 243-261.

Dewey, J. (1933). *How We Think: A Restatement of the Relation of Reflective Thinking to the Educative Process*. Boston: D.C. Heath.

Fenstermacher, G.D. & Sanger, M. (1998). What is the significance of John Dewey's approach to the problem of knowledge? *Elementary School Journal, 98*(5), 467-478.

Grant, G.E. & Huebner, T.A. (1998). The portfolio question: A powerful synthesis of the personal and professional. *Teacher Education Quarterly, 25*(1), 33-42.

Grimmett, P., Erickson, G., MacKinnon, A., & Riecken, T. (1990). *Reflective Practice in Teacher Education*. New York: Teachers College Press.

International Society for Technology in Education. (1997). National standards for technology in teacher preparation. ISTE accreditation and standards committee (Online). Retrieved October 25, 2002, from: http://www.iste.org/Resources/Projects/TechStandards/intro.html

Jackson, D. (1998). Developing student generated computer portfolios (Online). Retrieved October 25, 2002, from: http://www.coe.uh.edu/insite/elec_pub/HTML1998.pt_jack.htm

Jonassen, D.H. (2000). *Computers as Mindtools for Schools* (2nd ed.). Upper Saddle River, NJ: Merrill.

Jones, A.H. (1998). Editor's preface: Teaching portfolios in teacher education. *Teacher Education Quarterly, 25*(1), 2-3.

Lasley, T.J. (1992). Promoting teacher reflection. *Journal of Staff Development, 13*(1), 24-29.

Lyons, N. (1998a). *With Portfolio in Hand: Validating the New Teacher Professionalism*. New York: Teacher's College Press.

Lyons, N. (1998b). Reflection on teaching: Can it be developmental? A portfolio perspective. *Teacher Education Quarterly, 25*(1), 115-127.

Maddux, C.D. (1984). Breaking the Everest syndrome in educational computing: An interview with Gregory Jackson and Judah L. Schwartz. *Computers in the Schools, 1*(2), 38-39.

Maddux, C.D., Johnson, D.L., & Willis, J.W. (2001). *Educational Computing: Learning with Tomorrow's Technologies*. Boston: Allyn and Bacon, 96-115.

Montgomery, L.A. (2002). *Electronic portfolios for pre-service teachers: Merging technology, self-assessment, and reflective practice*. Paper presented at the American Association of Colleges for Teacher Education Conference, New York City.

Moss, P.A. (1997). *Developing coherence between assessment and reform in the licensing and professional development of teachers*. Paper presented at the annual meeting of the American Educational Research Association.

National Council for Accreditation of Teacher Education. (2000). Technology and the new professional teacher: Preparing for the 21st century classroom (Online). Retrieved October 25, 2002, from: http://www.ncate.org/accred/projects/tech/tech-21.htm

Niguidula, D. (1993). The digital portfolio: A richer picture of student performance. Coalition of Essential Schools (Online). Retrieved October 25, 2002, from: http://www.essentialschools.org/cs/resources/view/ces_res/225

Powers, S.M. (1998). Developing a need for the NCATE/ISTE standards for pre-service teachers (Online). Available from: http://www.coe/uh/edu/insite/elecpub/HTML1998/pt_powe.htm

Richert, A.E. (1990). Teaching teachers to reflect: A consideration of programme structure. *Journal of Curriculum Studies, 22,* 509-527.

Ross, E.W. & Hannay, L.M. (1986). Towards a critical theory of reflective inquiry. *Journal of Teacher Education, 37,* 9-15.

Schon, D. (1983). *The Reflective Practitioner: How Professionals Think in Action.* New York: Basic Books.

Schon, D. (1987). *Educating the Reflective Practitioner: Towards a New Design for Teaching and Learning in the Professions.* San Francisco: Jossey-Bass.

Sheingold, K. & Frederiksen, J. (1994). Using technology to support innovative assessment. In B. Means (Ed.), *Technology and Education Reform.* San Francisco, CA: Jossey-Bass.

Shulman, L.S. (1992). *Portfolios in teacher education: A component of reflective teacher education.* Paper presented at the annual meeting of the American Educational Research Association, San Francisco.

Stiggins, R.J. (1987). Design and development of performance assessments. *Educational Measurement, 6*(3), 33-42.

Stone, B.A. (1998). Problems, pitfalls and benefits of portfolios. *Teacher Education Quarterly, 21*(1), 105-114.

Taggart, G.L. & Wilson, A.P. (1998). *Promoting Reflective Practice in Teachers: 44 Action Strategies.* Thousand Oaks, CA: Corwin Press, Inc.

Valli, L. (1990). *Teaching as moral reflection: Thoughts on the liberal preparation of teachers (Report No. SP 033 712).* Milwaukee, WI: Association of Independent Liberal Arts Colleges for Teacher Education. (ERIC Document Reproduction Service No. ED344 853).

Van Manen, M. J. (1977). Linking ways of knowing with ways of being practical. *Curriculum Inquiry, 6*(3), 205-228.

Wolf, K. (1996, March). Developing an effective teaching portfolio. *Educational Leadership, 53,* 34-37.

Wolf, K., Whinery, B., & Hagerty, P. (1995). Teaching portfolios and portfolio conversations for teacher educators and teachers. *Action in Teacher Education, 17*(1), 30-39.

Yinger, R. & Clark, C. (1981) *Reflective journal writing: Theory and practice (Occasional Paper No. 50).* East Lansing, MI: Institute for Research and Teaching.

Zeichner, K.M. & Liston, D.P. (1987). Teaching student teachers to reflect. *Harvard Educational Review, 57,* 23-48.

Index